'Masaryk, our first President, based his politics on morality. Today, this moral spirit has been revived in our people. I believe that we now have a chance to make this our special contribution to European and world politics.'

Václav Havel
President

Czechoslovakia
Czech and Slovak Federative Republic
(CSFR)

PROSPECT *NEW EUROPE* GUIDES

CZECHOSLOVAKIA

General Editor

Laura McCaffrey

Czechoslovak Editors

Jana Novotná

Pavel Löffelmann

PROSPECT *NEW EUROPE* GUIDES

CZECHOSLOVAKIA

First published in Great Britain and Czechoslovakia in 1991 by Hawker Publications Ltd and Orbis, Prague under licence to
Prospect Publishing Ltd
Park House 13
140 Battersea Park Road
London SW11 4NB

English writing team: Laura McCaffrey, David Cumming, Adrian Slack, Alex Gammie.
Czechoslovak writing team: Jana Novotná, Pavel Löffelmann, Fedor Mikovič. Additional research: Jaromír Douda, Jan Rokyta, Dr. František Parkán, Stanislav Červenka.
Maps drawn by Jaromír Douda.
Typesetting and design: Helen White, Johanne Silby.
Printed and bound in Czechoslovakia.

The idea for this joint publishing venture between Czechoslovakia and Great Britain was conceived by Adrian Keefe of Prospect Publishing Ltd.

Prospect Publishing Ltd have made every attempt to ensure that the information contained in this guidebook is correct at the time of going to press. But it must be stressed that the situation in Czechoslovakia is changing so rapidly that we can take no responsibility for any errors of whatever nature.

British Library Cataloguing in Publication Data
McCaffrey, Laura
Czechoslovakia
1. Czechoslovakia. Travel
1. Title II. Novotná, Jana III. Löffelmann, Pavel
914. 370443

ISBN 0-9514649-3-0

CONTENTS

PART II

HOW TO USE THIS BOOK

MAPS

All place and street names are in Czech or Slovak depending on the region, on the basis that this is what you see on signposts. The symbols below are the same for each map. Monuments and places to see and visit are all numbered and outlined in the key of each town map. Hotels and other places to stay are shown in a circle, restaurants in a square.

Map symbols

- Tourist information
- Airport
- Bus station
- Train station
- Post office
- Parking
- Emergency medical aid
- Places of interest

Abbreviations

nábr. nábřeží/nábrežie embankment; nám. náměstí square; most bridge

ACCOMMODATION

The different types of accommodation in Czechoslavakia – hotels, tourist hostels, mountain chalets and campsites – are each divided into categories based on facilities and price range. These are only a guide and within each category there can be significant variations. Prices are escalating all the time, particularly in Prague. Hotel prices are for one person for one night and are usually quoted in $US. You can pay in any foreign currency equivalent to the $US price, but Korunas are not accepted from tourists. It's worth bearing in mind that Czechoslovaks pay less than visitors – a good reason to make friends quickly!

Hotels

A* de luxe — **$70 - 120 (approx. £41 - 71)**

These are the top class hotels. Rooms have en suite bathrooms or showers, tv and fridge. Each has a restaurant and bar, exchange bureau and parking.

A* — **$60 - 100 (approx. £36 - 60)**

Comparable to A* de luxe but generally with smaller rooms and restaurants and facilities some 10% cheaper. All have an exchange bureau and parking.

B* — **$40 - 80 (approx. £24 - 48)**

Not every room has en suite bathroom but all have a washbasin. Restaurants and wine bars are in the II price category (see below). All have an exchange bureau and most have parking.

B — **$30 - 50 (approx. £18 - 30)**

One, two or three bed rooms with washbasin. Toilet and bathroom on each floor. Rooms are basic without radios or phones but there is at least one restaurant. Parking spaces are not guaranteed.

C — **$ 20 - 40 (approx. £12 - 24)**

Rooms with two beds or more with washbasin but very little else. Toilet and bathroom are shared and the hotels serve breakfast but seldom have a restaurant. Parking spaces are not guaranteed.

Tourist hostels and mountain chalets

A A Generally these compare to C category hotels. **$30 - 80 (approx. £18 - 48)**

B B Dormitory accommodation with very basic facilities. **$5 - 50 (approx. £3 - 30)**

Campsites

Although graded in the guide these categories are becoming so blurred they are not very useful. Many campsites have pitches for both tents and caravans and some offer chalet accommodation as well. Prices for one night are around 90 Kčs per person, 150 Kčs per car, 150 Kčs per tent and 220 Kčs per caravan.

RESTAURANTS

The following price ranges are based on the typical cost of one main dish for one person.

I	100 - 200 Kčs	III	60 - 150 Kčs	V	20 - 40 Kčs
II	80 - 200 Kčs	IV	30 - 80 Kčs		

Detailed maps in Part II of this guide

1 Giant Mountains (Krkonoše)
2 Little Fatra (Malá Fatra)
3 Low Tatras (Nízke Tatry)
4 High Tatras (Vysoké Tatry)

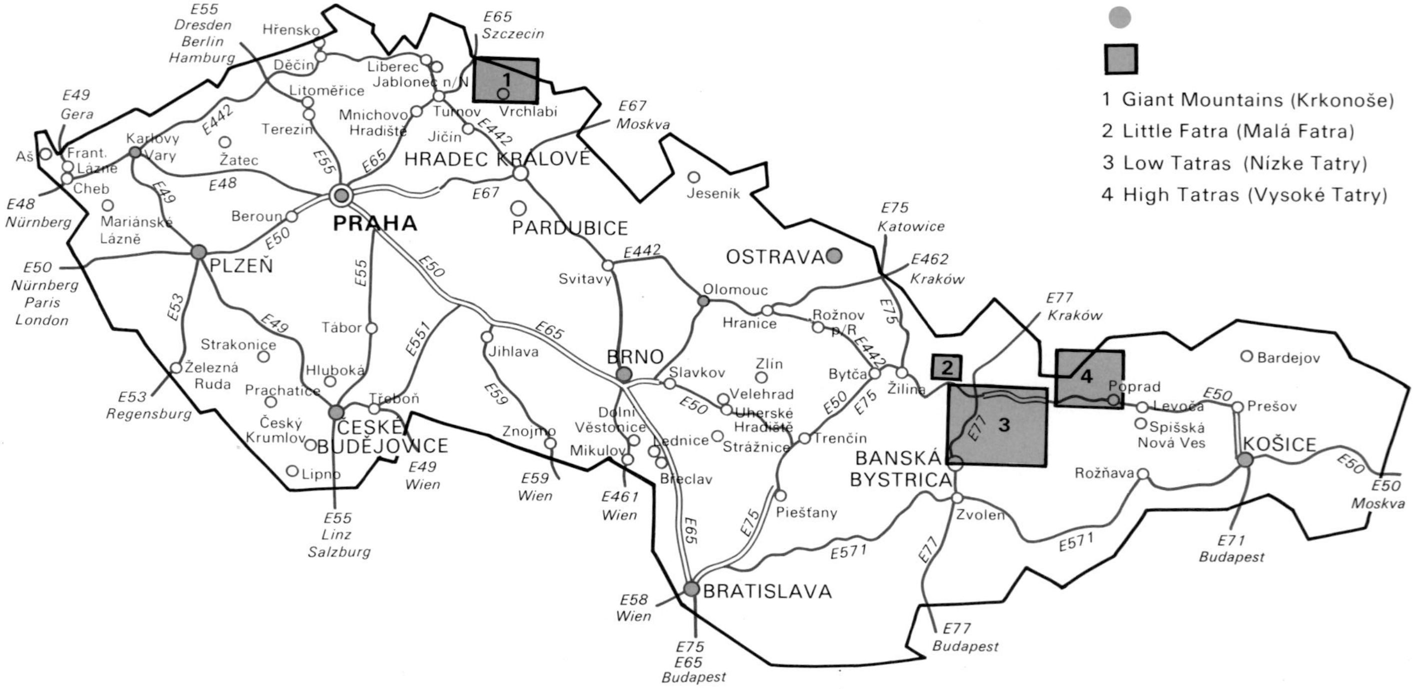

INTRODUCTION

The country we know today as Czechoslovakia first appeared on the maps of Europe after the Treaty of Versailles in 1918. Until then the Czech lands of Bohemia and Moravia had been under Austrian rule, while Slovakia had belonged to Hungary. Nationhood was short-lived in the painful, miserable years of the Depression. In 1938 Britain and France agreed to Hitler's demands for the Sudetenlands bordering Germany in return for peace — the notorious 'Peace in our time'. It was not to be. In March 1939 Hitler invaded Czechoslovakia and overran Bohemia and Moravia, granting Slovakia a measure of independence. The Czechs were treated harshly. When their Resistance assassinated the head of the German government, Heydrich, the Nazis retaliated by executing all the men in the village of Lidice and razing it to the ground.

Hitler invades

In 1942, disillusioned by Chamberlain's disastrous policy of appeasement towards the fascist powers, the Czechoslovak government in exile signed a treaty of friendship with the USSR. In 1945 it was Soviet forces who liberated Prague from the Germans, the Americans being prohibited from entering Czechoslovakia by the

Charles Bridge, Prague, its sculptures forming an open-air gallery

Opposite: a winter scene in the beautiful Šumava mountains

Treaty of Yalta. There then followed a half-hearted attempt at multi-party democracy, but the Communist Party soon gained the upper hand and by 1948 held the reins of power. With support from Moscow it ruled with an iron fist, stifling all opposition within its own ranks and in society at large. All non-idealogically-sound thoughts and ideas were forced underground and the economy was converted into a gigantic foundry to supply Moscow and its satellites with machinery for their factories.

Death of Stalin

Even after the death of the Party supremo Klement Gottwald and his political mentor Josef Stalin in 1953, the Czechoslovak Communist Party's consolidation of power continued unabated and unchallenged. In 1960 the new constitution reaffirmed its dominant role as the champion of Marxist-Leninism in Czechoslovak society.

Alexander Dubček

The tide began to turn in the 1960s when a new generation of young intellectuals started to question whether Czechoslovakia was on the right track. Economic failures also provoked debate within the Party. In 1967 Antonín Novotný resigned as Party leader and Alexander Dubček took his place. Dubček represented the reformist wing and championed its manifesto of reforms, the Action Programme, published in April 1968, in what has since become known as the 'Prague Spring'. Dubček wanted 'socialism with a human face' – Moscow did not.

1968

Fearful that liberalization might be contagious, Warsaw Pact forces entered Czechoslovakia that August. The liberals were disgraced and exiled while Dubček was posted to an ignominious job in the forestry department. Once again the country was subjugated to Moscow's rule.

Charter 77

In the next 20 years while the economy continued to stagnate, the seeds sown in the Prague Spring began to germinate, especially among the intellectuals. Soon they had a mouthpiece, the playwright Václav Havel. In 1975 he courageously wrote an open letter to Dubček's successor, Gustáv Husák, pointing out that the country was entering a terminal decline and that reforms were urgently needed to prevent disaster. The following year Havel was a founder of Charter 77, a group which openly opposed the abuse of human rights in Czechoslovakia. Instead of sparking off a dialogue, the Charter's signatories themselves became victims of Husák's repressive regime. Havel received a four-year prison sentence, others were exiled or lost their jobs.

THE VELVET REVOLUTION

In the 1980s the rise of Solidarity in Poland and the arrival of Gorbachev in Moscow boosted the dissidents' morale, as did Havel's nomination for the Nobel Peace Prize. Spurred on by Moscow – and unnerved by the collapse of the Communist Party in East Germany and Bulgaria – the Czechoslovak government adopted a more conciliatory stance, no longer turning a deaf ear to the pleas for reform and liberalization. But it was too late. On November 17, 1989 a student march in Prague developed into a huge anti-government demonstration in Wenceslas Square. The Communist Party felt the reins of power slipping away but there was little they could do. In desperation riot police were called in, with bloody results. Further marches followed and on November 19 an alliance of dissident groups, Civic Forum, was formed. In Slovakia a like-minded association was organised, Public Against Violence. Reforms and resignations were demanded from the government. Strikes and further demonstrations followed throughout the country. The government began to bow under the pressure; the crowds continued to gather, their demands growing louder hour by hour. Within days the Communists had been ousted from the seats of power and their places occupied by members of Civic Forum. The Party had been toppled and Havel was elected president. The 'gentle' or 'velvet revolution' – so called because it was a relatively peaceful operation compared to the bloodier uprisings in other East European countries – had triumphed.

Protest marches

Communists ousted

The early 1990s finds Czechoslovakia sound in heart but poor in body, and no one, not least the Czechoslovaks themselves, underestimates the tricky path ahead as they open their doors to comparatively wealthy Western consumers and more efficient and technologically advanced businesses. However Czechoslovakia is in a favourable position compared to other Eastern European countries, certainly as regards travel and tourism, and has the will and ability to forge the way ahead.

VISITORS' PARADISE

Czechoslovakia's scenery remains spectacular, despite the sulphurous emissions of its antiquated factories making it one of the most polluted countries in Europe. The lowlands of the majestic Danube valley give way to the towering peaks of the awe-inspiring Tatra Mountains of Slovakia, snow-clad in winter, covered in alpine flowers in summer. Nearly a third of the country is forest – though pollution is threatening thousands of trees – where you stand a good chance of seeing animals virtually extinct in other parts of Europe – bears and boars, wolves, lynx and foxes are just a selection. Among the forests are lakes and fast-flowing rivers teeming with fish to tempt the angler. There are fascinating caves and oddly shaped sandstone rock formations to visit, as well as bubbling mudpools and jetting geysers. Lovers of fairy-tale castles will not be

Lush forests

disappointed either – there are thousands of them, ranging from decrepit ruins to proudly restored majestic monuments with impressive museums.

Prague

And then of course there's Prague, the 'golden city', the jewel in the crown of Charles IV, who made it the capital of western Europe in the Middle Ages. Many refer to Prague as the most beautiful city they have ever visited and after a few hours' wandering among its narrow streets, it's easy to see why. The modern suburbs are an ugly concrete sprawl, but the historic centre retains its centuries-old charm and takes you a step back in time.

Czechoslovakia really does offer something for everyone – from the culture-vulture in search of opera and all things baroque and the battered soul in need of rest and recuperation at a hilltop spa, to the outdoor enthusiast – walker, climber, camper, angler or sailor – yearning for the open air and the inquisitive traveller merely in need of a cultural jolt.

Children enjoying the annual folk festival at Strážnice

FACTS AND FIGURES

CLIMATE

Although Czechoslovakia has four distinct seasons, its weather is as unpredictable as that of any other European country. Summers are generally warm and winters cold, with spring and autumn mild to chilly. Daytime temperatures in Prague can reach 32°C (the high 80°sF) in July and August, while in January they hover just above freezing, plunging well below at night. Southern Slovakia is the warmest area, the mountains the wettest and coldest with plenty of snow falling in winter for skiing. In the resorts of the Tatra Mountains, it's 12° to 15°C (54° to 60°F), higher up it averages 4°C (40°F).

Prague temperatures

These are average maximum temperatures. In winter it can get much colder, so be prepared.

January	1°C	(34° F)
February	3° C	(37° F)
March	3° C	(37° F)
April	13° C	(55° F)
May	18° C	(64° F)
June	22° C	(72° F)
July	25° C	(77° F)
August	25° C	(77° F)
September	18° C	(64° F)
October	12° C	(54° F)
November	5° C	(41° F)
December	1° C	(34° F)

Krkonoše (Giant) Mountains — perfect for skiing

Striking houses in Pařížská St, Prague, with the tower of the Old Town Hall

In December, January and February be prepared for freezing temperatures and treacherous snow and ice underfoot. Warm clothing should also be taken for the chilly months in spring and autumn. Light clothing is needed for summer – July and August are the hottest months. Remember that temperatures are lower in the mountains throughout the year and it can get cold even in summer, so take a sweater and a wind- and rain-proof jacket to be on the safe side.

HEALTH

Free treatment

No special injections or precautions are needed. There is a reciprocal health-care agreement between Britain and Czechoslovakia so medical treatment is free for British travellers, but prescribed medicines have to be paid for. DSS Form E111 is not required as treatment will be provided on production of a British passport. Even so it's advisable to take out a comprehensive insurance policy covering medical problems in case of an emergency which

Many rivers flow through the beautiful forests of Šumava

requires you being flown home. Throughout the country the telephone number for emergency medical aid is 155. Pharmacies (*lékárna*) can be found in all major towns, addresses are listed in Part II of this guide.

TIME

Clocks change

One hour ahead of British standard and summer time. Six hours ahead of American Eastern time. Clocks go forward one hour on the last Saturday in March and back an hour on the final Saturday of September.

ELECTRICITY

220V AC, 50 cycles. Most plugs are different from British and North American ones although the better hotels have two-pin razor sockets. Light bulbs have a screw-in fitting.

MONEY

Notes and coins

The local currency is the Koruna, abbreviated to Kčs. One Koruna is divided into 100 hellers. There are 1000, 500, 100, 50, 20 and 10 Kčs notes and 10, 5, 2 and 1 Kčs coins. Hellers are coins of 50, 20, 10 and 5. At the moment the Koruna is not a 'hard' currency – that is it cannot be brought into or taken out of the country and cannot be exchanged abroad.

Credit cards are not widely used outside tourist haunts. Access, Visa, Diners Club, American Express and

Japan Credit Bureau cards are accepted by hotels and Tuzex shops (duty-free shops which only accept foreign currency) and by large stores and restaurants in Prague.

Travellers' cheques

Travellers' cheques are accepted by exchange bureaux, hotels and banks. Foreign exchanges are widespread – in most hotels, banks and travel agencies. Many private ones are now springing up too. The majority shut at weekends but at border crossings and Prague airport they are open 24 hours. Banks are open Mon to Fri 08.00 - 14.00.

Sending money

If you need to get money to someone in Czechoslovakia the best way is to telex it to Československá obchodní banka, Na příkopě St 14, 115 20 Prague. Telex: 066 12 22 01.

Prices

The following prices will give you an idea of the cost of living – definitely cheap at the moment. They are, of course, subject to fluctuation upwards, possibly dramatically and at short notice. Three-course meal 150 Kčs, glass of beer 10 Kčs, glass of wine 15 Kčs, cup of coffee 10 Kčs, 20 cigarettes 14 Kčs, public transport in Prague 4 Kčs, theatre ticket 50 Kčs.

SHOPPING

Food shops are open 06.00 - 18.00, sometimes until 21.00 or 22.00, in the week, 06.00 - 12.00 on Saturdays. Others open 09.00 - 19.00 (shut 12.00 - 14.00) on weekdays, 08.00 - 12.00 on Saturdays. Department stores open 09.00 - 19.00 in the week, 08.00 - 13.00 on Saturdays. Most shops are closed on Sundays, although some baker's and food shops open in the morning. Supermarkets are a rarity but

A lovely preserved pharmacy in Bratislava

The Old Town Square, Prague. Look out for the pottery in the market

there are plenty of self-service shops. The prices of certain basic foods are fixed by the government but even these are being affected by inflation.

Cut glass, china, pottery, leather items (typical price of a woman's jacket is 5000 Kčs), books, records and CDs are all good value but style and quality are not up to Western standards. Note that you can only export 1000 Kčs worth of things (Tuzex goods excepted) before paying duty. If in doubt, check with Čedok.

Foreign currency shops

Tuzex are a chain of shops which only accept credit cards and foreign currency. They stock top-quality Czechoslovak and imported goods not available elsewhere. All are sold duty-free so there is no limit to what you can take home with you.

TELEPHONE

Local calls cost 1 Kčs from a payphone. Lift the receiver, insert the money and dial the number. For international calls, you can dial direct to many countries including Britain (code from Prague 0044) and North America (code from Prague 01142).

Phoning home

Phoning home from a main post office or telegraph office is much cheaper than from your hotel. Post offices are open Mon to Fri 8.00 - 18.00, 08.00 - 12.00 on Saturday. Telephone and telegraph offices are open longer, often 24 hours. There are international payphones in the centre of Prague. For international enquiries for Britain and North America dial 0132.

MAIL

Poste Restante

Mail can be sent Poste Restante to any main post office. If you don't know the address, simply add 'Posta 1' above the destination town or city. It's a good idea to print or underline the receiver's name. American Express in Prague (in the Čedok office, Na příkopě St 18, tel: (02) 22 42 51) will keep letters for cardholders or people using their traveller's cheques for one month free of charge.

THEFT

This is increasingly a problem, especially in Prague. Police HQ (VB, Konviktská 14, Staré Město) should be informed of any thefts or losses and a copy of their report kept if you're making an insurance claim. Throughout the country the police emergency number is 158.

TOILETS

Lavatories are marked WC or OO. Women's toilets are *Dámy* or *Ženy*; men's *Páni* or *Muži*.

LANGUAGE

There are two official languages — Czech, spoken in Bohemia and Moravia and Slovak, spoken in Slovakia. Czechs and Slovaks understand each other, so any Czech words you pick up can be used in Slovakia and vice versa. The languages of neighbouring countries are also spoken in the borderlands. German is widely understood and spoken. English is not but this is changing as it is now taught in schools. See page 200 for some useful phrases.

Dictionaries

It's worthwhile investing in a phrase book or dictionary. A comprehensive Czech-English, English-Czech dictionary is published by Bradt Publications, 41 Nortoft Road, Chalfont St Peter, Buckinghamshire SL9 0LA (in the USA by Hippocrene Books Inc, 171 Madison Avenue, New York, NY 10016). *Traveller's Czech* by M. Sova and English-Czech and Czech-English dictionaries by Hais and Poldauf can be bought in Čedok offices and bookshops in Czechoslovakia and abroad.

Learning the language

Most English-speaking people find Czech a difficult language to learn, but if you want a challenge, try *Czech for English-speaking Students* by M. Sára, J. Sárová and A. Bytel available from Čedok or Collets, Denington Estate, Wellingborough, Northamptonshire NN8 2QT. *Colloquial Czech* by James Naughton (Routledge - book and accompanying cassette) and *Teach Yourself Czech* (Linguaphone/Teach Yourself Books) could also help. There are no books teaching Slovak yet.

Courses The Polytechnic of Central London, 9-18 Euston Centre, London NWl 3ET, tel: (071) 911 5000, runs courses in Czech and the University of London's School of East European and Slavonic Studies, Senate House, Malet Street, London WClE 7HU, tel: (071) 636 8000, has courses in Czech and Slovak.

BACKGROUND READING

Pre-revolution books

The Double Eagle by Stephen Brook (Pan).
Utz by Bruce Chatwin (Cape (h/b), Pan (p/b).
Life with a Star by Jiří Weil (Collins (h/b), Fontana (p/b).

Post-revolution books

The Uses of Adversity and *We the People: The Revolution of 89* both by Timothy Garton Ash (Granta).
The Rebirth of History: Eastern Europe in the Age of Democracy by Misha Glenny (Penguin).
The Times Guide to Eastern Europe edited by Keith Sword (Times Books).

BUSINESS MATTERS

The economy In the inter-war years Czechoslovakia had one of the strongest economies in Europe. Since then a combination of poor management, inadequate investment and energy inefficiency has left it weakened. Since the 'velvet revolution' the government has committed itself to joining the European Community and to introducing a free market economy, with full currency convertibility planned for 1993. **Help needed** The government is currently seeking foreign assistance in metallurgy, electronics and electrotechnics, chemicals, environmental pollution control, energy (efficiency and control of waste), health care, science and technology, transport and communications, agriculture, nutrition. The many trade fairs and exhibitions which take place in Czechoslovakia throughout the year provide opportunities for making important contacts. Help can be provided by the Czechoslovak Chamber of Commerce and Industry (Argentinská 38, 170 05, Prague 7) which is compiling a database of all new businesses and organizations within Czechoslovakia.

EMBASSIES AND CONSULATES

Britain Embassy of Czechoslovakia, 28 Kensington Palace Gardens, London W8 4QY.

USA Embassy of Czechoslovakia, 3900 Linnean Avenue NW, Washington DC 20008.

The lovely Gothic interior of St Vitus' Cathedral, Prague

SETTING OFF

New deals

Travel to Czechoslovakia has improved greatly since the revolution, particularly as far as flights and package holidays are concerned. But remember that it's a rapidly changing scene and new deals and holiday ideas are likely to be introduced in the next few years.

VISAS

Every visitor needs a full passport which will be valid for three months after entry into Czechoslovakia. Following the relaxation of entry requirements in the autumn of 1990 American, Canadian and British passport holders do not need a visa.

ČEDOK

Information

The Czechoslovak Travel Bureau, Čedok, is a useful first port of call for up-to-date information on holidays and travel in Czechoslovakia. It has offices/representatives in most capital cities. As well as operating its own package holidays (see the section on Tours) it can help independent travellers with advice on itineraries and by booking accommodation, flights and excursions. Within Czechoslovakia Čedok owns many hotels and has offices in all major towns and cities which organize a wide range of trips and book guides, tickets and hotel reservations.

Britain

Čedok, 17-18 Old Bond Street, London W1X 4RB. Tel: (071) 491 9180.

USA

Čedok, 10 East 40th Street, New York, 10116. Tel: (212) 689 9720.

BY AIR

From London

The national airline, ČSA Czechoslovak Airlines (12A Margaret Street, London W1N 7LF. Tel: (071) 255 1366/1898. Fax: (071) 323 1633) and British Airways (156 Regent Street, London W1R 5TA. Tel: (071) 434 4606) operate a direct two-hour flight to Prague.They cost £422 (£502 Club/Business Class). PEX and APEX fares are cheaper, less flexible and carry heavy penalties for cancellation and alterations to travel arrangements. The PEX return fare is £222. An APEX return costs £194. Discounted APEX tickets are available from bucket shops and travel agents.

From the USA

ČSA flies twice weekly from New York to Prague.

A return business class ticket will cost about $2000, an APEX fare around $700. The cheapest way is to take advantage of any special tickets on offer to London or another European city and to carry on to Czechoslovakia from there by air or train.

Franz's Spring at Františkovy Lázně — one of 24 mineral springs in this popular spa town

BY TRAIN

Czechoslovakia is connected to the rest of Europe's international rail network with regular services. From London there's a daily train from Victoria Station via Paris to Prague's Hlavní nádraží station. It crosses the Channel between Folkestone and Boulogne and sleepers can be booked for the Paris-Prague section of the journey. An adult single costs £119 and a return £182 (valid for two months) – both allow you to break your journey. If you are under 26 there is a youth return fare of £145 (£82 single). Currently there are no reductions for people over 60 on this journey. For information on youth and student fares contact Eurotrain, 52 Grosvenor Gardens, London SWl 0AG, tel: (071) 730 3402 or Wastells Travel, 121 Wilton Road, London SWlV 1JZ, tel: (071) 834 7066.

Inter-Rail

Anyone taking in Czechoslovakia on their grand tour of Europe can cut costs with an Inter-Rail card. It covers unlimited rail travel in 24 countries in Europe and North Africa for one calendar month, along with good discounts on rail travel in Britain and Northern Ireland and on cross-Channel ferries and hovercrafts. It costs £175 and can be bought at main railway stations and some travel agents by anyone under 26 who has been living in Britain or Northern Ireland for at least six months. Anyone under 26, full-time students, teachers, academics and

Eurotrain

accompanying spouses and children can now get Eurotrain passes for Czechoslovakia as well as most other European countries (including Hungary and Poland). The Czechoslovak Explorer pass costs £18.50 (£26.50 for first class) and is valid for one week's unlimited travel on all trains. It's available from student travel offices, High Street travel agents or direct from Eurotrain, 52 Grosvenor Gardens, London SWlW 0AG. Tel: (071) 730 8518.

Timetables for the railways within Czechoslovakia are available from BAS Overseas Publications, 48-50 Sheen Lane, London SW14 8LP. Tel: (081) 876 2131.

BY CAR

London to Prague is about 1300km (807 miles). The easiest way is to cross the Channel between Dover and Ostend and head for Nuremberg via Brussels, Cologne and Frankfurt. The E50 from Nuremberg goes to Prague via Plzeň. Take your driving licence and vehicle registration document with you, together with a 'green card' from your insurance company. Vehicles without a green card have to pay an insurance premium at the border– currently 50 Kčs per month for a motorbike, 250 Kčs for a car. For more detailed information on driving within Czechoslovakia see **On the move** p 21.

Green card

Ski lift on Mount Chopok, Low Tatras

BY COACH

There are regular coach services between Czechoslovakia and its neighbours. From Vienna, for instance, they go every day to Bratislava and Brno.

BY BICYCLE

No extra charge

Most airlines will carry your bike for no extra charge provided you are within your baggage allowance (check with them beforehand; also on how you should prepare your bike for the flight). Most European rail networks transport bikes free of charge or for a small fee.

BY BOAT

A daily hydrofoil service operates from April to October between Vienna and Bratislava. The journey takes about an hour. Further information from Čedok, 17-18 Old Bond Street, London WlX 4RB. Tel: (071) 491 9180.

SPECIAL INTEREST HOLIDAYS

Czechoslovakia has a bit of everything. If you want an active trip there are plenty of opportunities for winter sports, walking, climbing, caving, watersports, hunting and fishing. If it's a slower pace you're after you can find rest and recuperation in a health spa.

Winter sports

Ski resorts are springing up all the time in Czechoslovakia but the facilities and skiing – both downhill and cross-country – are particularly good at Štrbské Pleso, Starý Smokovec and Tatranská Lomnica in the Tatra Mountains of Slovakia and Špindlerův Mlýn in the Krkonoše (Giant) Mountains of Bohemia. These resorts have instructors, equipment hire, lifts and good hotels. At the moment prices are reasonable.

Walking

Czechoslovakia must come close to being a walker's paradise – it can literally be crossed from west to east without ever having to go down into the valley. Countless miles of marked paths lead you through spectacular scenery, from the alpine beauty of the High Tatras to the more difficult routes of the Low Tatras, from the deep forests of the Šumava mountain range to the naked ridges of the Krkonoše (Giant) Mountains, from the canyons of the Slovenský Raj (Slovak Paradise) to the rocky Malá Fatra. Long-distance hikes can be planned around the network of campsites, hostels and self-catering huts.

Climbing

The Tatra Mountains, the highest in the country, offer the best all-year alpine climbing on ice and rock in Czechoslovakia while the sandstone rocks in North Bohemia offer more difficult routes and the Pálava region of South Moravia and the Malá Fatra have plenty of challenging limestone faces. You must have a valid membership card from a climbing club or you'll need a guide – the more difficult the climb, the higher the price. In protected regions, nature reserves and national parks in Slovakia a guide is obligatory. Make sure you have insurance which covers emergency help from the mountain rescue service.

Caving

If you're into caves, then there's lots for you to do in Czechoslovakia. Many caves have guided tours for the public through such wonders as the spectacular Dobšinská ice cavern in East Slovakia, the Demänovské caves in the Low Tatras, Domica in the Slovenský Kras and various systems in the Moravský Kras near Brno. You need permission to explore the many other cave systems on your own and must be a member of a caving club. Consult Čedok on how to go about it.

Watersports

Considering Czechoslovakia is a land-locked country there are incredible opportunities for watersports fans. Canoeists can enjoy paddling beautiful rivers of all grades of difficulty including the Otava, Lužnice, Sázava and Vltava in Bohemia and the Hornád, Hron and Váh in Slovakia. Throughout the country the many rivers, lakes and reservoirs offer opportunities not only for canoeing but also for swimming, windsurfing and sailing.

Hunting

Hunting, a centuries-old tradition, is expensive and only for the dedicated rather than the happy-go-lucky tourist. Licences and insurance are compulsory, as are a string of other charges and bureaucratic requirements. Further details from Čedok in London (address on p. 19) for hunting in Bohemia and Moravia, Tatratour for Slovakia, Zahradnická 34, 821 08 Bratislava.

Fishing

Anglers require a fistful of documents including an official fishing card, a fishing permit and a list for recording their catch for statistical purposes. Having acquired them all (Čedok will help, address on p. 19), there are carp, pike, trout, chub, grayling and bream to be caught in the rivers and lakes.

Spas

Visiting health spas has become a way of life for many Czechoslovaks and is now an attraction for increasing numbers of foreigners. Poor blood circulation, what's quaintly referred to as 'women's problems' and all manner of nervous, respiratory and abdominal disorders are dealt with using hydrotherapy, electrotherapy, mud baths and, perhaps not for the squeamish, 'subcutaneous gas injections'. All-inclusive packages can be arranged through Čedok or BALNEA Spa and Travel Service, Pařížská St 11, 110 01 Prague 1.

TOUR OPERATORS

In Britain

Brochures and information for the following companies who offer a wide variety of package tours (weekend breaks, walking tours, special interest trips etc) should be

The caves of the Moravský Kras are quite spectacular

available from most high street travel agents. Failing this write or phone the head offices of the relevant companies who will be able to put you on the right track.
Čedok, 17-18 Old Bond Street, London WlX 4RB. Tel: (071) 491 9180.
Thomas Cook/Travelscene, 11-15 St Ann's Road, Harrow, Middlesex HA1 1AS. Tel: (081) 427 8800.
Cosmos/Tourama, Tourama House, 17 Homesdale Road, Bromley, Kent BR9 9LX. Tel: (081) 464 3444.
Explore Worldwide Ltd, 1 Frederick Street, Aldershot, Hampshire GU11 1LQ. Tel: (0252) 319448.

Adventure travel

Simon Hayman, who has written and travelled widely throughout Czechoslovakia, is planning to lead small groups of more adventurous people to the parts other tour operators fail to reach. Contact 41 Nortoft Road, Chalfont St Peter, Buckinghamshire SL9 0LA.
Page & Moy Travel Ltd, 136-140 London Road, Leicester LE2 1EN. Tel: (0533) 552521.
Peltours, 156 Oxford Street, London W1N 9DL. Tel: (081) 346 9144.
Progressive Tours, 12 Porchester Place, London W2 2BS. Tel: (071) 262 1676.
Ramblers Holidays Ltd, Longcroft House, Fretherne Road, Welwyn Garden City, Herts. AL8 6PQ. Tel: (0707) 331133.
W H Smith Travel, 9 Havelock Square, Swindon SN1 1LE. Tel: (0793) 531992, or your high street shop.

Sovereign Holidays, Groundstar House, London Road, Crawley, West Sussex RH10 2TB. Tel: (0293) 560777.

In the USA
Dailey-Thorp Travel, 315 West 57th Street, New York, NY 10019. Tel: (212) 307 1555. (Exclusive tours for music buffs.)
ETS Tours Inc., Box 1568, 450 Harmon Meadows Boulevard, Secaucus, NJ 07096-1568. Tel: (800) 346 6314.
Globus-Gateway/Cosmos, 95 Queens Boulevard, New York, NY 10022. Tel: (212) 223 177.
Health and Pleasure Tours Inc., 165 West 46th Street, New York, NY 10036. Tel: (212) 586 1775. (Health spa holidays.)
Orbis, the Polish national tourist body, 500 Fifth Avenue, New York, NY 10110. Tel: (212) 391 0844.
Travcoa, 4000 MacArthur Boulevard, Suite 650E, Newport Beach, CA 92660. Tel: (800) 992 2003.
Hemphill Harris Travel Corp., 16000 Ventura Boulevard, Encino, CA 91436. Tel: (818) 906 8086.

WHAT'S ON WHEN

The major sports and cultural events are listed below. More detailed information is available from Čedok.

January
Bohemia ski jump championship, Harrachov and Liberec.
Jizerská padesátka, a huge 50km (31 miles) cross-country skiing race. It starts in Bedřichov.

May
Festival of children's films, Zlín.

June
Olomouc Flower Festival.
Barum Car Rally, Zlín.
International TV festival, Prague.
Strážnice folk festival, June/July.
Terchová folk festival, near Žilina (last weekend in June).
Hungarian folk festival in Gombasek (near Rožňava), last weekend in June.
Festival of Ukranian workers, Svidník, 3rd or 4th weekend in June.

July
Music festival, Bratislava.
Východná folk festival.

August
Chopin festival, Mariánské Lázně.
Open tennis tournament, Prague.
Jánošík Days festival, Terchová, Malá Fatra.
Motorcycle Grand Prix, Brno.

September
Flora Olomouc, flower festival.
Children's TV festival, Bratislava.
International music festival, Brno.

October
Grand Pardubice steeplechase horse race, Pardubice.

ON THE MOVE

Public transport

There is a good, reliable, inexpensive public transport system throughout the country which makes life easy for the independent traveller. The rail network is extensive and its fares low but the carriages are basic and always crowded. Long distance buses are plentiful too but are usually full and more expensive than the train. For both it's best to reserve seats as far ahead as possible, especially for long journeys. There's a very good domestic air service linking all the main cities with regular flights. If you're planning on driving, you'll find the roads are usually in good condition and outside the main centres the traffic is light. There's only one motorway which connects Prague, Brno and Bratislava.

The Singing Fountain, Mariánské Lázně — listen to the music play

BY AIR

Internal flights are operated by Czechoslovak Airlines (ČSA) from their home-base at Prague's Ruzyně airport to Banská Bystrica (Sliač), Bratislava, Košice, Ostrava, Piešťany and Poprad-Tatry; also services to Brno and Karlovy Vary during the summer season. There are ČSA booking offices in all these cities. Availability and prices are currently subject to change so do check locally. Further information from Čedok in Prague or ČSA Revoluční St 25, Prague. Tel: (02) 23 17 39 5.

Fares

Sample fares from Prague are Bratislava 620 Kčs, Košice 800 Kčs, Ostrava 580 Kcs, Poprad-Tatry 720 Kčs.

BY BUS

Remote villages

Buses serve even the most remote mountain villages – wherever the road goes, the bus follows. Most of the routes are operated by the state bus company ČSAD but on some of the long distance journeys private firms such as ČEBUS in Prague are starting to compete. The buses are basic but comfortable. Tickets are normally bought from the driver but reservations can be made for some journeys. Consult Čedok.

BY CAR

You drive on the right as in the rest of continental Europe. Keep to the right except when overtaking. The maximum speed limit for cars is 60 kph (37 mph) in built-up areas, 90 kph (56 mph) outside them and 110 kph (68 mph) on the motorway. Motorbikes are restricted to 80 kph (50 mph) and must keep their headlights on all the time. Radar checks are common with on-the-spot fines of up to 500 Kčs for offenders. Use dipped headlights, not sidelights, in poor visibility. At crossroads give way to traffic from the right. Don't enter bus lanes and always wait behind a tram when it's at a stop.

Drunk driving

It's a severe offence to drink any alcohol and drive with heavy penalties if you're caught. Seat belts are compulsory in the front seats outside built-up areas. Children under 12 must travel in the back. You must not stop in the following places: before the brow of a hill; within 5m (16ft) of a pedestrian crossing; before intersections; before bus or tram stations without a safety zone; on bridges; within 15m (50 ft) of a level crossing; within 3.5m (11.5ft) of tram rails.

Petrol

The price of petrol and diesel is fixed and they're only available through state-owned petrol stations. However all this could change if privatization creeps into the system. Petrol is sold as Special (90 octane) or Super (96 octane); unleaded is also available although it's not widespread – it becomes rarer the further east you go. Čedok has a list of the towns with unleaded garages. The quality of fuel is better at motorway services than elsewhere. Foreigners can buy petrol and diesel coupons which are meant to give a discount on prices, but at the time of writing it's cheaper to pay cash at the pumps! Note however that diesel can only be bought by coupon. The coupon price of a gallon of petrol is £2, while Czechoslovaks pay 18 Kčs a litre for Super – the equivalent of £1.56 a gallon. Coupons are available from the Živnostenská Bank in London (18 King William Street, London EC4N 7BY, tel: (071) 283 3333), at border crossings, from major banks in Czechoslovakia and Tuzex (foreign currency) shops.

Where roads go buses follow — through a deep gorge in the Malá Fatra

On the motorway and major roads there's usually a 24-hour filling station every 50km (31 miles) or so, where you can buy motor accessories such as oil and snacks. Most garages shut at night so fill up your tank before setting out and top it up where you can.

Autoturist will come to your help if you break down or are involved in an accident. The phone number of their nearest office is available from garages and police stations (look for the sign VB) or from the Autoturist offices at Limuzská St. Prague, tel: (02) 77 34 55 (24 hour) or Halášova St, Bratislava, tel: (07) 21 54 59/24 40 13. There are SOS phones on the motorway and throughout the country you can get assistance by phoning 154.

Car repairs

Owners of a Škoda, Lada, Renault, Fiat and VW in a town should have no problem in finding a garage to fix their cars. Except when major surgery is needed, spares are available. Others will have to rely on a mechanic's intuition until other makes become more widespread. Čedok can tell you where the garages are.

Roads

By and large the roads are good with internationally recognised signs. The motorway is toll-free. Note that lorries are banned from travelling on the motorway and dual-carriage highways Friday afternoon, Saturday morning and Sunday afternoon. Even so roads into and out of Prague and other major cities clog up at weekends. Parking is a problem in Prague (information on p. 65).

Car hire

Car hire can be arranged through Pragocar which has an office in all the large towns and cities or through Brnocar which operates only in Moravia. Once again things are on the move and private firms are springing up all over the place but they tend to have only small cars such as the Škoda Favorit or Lada. Pragocar has a wide range including Opel Kadetts and Omegas and Renault 21s and Trafic minibuses. Rental varies from the equivalent of £16-£35 per day plus 16-35 pence per km travelled. Per week it's £99-£207 or £196-392 for unlimited mileage. You pay in foreign currency.

BY TRAIN

The rail network is run by the state railway ČSD and the bulk is electrified. It's as comfortable as any other system in Europe but much in demand, so try to book ahead especially at weekends and in holiday periods

Booking

Express and fast trains have first and second class accommodation including sleepers and couchettes on the longer routes, as well as restaurant cars. Most of the compartments are non-smoking. There's a 16 Kčs surcharge for these trains, first class is 50 per cent extra. Advance reservation costs a further 4 Kčs. Tickets can be booked at any major station as they are all linked by computer – look for the sign saying *místenka*. Sleepers should be booked through Čedok. First class costs 80 Kčs, second class 50 Kčs and couchettes 30 Kčs. Ordinary trains are exclusively second class and all their compartments are non-smoking. They cannot be booked in advance, nor do they have any sleepers.

Fares

Fares are very reasonable. Tickets are usually valid only for a day. However for journeys of more than 200km (124 miles), they're valid for three days which means you can have a stopover en route. All the major stations usually have a waiting-room, left-luggage office and a snackbar or restaurant. Note that some left-luggage offices have a weight limit of 15 kg (33lbs), which may be a problem for backpackers.

Left luggage

If you have to use a left-luggage locker, be prepared for the combination locks. You set your own numbers on the inside, close the door and revolve the knobs on the outside. Don't forget to write down the combination you've chosen because when you return you have to set the numbers on the outside to open the door. Lapses of memory will cost you 20 Kčs.

BY BIKE

Country roads

Czechoslovakia is not geared up for the cycling tourist. Bike lanes/paths are almost unheard of so it's no fun in the cities but the country roads have little traffic and plenty of refreshment stops. Most trains take bikes.

BY THUMB

In Czechoslovakia the thumb is replaced by a more assertive downward flap of the arm with an open palm facing the traffic. As ever lifts are unpredictable. Country roads tend to be easier than the major highways and getting into a town or city is much easier than trying to escape from it. Women hitchers should have no problems.

LOCAL TRANSPORT

Public transport is provided by trams and buses while Prague has an underground as well. Tickets cost 2-4 Kčs per journey and must be bought before boarding at a PNS (newsagent's) kiosk. You need a separate ticket for each journey and make it valid by punching it in a machine by the door. Travelling without a ticket is illegal and you'll

A Prague tram trundles over cobbled streets

be fined on the spot, irrespective of nationality. Tickets are only usable in the town of issue.

Taxis

Taxi numbers have been increasing recently but in the smaller towns they're still rare. All the cities and major towns have at least one radio-cab firm which a hotel or restaurant can contact for you. There are also taxi stands outside most major railway stations, in town centres and near the nightlife areas. Passing taxis can also be hailed in the street – unoccupied ones will usually have an illuminated sign. Fares vary but should be in the region of 4-8 Kčs per km. In tourist areas drivers may try to fleece you – meters may be mysteriously out of order or 'accidentally' not turned on. At night it's a good idea to check how much a journey will cost in advance. Don't worry about haggling!

TRAVEL FOR THE HANDICAPPED

Facilities are rare and extremely limited. Wheelchair-bound travellers will be particularly hard hit. There have even been reports of downright hostility from some officials when help has been requested.

WOMEN TRAVELLING ALONE

Czechoslovak men generally treat women with great courtesy so it's unlikely solo travellers will have any

Be alert

problems. Nevertheless it pays to be alert as there have been reports of single women travellers being harassed at night by drunks, especially in Prague and Bratislava.

ACCOMMODATION

There's a wide choice – hotels in all price ranges, camp–sites, hostels, mountain chalets and private homes. Even so rooms are much in demand, especially during the height of the summer season in popular locations such as Prague, the Krkonoše (Giant) Mountains, Bratislava and the resorts of the High Tatra Mountains.

Booking ahead

It's advisable to book hotels as far ahead as possible. You can contact your choice direct – many hotels now have a fax facility (see the respective city or town entries). Otherwise you can book through Čedok for a £15 fee or other travel agencies (their head offices are listed under Prague). Čedok will also give you a list of hotels with their addresses and phone numbers.

Hotels are divided into five categories - see p. (vii) for how these are represented in this guide.

Private lodging

Lodging with a family in Prague (minimum stay of 3 nights) costs £10.70 per person for a double and £13 for a single room, inclusive of a voucher for breakfast at a local restaurant. Contact Pragotour, U obecního domu 2, 110 00 Prague 1 and Toptour, Rybná 3, 110 00, Prague 1.

The ski resort of St Peter in the Krkonoše (Giant) Mountains

CKM (Cestovní Kancelář Mládeže/the Youth Travel Bureau) has accommodation for students and young people in high standard hotels, campsites and hostels. It caters for groups and independent travellers. Groups of more than five people should make a reservation as far ahead as possible through the CKM office in the region where they plan to stay (addresses under individual towns and cities in Part II). Individuals can take pot luck on arrival in a town or make bookings in Prague at CKM's HQ at Žitná 12, 121 05 Prague 2.

Campsites

There are two categories of campsites, A and B depending on the facilities available (see p. (vii) for an explanation). Many also have chalet accommodation if you don't fancy camping. They're usually open for a limited season, often May to September. Category A sites, usually signposted as 'Caravan Camp', have electrical connection points. Prices are around 15-30 Kčs a tent, plus 8-30 Kčs a person and a vehicle charge. Čedok and Autoturist have a list of sites with phone numbers.

Reservations can also be made through Autoturist, Opletalova St 29, Prague 1. Tel: (02) 22 35 44-9. Open Mon to Fri 09.00 - 12.00, 13.00 - 16.00.

Tourist hostels

Turistická ubytovna or *TU* are usually just places to sleep with limited washing facilties and no kitchen. Accommodation is in dormitories, the number of beds in each one determining their category. A class hostels cost about 50 Kčs a night, B class cost 40 Kčs. Motels are rare but comfortable and quite pricey.

Other options

Mountain huts and chalets (*Horská chata* or *Cz*; *Turistická chata* or *SI*) come in two categories. A class corresponds to C-class hotels while B class offer more rudimentary dormitory accommodation.

Forest cabins (*Chatová osada* or *CHO*) are mainly found in Slovakia. You usually pay for the whole cabin (2 to 4 beds) rather than per person. There are three categories – A*, A and B.

Some pubs have rooms to let. Look for a sign saying *Ubytovací hostinec* or the initials *UH*. They're usually quite basic and cheap.

FOOD AND DRINK

Restaurants

The food in many restaurants is uninspiring except in Slovakia but most people rate the beer the best in the world. A typical meal in a restaurant will begin with soup, followed by roast pork, duck or goose accompanied by dumplings in a rich gravy and sauerkraut, washed down with beer. Fresh green vegetables are rare, but there are plenty of the pickled variety. Tea is made with a bag and is generally drunk with lemon. Coffee is usually Turkish.

All restaurants are graded according to quality and comfort from I to IV (see p. (vii) for an explanation). Lunch is generally served between 12.00 and 14.00, dinner from 18.00 to 22.00. Smoking is not allowed during the busiest periods. Restaurants in the top two categories fill up quickly so it's best to reserve a table.

Where to drink

It's said that Bohemia makes the best beer, Moravia the best wine and Slovakia the best spirits. The famous Pilsner beer originally came from Plzeň and Budweiser (Budvar) from České Budějovice. The bars (*pivnice*) tend to be down-to-earth as the clientèle is more concerned about the quality of the beer than the surroundings. They often serve good value food.

Wine bars

Wine bars (*vinárna/vináreň* in Slovakia) are just as popular as the bars. They usually serve local wines and food. Foreign wines can be bought in restaurants. The bars and wine bars also sell two lethal spirits – *slivovice*, a plum brandy, and *borovička*, a vodka-like beer chaser. Bars and wine bars often open throughout the day until 23.00 or midnight, sometimes until 03.00 in a city. If you want to keep away from alcohol, then there are a growing number of coffee shops and snackbars to tempt you.

TIPPING

This is expected. In cheaper restaurants leave 3-5 Kčs, in expensive ones 10 per cent of the bill. Give taxi drivers about 5 Kčs, hotel staff 2-5 Kčs for each piece of luggage.

Beer production is a serious business in Plzeň

THE HISTORY OF CZECHOSLOVAKIA

Until 1918 the Czech and Slovak lands were completely independent of each other. It was only then, after the collapse of the Austro-Hungarian Empire, that their unification into a single nation came onto the agenda. Up to that date both had co-existed as separate entities within the ill-fated Empire, with the Czech lands under the influence of Austria and Slovakia controlled more from Hungary.

THE CZECH LANDS (BOHEMIA AND MORAVIA) PRE-1918

Bohemia and Moravia have been inhabited since earliest times, certainly since 70,000BC. The first people to have had any significant impact on the region were the Celts, who began arriving around 400BC. They were expert artisans and traders who lived in fortified settlements and minted their own coins. Between 623-658AD the Celtic lands were absorbed into a state under the control of Samo, a merchant from an area of modern-day Germany. After his death the state disintegrated and the Czech lands were absorbed into the Great Moravian Empire, which also comprised large chunks of Slovakia and Hungary, Austria, Germany and Poland. The Moravian Empire emerged in the 9th century and lasted some 70 years before being conquered by the Magyars from Hungary. By then the local Přemyslid dynasty had consolidated its power in Bohemia and early in the 11th century it also took over Moravia. Václav was one of the Bohemian kings who stoutly defended the spread of Christianity. He was assassinated and later canonized, becoming St Václav or, more familiarly, St Wenceslas of Christmas carol fame (seen today astride his horse in the middle of Prague's Wenceslas Square). In 1212 the skilful diplomacy of Přemysl Otakar I engineered the Golden Bull of Sicily, a document making the Přemysls the hereditary monarchs of Bohemia and its territories.

Great Moravian Empire

Wenceslas assassinated

At the start of the 14th century the Přemyslid dynasty came to an end when Václav (Wenceslas) III was assassinated in childhood leaving no heir to the throne. In 1310 the Bohemian nobility chose John of Luxemburg as their new king. In 1346 he was succeeded by his son Charles IV who was also elected Holy Roman Emperor in 1349. Under his rule Prague became the political and cultural hub of Europe.

In the 14th century hostility to the lax lifestyle in the

Hussite rebellion

monasteries grew throughout Europe. In Bohemia the cause was championed by Jan Hus (John Huss), a professor at Prague University who incurred the wrath of the clergy but the support of the people and the king. The debate soon escalated from a theological squabble to take on social and political overtones, stirring up the nobility and threatening the status quo. Hus was arrested and burnt at the stake on July 6, 1415. This provoked only further unrest. On July 30, 1419 furious Hussites stormed the town hall in Prague's New Town and hurled government officials out of its windows. The Hussite wars had begun. The movement was quashed in 1434 at the Battle of Lipany, although it struggled on impotently for a couple more years.

The picturesque château at Konopiště near Benešov

Society may have stabilized, but equilibrium in Bohemia was not restored until the reign of George of Poděbrady (1458-71). He was succeeded by the Jagellon dynasty from Poland who ruled until 1526 when Ferdinand I of Habsburg became King of Bohemia and King of Hungary. His reign was marked by bitter battles with the Czech nobility who had put him in power but objected to the constraints imposed on their powers and fortunes. Over the years the struggle transformed into a religious dispute between Catholic and Protestant. In 1618 the nobles began a revolt that was not put down until their bloody defeat at the Battle of White Mountain on November 8, 1620. The following year its 21 leaders were executed by the Austrians and all signs of a nascent nationalism were crushed -- the Czech language was suppressed and the people stripped of all power and reduced to little more than the rulers' serfs.

Nationalism crushed

At the Treaty of Westphalia in 1648 ending the Thirty Years' War which had raged throughout Europe, Bohemia remained part of the Austro-Hungarian Empire. Thereafter the Austrians consolidated their stranglehold of Bohemia and the deteriorating social and living conditions triggered off many uprisings. The largest broke out in north-west Bohemia in 1775 and spread into Moravia. Maria Theresa, then Queen of Bohemia, introduced economic and social reforms to placate the

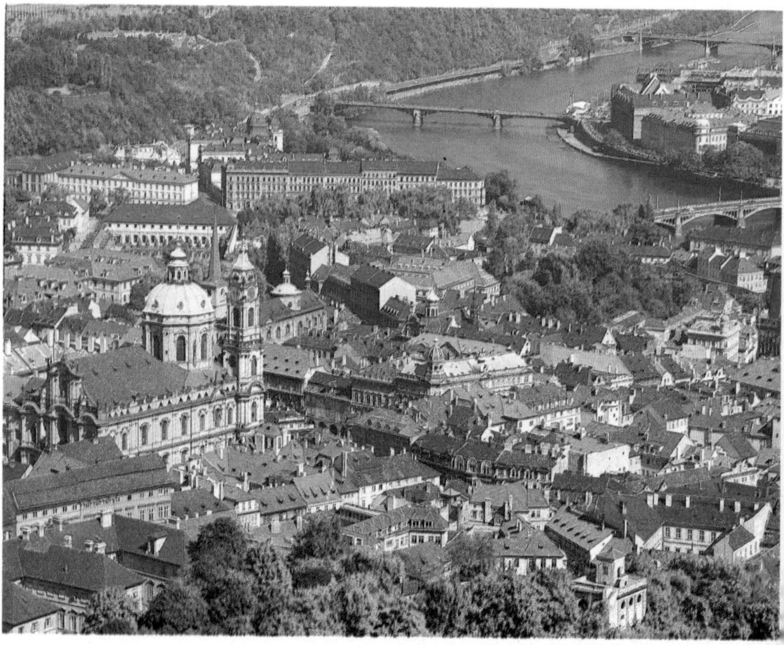

Prague — the Vltava River

masses, ensuring the continued dominance of the Austrians at the same time. Her son Emperor Joseph II followed her example and in 1781 abolished serfdom and issued the Edict of Tolerance which ended religious persecution. This was the beginning of a Czech renaissance – the language and culture started to flourish again, encouraged by the publication of the first Czech newspaper (1789) and the founding of the first permanent theatre in Prague. By the start of the 19th century the foundations of an industrial base had been laid. It grew rapidly throughout the century, boosting the Czechs' self-esteem and bolstering their increasingly vociferous demands for an autonomous existence away from the influence of Austrian rule.

Czech renaissance

SLOVAKIA PRE-1918

People have been living in Slovakia since prehistory – evidence of the existence of Neanderthal man from about one million years ago has been unearthed near Gánovce. We know too that a region called Nitra, ruled by a prince, emerged at the beginning of the 9th century. By the start of the 10th century Nitra had been taken over by the neighbouring Great Moravian Empire. In the 11th century it was overrun by the Magyars and so began the Hungarian domination of Slovakia which was not to end until 1918. Feuding between monarchs and nobles fragmented the kingdom and it was not unified until the reign of King Ludvík I (1342-82).

Hungarian domination

In the early part of the 15th century Hungary opposed the Hussites in Bohemia, even launching attacks on them from Slovakia. In retaliation the Hussites invaded Slovakia and occupied several towns. They won over the support of the local people and soon controlled the whole of eastern and part of central Slovakia.

King Mathias (1458-90) recaptured the Slovak areas held by the Hussites and reasserted Hungarian control, annexing the whole of Moravia at the same time. Under his rule trade, culture and scholarship flourished in Slovakia. In 1526 the Austrian Habsburgs took over the Hungarian throne, uniting Czechs and Slovaks within one empire if not within one nation.

One Empire

In the 16th century Slovakia was suffering a similar fate to the neighbouring Czechs with religious strife, feuds between king and nobles, peasant uprisings and imperialistic Austrians hindering the development of its towns and industries.

In the second half of the 17th century the Turks invaded the lower Danube lands and the centre of Hungarian power shifted to Slovakia. For a time Bratislava became the capital of Hungary.

Peace treaty

Following the Karlovci peace treaty in 1699 the Hungarian occupying forces left southern Slovakia although many individuals chose to remain. In 1711 a rebellion in Rákoczi led to a pact between the Slovak nobility and their Hungarian king. While this benefitted the nobles, the lot of the peasantry hardly improved and many took to the mountains, preferring banditry to serfdom. Some, such as Juro Jánošík, became local heroes with their escapades providing the plot for books and many a fireside tale.

Serfdom abolished

Serfdom was finally abolished in 1785. By the end of the 18th century a nationalist movement began to form but it lacked strength and soon fizzled out. A more self-assured group assembled in 1861, publishing the Memorandum of the Slovak Nation with proposals for independence.

Proposals for autonomy

Two years later the Slovak Foundation was set up to promote Slovak literature and art. Despite Hungarian attempts to quash it – the Slovak Foundation was closed in 1874 – the movement gathered momentum. Its growth continued throughout World War I, during which many strikes and mutinies were harshly suppressed. Finally on October 30, 1918 the Slovak National Council met and agreed to the merging of the Czech and Slovak lands into one country.

One nation

Within 30 years the reins of power in the newly independent republic were held by the Moscow-backed Communist Party and Czechoslovakia once more returned to being subjugated by a foreign power from whose shackles it has only just broken free. The history of Czechoslovakia since 1918 in the introduction gives details of this period.

IMPORTANT DATES AND EVENTS

70 000BC First human settlements.
400 BC Arrival of the Celts.
623-659AD First Bohemian state ruled by Samo, a Frankish merchant.
830-907 The Great Moravian Empire.
924-c.935 Reign of Prince Václav (Wenceslas), later to become the patron saint of Czechoslovakia.
995 Bohemia united under the Přemyslid dynasty.
1018 Slovakia annexed by the Magyars: the start of Hungarian rule which was not to end until 1918.
1200-1400 The time of early Gothic architecture.
1212 Frederick II issued the Golden Bull of Sicily which acknowledged Bohemia as a hereditary kingdom.
1300-50 The golden age of Gothic architecture and painting.
1306 Assassination of Wenceslas III and the end of the Přemyslid dynasty.
1310-1437 Kings of Luxemburg ruled the Czech lands.
1346-78 Reign of Charles IV.

1360-90 The high point of Czech medieval culture.
1415 Jan Hus (John Huss) burnt at the stake.
1419-37 Hussite wars.
1471-1526 Rule of the Jagellon dynasty from Poland.
1526 Ferdinand I of Habsburg elected King of Bohemia – beginning of Austrian rule of the Czech lands, which finally ended in 1918.
1618-48 Thirty Years' War.
1618-21 Czech nobles rebel.
1620 Defeat of the nobles at the Battle of White Mountain.
1621 Execution of 27 leaders of the revolt in Prague.
1624 Re-Catholicization of Czech territory; Protestant clergy expelled.
1648 Peace treaty of Westphalia ended the Thirty Years' War. This bloody conflict involved Austria, Denmark, France, the Netherlands, Germany, Spain and Sweden and brought central Europe to its knees. It began as a war between Protestants and Catholics but developed into a German struggle for supremacy.

Prague — the Týn Cathedral and statue of Jan Hus in the Old Town Square

The famous astronomical clock,the Old Town Hall in Prague

1699 Treaty of Karlovci.
1711 Rákoczi uprising leads to pact between Slovak nobles and their Hungarian king.
1740-80 Reign of Maria Theresa.
1780-90 Reign of Joseph II.
1848 Both Czechs and Slavaks demand greater autonomy, spurred on by other revolutions in Europe.
1861 Memorandum of the Slovak Nation published proposing independence from Hungary.
1862 Slovak Foundation set up to promote Slovak culture.
1918 National Committee set up in Prague and the Slovak National Council in Slovakia. Czechoslovak Republic proclaimed October 28 and Tomáš Masaryk became the first president November 14.
1921 Communist Party of Czechoslovakia founded.
1935 Edvard Beneš elected president.
1938 Czechoslovak government forced into accepting Hitler's demands for the Sudetenland. Beneš resigned and replaced by Emil Hácha.
1939 Sudetenland occupied by Nazi Germany and the German Protectorate of Bohemia and Moravia established.
1940 Czechoslovak government in exile formed in London under Beneš.
1942 Assassination of Reichsprotektor Heydrich; Lidice and Ležáky razed to the ground in retaliation.

1945 Prague liberated by Soviet forces.
1946 Beneš again elected president, with Communist Party leader Klement Gottwald as prime minister.
1948 Communists took control of the government; Gottwald became president.
1953 Death of Gottwald; Antonín Zápotocký made president.
1960 New constitution changed the country's name to the Czechoslovak Socialist Republic.
1968 Alexander Dubček elected First Secretary of the Communist Party. Ludvík Svoboda made president. August 21 Warsaw Pact armies entered Czechoslovakia.
1975 Gustáv Husák elected president.
1977 Charter 77 formed.
1989 Velvet Revolution (November 17) and the setting up of Civic Forum. Václav Havel elected president.
1990 Parliamentary and local government elections.

FAMOUS NAMES

St Agnes (Anežka Přemyslovna) (1205-82) Founder and first abbess of a Franciscan convent in Prague's Old Town. Proclaimed a saint in 1990.
Banič, Štefan (1870 - 1941) Inventor of the parachute (1913).
Beneš, Edvard (1884 - 1948) Politician and co-founder (with Masaryk and Štefánik) of Czechoslovakia in 1918. Later president and leader of its government in exile in World War II.
Čapek, Karel (1890 - 1938) Dramatist and novelist. His play *R.U.R.* (1921) introduced the word 'robot'.
Dvořák, Antonín (1841 - 1904) Composer of the famous *Symphony No. 9: From the New World.*
Forman, Miloš (Born 1932) Director of such award-winning films as *Closely Observed Trains, One Flew Over the Cuckoo's Nest* and *Amadeus.*
Freud, Sigmund (1856 - 1939) The famous psychiatrist was born in Příbor, north Moravia.
Hašek, Jaroslav (1883 - 1923) Satirical novelist and journalist, author of *The Good Soldier Schweik.*
Havel, Václav Playwright and leading dissident in the 1970s and 1980s who captured the heart of the people during the 'velvet revolution', becoming their first democratically elected president on December 29, 1989.
Heyrovský, Jaroslav (1890 - 1967) Scientist awarded the Nobel Prize for chemistry in 1959 for his discovery of polarography, a technique of analyzing ions in solution.
Janáček, Leoš (1854 - 1928) Composer of the operas *Jenufa* (1904) and *The Cunning Little Vixen* (1924).
Janský, Jan (1873 - 1921) Doctor who discovered the four blood groups in 1907.
Kundera, Milan (Born 1929) Novelist whose works

include *The Unbearable Lightness of Being* and *The Book of Laughter and Forgetting.*
Komenský (Comenius) Jan Amos (1592 - 1670) Priest, philosopher and educationalist who laid the foundations of modern teaching. His birthday, March 28, is commemorated as 'Teachers' Day'.
Lendl, Ivan (Born 1960) Champion tennis player from Ostrava, north Moravia.
Mahler, Gustav (1860 - 1911) The famous composer and conductor was born in Kaliště, near Jihlava, Moravia, where he spent much of his childhood, He later became a conductor in Prague and Olomouc.
Masaryk, Tomáš Garrigue (1850 - 1937) Philosopher and politician instrumental in the foundation of Czechoslovakia (with Beneš and Štefánik) and its first president (1918-35). His son **Jan** (1886 - 1948), foreign minister from 1941, died in mysterious circumstances after the communists took control.
Mendel, Johann Gregor (1822-84) Austrian monk and botanist, the founder of genetics. Most of his pioneering work done as abbot of the Augustine monastery in Brno.
Martinů, Bohuslav (1890 - 1959) Composer of six symphonies, operas, concertos and one ballet. He spent most of his life away from his homeland.
Murgaš, Josef (1864 - 1929) Inventor, pioneer of wireless telegraphy and butterfly collector.
Navrátilová, Martina (Born 1956) International championship-winning tennis player born in Revnice, near Prague. She emigrated to the USA in 1975.
Němcová, Božena (1820-62) Author of *Babička* (*Grandmother*), a book of fables close to the heart of every Czechoslovak.
Neruda, Jan (1834-91) Poet, journalist and novelist, fervent critic of hypocrisy in public and private life.
Ressel, Josef (1793 - 1857) Inventor of the ship's propeller.
Seifert, Jaroslav (1901 - 1985) Nobel Prize-winning poet (1984).
Škvorecký, Josef (Born 1924) Bohemian novelist and academic who emigrated to Canada in 1968. His works include *The Bass Saxophone, The Engineer of Human Souls* and *The Miracle Game.*
Smetana, Bedřich (1824-84) Composer of symphonic poems *My Fatherland* and the opera *The Bartered Bride.*
Štefánik, Milan Rastislav (1880 - 1919) Astronomer and politician. Co-founder with Beneš and Masaryk of Czechoslovakia and its first defence minister. Killed in a plane crash.
Tyl, Josef Kajetán (1808-56) Author, playwright and journalist who wrote the lyrics to the national anthem.

THE ARTS

It's impossible to quantify the importance culture plays in the everyday life of the Czechoslovak people. Their love of music and literature, of fine art and architecture and their patronage of the theatre has endured despite the sweeping attempts made to suppress it by successive oppressive regimes. If evidence other than the myriad restored buildings, theatres and galleries in every Czechoslovak town were necessary you need look no further than the dictionary. Even the very word Bohemia has the definition 'a district frequented by unconventional people, especially writers and artists'. A glance at the present elected government headed by a playwright and including a rock musician clearly demonstrates the special place reserved for artists and their work in the hearts and minds of the Czechoslovak people.

ART AND ARCHITECTURE

Czechoslovakia has an extraordinarily rich architectural heritage and it was not for nothing that Göethe described Prague as 'the prettiest gem in the stone crown of the world'. The country largely escaped bombing during the Second World War and the centre of Prague and many other provincial cities and towns have survived more or less unchanged since the early years of this century.

An early baroque palace, the Valdštejnský (Wallenstein) in Prague

The magnificent basilica of St Vitus, Prague

The earliest archaeological evidence is of the fortified settlements of the Great Moravian Empire of the 9th century. Some evidence remains of the Romanesque building under the subsequent Přemyslid dynasty, notably the Vyšehrad complex in Prague, but the first real flowering of the arts took place under the rule of Charles IV, son of the last Přemyslid princess.

Charles IV

Gothic influences

Gothic influences from Germany and France had begun to creep into architecture in Prague from the mid-13th century, as seen in the St Agnes Convent and the Old-New Synagogue. Charles was in Paris in 1323 at the peak of the High Gothic period and on his return had the Hradčany rebuilt along French lines and commissioned well-known architect Matthias of Arras to rebuild the basilica of St Vitus into a three aisled nave cathedral church in 1344. In 1352 the work was taken over by native Petr Parléř who completed the famous vaulting and built the astonishing Wenceslas Chapel with its gilt walls inlaid

Petr Parléř

with semi-precious stones. However the cathedral was not actually completed until 1929 which accounts for some very 20th century stained glass. Petr Parléř also built the Týn Church which dominates the Staroměstské náměstí (Old Town Square) in Prague and Charles Bridge. He also had a hand in the imposing castle overlooking the River Ohře at Loket outside Prague.

Charles Bridge

The Old Town Hall was created in 1381 by joining several houses in the Old Town Square and adding a chapel. This chapel, seen as a symbol of Czechoslovak nationhood, was callously blown up by the retreating Nazis and has now been reconstructed with modern stained glass. Civic pride was expressed in many other town halls such as the 13th century Old Town Hall in Brno with its magnificent Gothic portal.

Fortified castles

The Tartar invasions from 1241 meant that cities throughout Central Europe had to concentrate on heavy fortification rather than decorative architecture and the upheavals over the next centuries made sure that castles such as Spišský Hrad (13th century, rebuilt 15th) in Slovakia and the castle at Český Krumlov in south Bohemia became a feature of the landscape. The huge, much restored castle at Karlsbad is the exception because it was built to protect the Bohemian crown jewels rather than repel invaders. Many of the new towns from this period such as Levoča in Slovakia were built with massive walls. They had very ordered grid street plans as seen in the capital of South Bohemia České Budějovice and to a certain extent the Moravian town of Jihlava.

In Prague the legacy of Charles IV's far sighted town planning of the Nové Město (New Town) meant that by the end of the 14th century the area of the four 'towns' of Prague had been doubled and included around 100 monasteries, churches and chapels, many of which remain.

The castle at Český Krumlov, South Bohemia

Painters and sculptors

Religious foundations also provided the vast majority of work for painters and sculptors during this time of building – wall paintings and illuminated manuscripts such as the Vyšehrad Codex, altarpieces such as the 11 late Gothic examples in the amazing St Egidius' Church in Bardejov, statuary for churches such as the figure of St Wenceslas in his chapel within St Vitus' cathedral and the thriving workshops producing a distinctive Czechoslovak school of madonna figures.

Hluboká near České Budějovice

However the rule of Charles' weak son Wenceslas IV and the Hussite Wars put a stop to any major building in Prague until George of Poděbrady came to the throne in

1458. This is when the Týn Church gained its distinctive towers, the famous chiming horloge was added to the Old Town Hall and the second tower on Charles Bridge built.

Renaissance

George's successor Vladislav was responsible for the introduction of the first Renaissance characteristics into a Prague building when he commissioned Benedict Rejt to design and build Vladislav Hall as part of the renovation of the Hradčany (1486 - 1502). This huge vaulted hall was big enough for jousting matches. The other major architect of the time was Matouš Rejsek who in 1475 built the Powder Tower in the Nové Město which was completely reconstructed in 1880.

The beginning of the rule of the Catholic Austro-Hungarian monarchs with Archduke Ferdinand I in 1526 marked the return of the power of Rome to Bohemia and the introduction of Renaissance forms in the architecture of Prague. In 1536 northern Italian sculptors worked on Ferdinand's new summer palace, the Belvedere, which provided the model for a succession of Renaissance palaces such as the the Schwarzenburg in the Malá Strana (Lesser Town) below the Hradčany. In the exterior stucco and sculpture of palaces such as the Morzine in the Malá Strana you can see the continuation of a tradition of exterior decoration characteristic of so many buildings in Prague. The growing popularity of frescoes inside and out is part of this same tradition.

Italian sculptors

Frescoes

Hungarian kings adopted Bratislava as their capital in 1541 and enriched the architecture of the city by founding a university, rebuilding the palace (now restored) and making St Martin's a coronation cathedral.

Rudolf II

The period under Rudolf II from 1583 is often seen as another blossoming period for Prague. He was an obsessive, if indiscriminate, collector and amassed a fine collection of paintings and drawings, largely dispersed during the Thirty Years' War. His court was a great patron of Mannerist art rivalling the Medici in Florence and commissioning work by painters such as Bartholemew Spranger, Giuseppe Archimboldo and Hans von Aachen, many of whose paintings can be seen in Prague galleries. However the period was marked by religious strife and Catholic oppression was symbolized by the late Gothic St Saviour's Church (1578) and other Jesuit churches in Bohemia, Moravia and Slovakia.

Baroque

The architectural expression of Counter-Reformation zeal across Europe was the baroque style and Czechoslovakia is rich in Baroque buildings. The first major baroque church, the Church of Our Lady Victorious (1611-12) in the Malá Strana in Prague, clearly shows the influence of Italian architects. It is no surprise that the 19th century French sculptor Auguste Rodin described Prague as 'the Rome of the North'.

One of the earliest of the many baroque palaces in the capital and throughout the country was the Valdštejnský palác (Wallenstein Palace), a huge building in the Malá Strana with an Italian-style loggia. Another fine example is the Mirbach Palace in Bratislava.

Kilian Dientzen-hofer

More Italian architects followed through the century bringing Palladian (Černín Palace in the Malá Strana) and Roman (Strahov Monastery also in the Malá Strana) elements but the most famous baroque architect was Kilian Dientzenhofer in the first half of the 18th century. Kilian was Bavarian and provided the model for a style which would be continued by his followers for 50 years. His most eminent building is St Nicholas' Church in Prague's Old Town Square, a gorgeous confection with superb acoustics. Among his many projects Dientzenhofer unified the complex of buildings around the Loreta convent and added the two-storey walkways.

Baroque sculptures were added to Charles Bridge in the early part of the 18th century, many executed by the Austrian Matthias Bernard Braun and the Bohemian Max Brokoff. In architecture baroque, derivative of Dientzenhofer and his followers, dominated the rest of the century, gradually incorporating rococo elements such as the Kinsky palace in Prague's Old Town Square.

Rococo

Neo-classical

The neo-classical influence of the French empire style began to creep in at the beginning of the 19th century, most in evidence in the West Bohemian spa towns of Karlovy Vary and Mariánské Lázně, full of wonderfully elegant boulevards and colonnades.

Under Empress Maria Theresa (1740 - 1789) and her son Joseph (1780 - 1790) religious tolerance began to re-emerge and with it a consciousness of Czech nationalism. Architects harked back to the glorious days of Czech culture under Charles IV through a revival of the Gothic. An extension of the Old Town Hall was built in the early 19th century but was destroyed with the chapel at the end of the Second World War. Another extraordinary product of this neo-Gothic trend is the palace built by the Schwarzenburgs between 1841-71 at Hluboká nad Vlatavou near České Budějovice.

Neo-Gothic

National pride was also expressed in a rash of restoration work such as of the nave and façade of St Vitus' cathedral and the castle at Karlštejn.

However nationalism transcended stylistic boundaries and the greatest symbol of national culture for the Czechs at the end of the 19th century was the building in Prague of the neo-Renaissance National Theatre in 1881 by Josef Zítek. The construction work was funded by public donations – twice, as the original burnt down soon after it was built. In a similar style and for similar reasons the Bohemian National Museum on Wenceslas Square was built in 1893.

More general revivalist styles took over by the end of the century, to be succeeded by a Vienna Secessionist style related to Art Nouveau as evident in the 1900 Hotel Europa on Wenceslas Square. Prague was in some senses equal to Paris, Vienna and Berlin in its status as part of the avant garde in architecture at the beginning of the century. Even Jan Kotěra, the most famous Czech exponent of this style, was the pupil of a Viennese architect. One example of his work is the so-called Urbánek House on Jungmannova in Prague, built in 1912 and displaying a new, distinctly modernist restraint in the use of ornament.

Avant garde

A wealth of towers in Prague's Old Town

An even more pure and restrained modernist style is expressed in the 1928 building on the river in the Nové Město, the Manes House of Architects designed by Novotný. But perhaps the most famous architect to practise in Czechoslovakia was Mies van den Rohe who built the Villa Tugendhat in Brno in 1932.

Post war building

Post-war building is remarkably limited in the centre of Prague, with the exception of the Máj department store (1968) on Národní St, the sail-shaped buttresses added to the Emmaus Monastery – one of the few WWII bombing victims – in 1967, the all-glass New Scene Theatre next to the National Theatre from 1983 and the very new Palace of Culture begun in 1981.

MUSEUMS AND GALLERIES

For a country with such a history of cultural achievements and respect for the arts it is not surprising that Czechoslovakia is rich in museums and galleries. Ever since the time of Charles IV in the 14th century Prague has been a major European cultural centre, partly due to the founding in 1348 of one of Europe's earliest universities, Charles University.

Cultural centre

Today the history of the people and lands that make up modern Czechoslovakia is enshrined in a vast network of museums on a national, regional and local level. There are also large collections of paintings and folk art in civic galleries across the country and smaller private galleries are also on the increase.

MUSIC

By the 18th century learning music had become an intrinsic part of the education system in Czechoslovakia – a policy which in the following century yielded Czechoslovakia's four most famous musicians – Bedřich Smetana (1824 - 84), Antonín Dvořák (1841 - 1904), Leoš Janáček (1854 - 1928) and Bohuslav Martinů (1890 - 1959).

Famous musicians

The country has also attracted musicians from neighbouring countries. Unappreciated in his native Austria, Mozart went to Prague where his opera *The Marriage of Figaro* had received a rapturous reception and where he went on to compose *Don Giovanni*, premièred at the present-day Stavovské Theatre on October 29, 1787. Mozart himself conducted the performance. Today he is still held in great affection by a city and people justifiably proud of his remarkable contribution to their musical heritage and traditions.

Mozart

Today every city has its own symphony orchestra – Prague has four – and annual music festivals attract celebrities from all over the world. Concert halls are popular too, and in the bars and clubs anything goes.

Folk

Every town has its folk festival and songs have been handed down through the centuries. Under the Communists many singers used their lyrics to oppose the regime – and were banned for their pains. Marta Kubišová, a highly acclaimed singer before the invasion of 1968, was persona non grata for 20 years, though her old recordings continued to sell on the black market. During the 'velvet revolution' folk singers performed at demonstrations and were played on TV and radio.

Pop and rock

Rock has a high profile. Michael Kocáb, a prime mover in expelling the Russians from Czechoslovakia and now a member of parliament, is also leader of the band Pražský výběr (Prague's Choice). No one sees anything strange in Kocáb's ability to lead two lives. One of Havel's advisers, Jiří Černý, is a pop music publicist. Rock bands perform in the clubs and bars of larger towns. Western music is popular, but there are plenty of endemic bands such as Elán, Orlík and Laura and Her Tigers.

Opposite: an open air concert below Prague Castle

There has always been a healthy jazz scene in Czechoslovakia. In his book *The Bass Saxophone* (see Literature on p. 48), Josef Škvorecký explains why he feels jazz and revolution are inextricably linked. He

Every town has its folk festival

argues that jazz is offbeat and unpredictable and so is a thorn in the side of a regime bent on the imposition of order. Some of the better-known jazz bands today include Emil Viklický's group and the Baroque Jazz Quintet, but there are plenty of good bands to be found in the clubs or busking in city squares.

LITERATURE

The Czechoslovaks have always valued their writers and intellectuals, all the more because they have suffered so much at the hands of various regimes.

Franz Kafka

The most famous Czechoslovak novelist from the past is Franz Kafka (1883-1924) whose books, written in German, are widely available in translation.

Emigré writers

The West has also had access to modern, emigré writers such as Josef Škvorecký (*The Bass Saxophone*, *The Miracle Game*), Milan Kundera (*The Incredible Lightness of Being*, *The Joke*) and the writer/film director Miloš Forman (see Film and TV on p. 52). These artists have flourished in the West both before and since the Warsaw Pact invasion of 1968.

But what of the writers who remained in Czechoslovakia under Communist rule? All have had their troubles with the authorities, many being forced to take menial jobs (one firm of window cleaners would only accept workers with PhDs!)

Ivan Klíma

The writing of Ivan Klíma was banned for years but is now widely published all over the world. His latest book *Love and Garbage* is based on his experiences working as a garbage collector.

Bohumil Hrabal

The leading Czechoslovak novelist is Bohumil Hrabal, now in his seventies and living in Prague. The film of his book *Closely Observed Trains* had a cult following in the late sixties. His later novel *I Served the King of England* mixes the political, the personal and the fantastic in a story which Kundera describes as 'one of the most authentic incarnations of magical Prague'. It's widely known that Hrabal collects his fantastic stories by sitting in the bars in Prague every afternoon and just listening to the people talk.

Miroslav Holub

While Miroslav Holub has long been admired as a poet both at home and abroad, the Communists were more interested in his work as an immunologist. During those dark years Holub still managed to produce a constant flow of poetry – his book *Poems Before and After* was translated into English in 1984. He is rarely in Prague now – as a respected scientist and a poet he is in constant demand abroad.

The new generation

Recently there has been an explosion of Czech and Slovak talent in the fields of poetry, fiction and journalism. Although few have been translated yet, one young poet, Sylva Fisherová, is already in print in Britain and attracting a great deal of critical acclaim.

THEATRE

Theatre, in Czechoslovakia as elsewhere, has always been a useful outlet for those opposing oppression, so it's hardly surprising that a solid band of actors stood side by side with the students during the 'velvet revolution'.

Hard times

Ironically the economic changes following the revolution have meant that many theatrical companies have fallen on hard times. Directors are having to look to industry and business for funding in the same way as theatrical companies in the West. Audiences are down 30 per cent compared with pre-revolution figures, probably because the drama of everyday life satisfies all but the most devoted theatre goer, and now that television is free from political control, an evening in has become a more acceptable alternative.

Early days

The tradition of Czechoslovak theatre dates back to medieval times, but it wasn't until the 19th century that it really got under way. The year 1883 saw the opening of

National Theatre

the National Theatre, rebuilt from public donations after a fire razed it to the ground. The first perfomance there was *Libuše*, a national opera written by Bedřich Smetana. Today the National Theatre puts on a wide variety of plays by Czechoslovak and foreign playwrights as well as staging performances of opera and ballet.

Between the wars

After the First World War many new theatres opened. One of the country's most distinguished playwrights, Karel Čapek (1890 - 1938), became very popular between the wars – particularly with his symbolic fantasy *RUR (Rossum's Universal Robots)* – as did Jan Werich (1905-1980) and Jiří Voskovec (1905 - 1981), whose plays were shown at the Osvobozené divadlo (the Liberated Theatre). Jaroslav Hašek (1883 - 1923) wrote his novel *The Good Soldier Schweik* which laughed at the infamy, idiocy and inhumanity of war in 1921, but did not receive world-wide acclaim until it was produced as a play in Berlin in 1928. Hašek's hero knew every trick in the book for getting out of trouble and has come to epitomize the resourceful Czechoslovak character.

These days most good theatre companies are based in the capital, but all regional towns and many small towns have a theatre – some have several, and theatrical companies tour the country.

Experimental theatre

Experimental theatre has always been important in Czechoslovakia. Divadlo Na zábradlí (Theatre on the Balustrade) is the Prague company which put on Václav Havel's early plays. These included *Vyrozumění (The Memorandum)*, and *Zahradní slavnost (The Garden Party)*. Havel is widely regarded as the most important Czechoslovak playwright since Čapek.

Then there's the Realistické divadlo (The Realistic Theatre) and the Divadlo na Vinohradech at Vinhohrady. Also in the capital is The New Scene, a contemporary theatre company with its own modern building from 1983.

But perhaps the theatre best known to the West is the Laterna Magika (Magic Lantern) in Prague. It was from the basement of this theatre that Václav Havel and his colleagues planned the 'velvet revolution' of 1989. It is just as famous as a high calibre theatrical company which regularly travels abroad.

Opposite: the famous Magic Lantern Theatre in Prague

Puppets are popular with adults and children alike. The best known puppet theatre is Divadlo Spejbla a

Puppets are popular with adults and children alike

Hurvínka. The company travels all over the world and performs in several languages. Its puppets even appear in TV programmes now, and their entertaining voices can be heard on cassette recordings.

FILM AND TV

Miloš Forman

Without doubt the most famous name in Czechoslovak film is Miloš Forman, director of *One Flew Over the Cuckoo's Nest* and *Amadeus*, filmed in Prague. He escaped from Czechoslovakia after the 1968 invasion and arrived in New York with just a few dollars in his pocket. He went on to win several Oscars.

Today the Czechoslovak film industry is conservative rather than experimental – again the feeling is that when reality is absurd, it is hardly necessary to picture the bizarre on celluloid. Although there are plenty of cinemas, audiences have switched allegiance to the small square box. However, in the field of animation the Czechoslovaks excel and they have sold many animated films to the West in recent years.

Animation

American films are popular and plenty of these are imported for the cinema and TV. Crime series abound, and so, funnily enough, do British comedy shows.

DAILY LIFE

The recent political and economic changes have affected the routine of all Czechoslovaks and will continue to do so for years to come. The lowering of State subsidies is already raising prices, threatening inefficient industries and ushering in the twin ogres of the West – unemployment and inflation. On the other hand new businesses are springing up every week as entrepreneurs scent the profits of capitalism and the privatization of State organizations will open up further opportunities across the board. Inevitably there will be strains and stresses throughout society in the face of such massive change, but after centuries of oppression the Czechoslovaks have an in-built resilience which will no doubt see them through the turbulent times ahead.

New business

POPULATION

Out of a population of 15,651,000 the largest group is Czech (9,808,000), the next largest Slovak (4,984,000). The centuries-old rivalry between the two smoulders on even today. Several other nationalities live in the borderlands, the most important groups being Hungarians (599,000), Poles (73,000), Germans (53,000), Ukrainians (48,000) and Russians (7,000). In recent years the rate of population growth has declined in the wake of more liberal legislation on abortions and a trend towards families with fewer children. The average life expectancy is one of the shortest in the whole of Europe, especially among men, who tend to die five years earlier than in most other industrialized countries.

Prague — eating al fresco in the garden of U Fleků restaurant.

Netting carp

THE WORK FORCE

About half the population (7,558,000) work and 50 per cent of the workforce are women – a high figure compared to much of Europe. Almost three million people work in manufacturing industry, two million in the service sector of education, health, transport, etc. Agriculture is the next major employer with some 800,000 workers.

Second jobs

Most men top up their salary with second jobs, either after work or at the weekend. Women have a second job too – running the home. The day starts early with some people beginning work at 06.00 or 07.00 and schools opening at 08.00. The working week is 42.5 hours and some companies are beginning to introduce more flexible structures for their employees.

HOUSING

Most families live in State-owned apartments. A typical three-roomed flat costs between 400 and 700 Kčs a month to rent, depending on age and condition. Services such as telephone, gas and electricity are extra. Many people are

Home buying

now buying their flats with the help of loans from the State. Some people also live in flats owned by their firm or trade union. These are usually run like a co-operative with members from around 25,000 Kčs for a three-roomed flat and then a monthly rental. A high divorce rate (40,000 in 1989) and a tradition of people marrying

Housing shortage

young has contributed to the current chronic shortage of housing which the State is trying to put right. The lack of housing and escalating costs are encouraging young people to live at home longer and marry later.

EDUCATION

Education reforms

In the decades before the 'velvet revolution' the education system suffered at the hands of the State and the Communist Party. Ideological pressure dictated that religion and Western languages were banned from the syllabus and teachers who didn't tow the line were dismissed. History consisted only of Party-approved people and events. Much has changed since November 1989. Today, Marxist-Leninism is no longer a compulsory course in universities and colleges. The Russian language is no longer obligatory and has now been largely replaced with English, French, German and Spanish. Although a free State system is still the only choice for most parents, fee-paying schools are opening for the better off. Most children begin their education in nursery schools, progressing to an elementary school at the age of 6 where they remain until 15. Students then take exams and go on to a vocational secondary school or to a gymnasium (grammar school) to prepare for university.

RELIGION

There is freedom of worship in Czechoslovakia and 65 per cent of people are Roman Catholics. There are also members of the Evangelical Church, Czechoslovak (Reformed) Church and the Orthodox Church, plus small communities of other denominations including Baptists.

Prague — a face in the crowd

There is a Jewish synagogue in Prague. Places of pilgrimage isolated under Communist rule such as Velehrad and St Hostýn in Moravia and Svatá Hora in Bohemia are now coming back into the limelight.

THE ROLE OF WOMEN

Although guaranteed equal rights by law, in practice women are paid and promoted less than men. Even so they are expected to work to help make ends meet as well as run the home. Increasingly this has placed an intolerable burden on them, something which even President Havel has acknowledged and which is reflected in the high divorce rate. Divorced and single mothers do receive some preferential treatment but their standard of living is lower than for women in a couple. There is no doubt that the Czechoslovak male still sees himself as the protector of the weaker sex. In bars and restaurants a man always pays the bill – he would be insulted and the waiter embarrassed if the woman tried to pay.

High divorce rate

SEXUALITY

The liberal political climate since the 'velvet revolution' has led to a relaxation of many sexual taboos. Contraceptives are now available but only on prescription. Street stalls selling soft and hard pornography have mushroomed in the last couple of years and a political party, the splendidly named Independent Erotic Initiative, has been championing the cause of sexual freedom. Homosexuals now have their own pressure group – the Movement for the Equality of Homosexual Citizens – which has brought the issue of gay rights into the public arena.

Relaxation of taboos

RECREATION

The Czechoslovaks enjoy the great outdoors, taking full advantage of any opportunity to head off to the mountains, forests and lakes for skiing, hiking or watersports. While a few may have their own country houses or mountain chalets the majority are well catered for by the many inexpensive hotels, hostels and campsites run by their firms or trade unions. Horse racing, riding and tennis are also popular while spectator sports include football, ice hockey and skiing. Popular hobbies include gardening, stamp and coin collecting.

Outdoor people

At home people are great readers and, in spite of the high prices of books, city bookshops still do a very healthy trade with many avid readers eager to buy new titles. The many libraries are also kept busy.

Music and the theatre, both classical and modern, are very popular too and performers can usually be confident

Opposite: children learn to skate and ski from an early age in the mountains

Buskers on Charles Bridge in Prague find appreciative audiences

of playing to an enthusistic full house. There are many high calibre amateur orchestras, jazz bands, brass bands and choirs as well as folk song and dance groups.

CUSTOMS AND COURTESIES

Shaking hands

Etiquette is important to the Czechoslovaks as to the rest of continental Europe. They always shake hands when they meet and relatives and close friends kiss both cheeks. In restaurants it's customary for the man to take charge. If you're invited to a Czechoslovak household it's usual to take a small present for your hosts.

FOOD

The Czechoslovaks tend to have their main meal of the day at lunchtime when adults eat at work and children at school – both are subsidized. In the evening people tend to have a light dinner such as an omelette with sausages and cheese and only cook substantial meals at the weekend. A typical meal then would revolve around a main course of meat in a thick sauce (preferably pork, with mutton at the bottom of the list), accompanied by dumplings or potatoes and cabbage. In Slovakia, pasta and sheep's cheese (*halušky/brynza*) is a popular regional dish. Fresh fruit and vegetables are still scarce (and therefore expensive) and limited in variety, which encourages people to do a lot of pickling and preserving. The Czechoslovaks have a sweet tooth for desserts, cakes and pastries, which are usually homemade.

Typical meals

PRAGUE

PRAGUE – it's been called the city of a hundred spires, the golden city, the mother of cities. If you've never been there, you may be forgiven for thinking the Czechoslovaks have a disproportionate pride in their beautiful capital. However, you need only stand on the castle's ramparts to gaze at the breath-taking panorama below you to appreciate that this pearl among European cities more than deserves the lavish praise heaped upon it by visitors and residents alike.

Prague lies in the very heart of Bohemia astride the River Vltava and archaeological finds confirm that a settlement was built here by the Slavs – the ancestors of the Czechs – as early as the 5th century AD. By the turn of the 10th century Prague had become a major trading town. Soon after the first of many fine churches and monasteries were constructed, confirming the religious significance as well as the commercial importance of the city.

The 14th century saw Prague entering its golden age when Charles IV, King of Bohemia and Moravia and Holy Roman Emperor, made it his capital. With 40,000 inhabitants

The steeples of St Vitus' Cathedral dominate the skyline above Charles Bridge

it was one of the biggest cities of the time and soon developed into the cultural and political centre of Europe – a role reflected in the noble architecture of the buildings and monuments erected by Charles IV. After his death in 1378 Prague lost its influence and religious squabbles plunged the city into decline. It recovered briefly at the end of the 16th century when the Austrian Emperor Rudolf II restored it to its former glory and encouraged traders, artists, artisans and scientists to return. After his death and the outbreak of the Thirty Years' War in 1618 the city was once more the victim of embittered religious factions. After the defeat of the Czech forces at the Battle of White Mountain in 1620 Austria reasserted its dominance and great chunks of Prague were soon knocked down to make way for the ostentacious palaces of the nobility. During the next 200 years the demands for independence from Austrian rule escalated. Autonomy was finally granted in 1918.

Five towns were drawn together over the centuries to create Prague – Hradčany, Malá Strana (the Lesser Town), Staré Město (the Old Town), Nové Město (the New Town) and Josefov (Joseph's Town or the Jewish quarter). Each area has managed to retain its own identity and the many wonderful restored buildings and monuments provide the visitor with a fascinating insight into bygone ages. Today they are the nucleus of a city of 1.2 million people which is the political, commercial and cultural hub of the country.

SETTING OFF

By air

Ruzyně airport is 20km (12 miles) from the city centre. Taxis take about 30 minutes and cost around 260 Kčs. Alternatively there's a regular bus service operated by Czechoslovak Airlines to its terminal and booking office at Revoluční St 1, in the Old Town next door to the Kotva department store. Tel: (02) 23 17 39 5 for bus times. The service is free to domestic flight users, about 9 Kčs to others. There's also a shuttle bus to the main hotels – buy your 50 Kčs ticket before boarding. You can also use a number 119 city bus to Dejvická metro station for 4 Kčs and catch a train into the city centre. If in doubt help is available from the Čedok desk at the airport, open Mon to Fri 07.00 - 18.00, Sat and Sun 08.00 - 16.00.

By bus

Most domestic and international long-distance coaches arrive at Florenc bus station on Na Florenci, Florenc station on metro line C. An express bus to Bratislava takes 5 hours and costs about 150 Kčs; to Brno it's 100 Kčs. For information tel: (02) 22 14 45/22 14 40.

For more detailed information on international connections see Setting Off on page 14.

By train

The majority of international and domestic trains arrive at the main railway station Hlavní nádraží near Wenceslas Square, metro line C. It's also called the Main-Wilson station and is an impressive, restored, art nouveau-style building worth more than a second glance. Reservations can be made at the *místenky* which is open 24 hours. There's also an accommodation desk in the main concourse, open Tues to Sun 07.00 - 12.00, 18.00 - 21.00. The other important station is Masaryk on Hybernská St, Republiky Square station on metro line B. You can get express trains from here to

Bratislava, Brno, Děčín, Ostrava and Pardubice. For train information tel: (02) 23 64 44 1/ 26 49 30.

ON THE MOVE

There's a good, cheap public transport system with a metro underground railway, trams and buses. You can use the same ticket for all three. A ticket for a single journey costs 4 Kčs, a day pass 25 Kčs and a tourist ticket starts at 40 Kčs for two days up to 70 Kčs for five days' travel. Tickets can be bought at metro stations, PNS shops (newsagent's) and tobacconist's, as well as at some food shops, restaurants and hotel receptions.

Metro

The metro has three lines – A which runs east to west and B and C which both run north to south. The metro is easy to use, spotlessly clean and the quickest way to get round the city. It's open 05.00 - 24.00. Entrances are marked *Vstup* and exits *Výstup*. Recorded announcements on the trains tell you where you are. Note that complete maps of the metro system are a rarity, even at the stations – see the map on page 66. There are ticket machines and change machines at the stations. Punch your ticket in the machine at the entrance for every journey or you will be liable to an instant fine, foreigner or not.

PRAGUE

1 Prague Castle/St Vitus' Cathedral/St George's Church/ Lobkowicz Palace/St George's monastery
2 Vikárka restaurant
3 Schwarzenberg Palace
4 Sternberg Palace
5 Černín Palace
6 Loreta/Church of the Nativity of Our Lord
7 Strahov monastery/ House at the Golden Tree/Museum of Czech Literature
8 Petřín Tower
9 Hunger Wall
10 Nebozízek restaurant
11 U kocoura beer bar
12 British Embassy
13 Wallenstein Palace
14 U sv Tomáše brewery
15 U Schnellů bar
16 St Nicholas' Church
17 Malostranská beseda
18 US Embassy
19 U tri pstrosu hotel
20 Charles Bridge
21 Diplomat hotel
22 Klementinum
23 Old Town Hall
24 Church of Our Lady of Týn
25 Old-New Synagogue
26 Jewish cemetery
27 Pinkas Synagogue/House of Ceremonies
28 Maisel Synagogue
29 Jewish State Museum
30 House of Artists/Dvořák Hall
31 Intercontinental hotel
32 St Agnes' Convent/National Gallery
33 ČSA
34 ČSA
35 Kotva department store
36 Paříž hotel
37 Municipal House/Smetana Hall
38 Powder Tower
39 U supa bar
40 Vegetárka restaurant
41 Ungelt hotel
42 Atlantic hotel
43 Department store Bílá Labuť
44 Museum of the City of Prague
45 Atrium hotel
46 Tennis courts Štvanice
47 National Technical Museum
48 Karolinum
49 U zlatého tygra bar
50 Smetana Museum
51 Theatre on the Balustrade
52 Bethlehem Chapel
53 Police
54 U dvou koček bar
55 Pharmacy
56 Pelikán
57 Dětský Dům
58 South Bohemian restaurant
59 Sluna
60 Koruna restaurant
61 Revue Alhambra
62 Staročeská rychta restaurant
63 Dům Obuvi
64 Družba hotel/ Tabarin bar
65 Tatran hotel/ bar
66 Sluna
67 Sofia restaurant
68 Rybárna restaurant
69 Jalta hotel
70 National Museum
71 Smetana Theatre
72 Esplanade hotel
73 Pragocar
74 Palace hotel
75 U Pinkasů restaurant
76 Department store Máj
77 Reduta
78 National Theatre/ Laterna Magika
79 Varieté Praga
80 British Airways
81 Beograd restaurant
82 U Fleků bar
83 Boat transport harbour
84 Juniorhotel
85 Antonín Dvořák Museum
86 U kalicha bar
87 Spejbl and Hurvínek Theatre
88 TJ Dolní Měcholupy hostel
89 Slavia stadium
90 Palác kultury night club
91 Club hotel
92 Forum hotel
93 Vyšehrad/Slavín cemetery
94 Horse track
95 Balkán hotel
96 Golf course
97 Mozart Museum
98 Sportcamp Motol
99 Praha hotel
100 Canadian Embassy
101 Holešovice stadium
102 Troja Castle
103 Prague Zoo
104 Moravan hotel
105 Music Theatre at Karlín
106 TJ Čechie hostel
107 Tichý hotel
108 Passport and visas

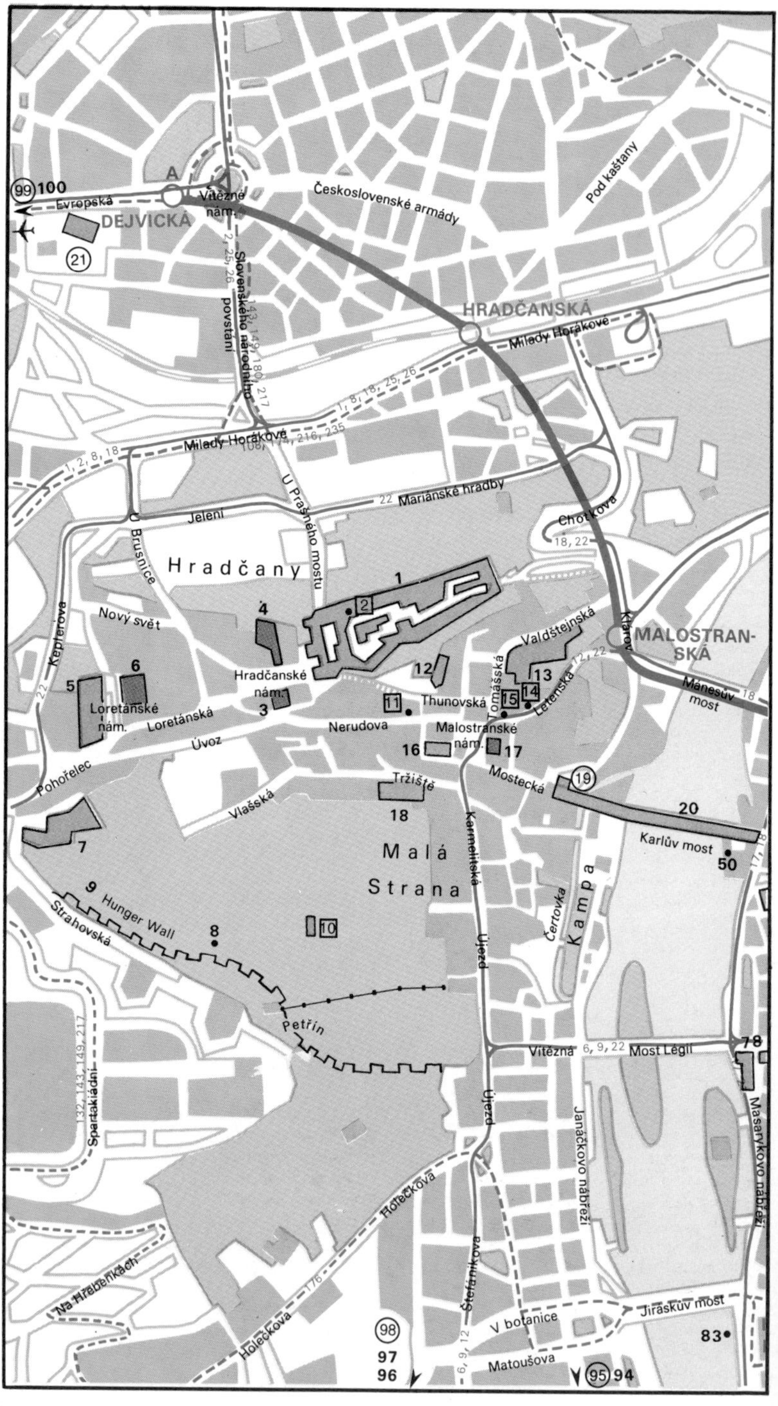

DEJVICKÁ
HRADČANSKÁ
MALOSTRANSKÁ
Evropská
Vítězné nám.
Československé armády
Pod kaštany
Slovenského národního povstání
Milady Horákové
Mariánské hradby
Jelení
Chotkova
U Prašného mostu
U Brusnice
Hradčany
Nový svět
Keplerova
Hradčanské nám.
Loretánské nám.
Loretánská
Úvoz
Pohořelec
Nerudova
Thunovská
Valdštejnská
Tomášská
Letenská
Klárov
Mánesův most
Malostranské nám.
Mostecká
Tržiště
Vlašská
Karlův most
Malá Strana
Karmelitská
Kampa
Čertovka
Hunger Wall
Strahovská
Petřín
Újezd
Vítězná
Most Legií
Janáčkovo nábřeží
Masarykovo nábřeží
Spartakiádní
Holečkova
Na Hřebenkách
Štefánikova
V botanice
Jiráskův most
Matoušova

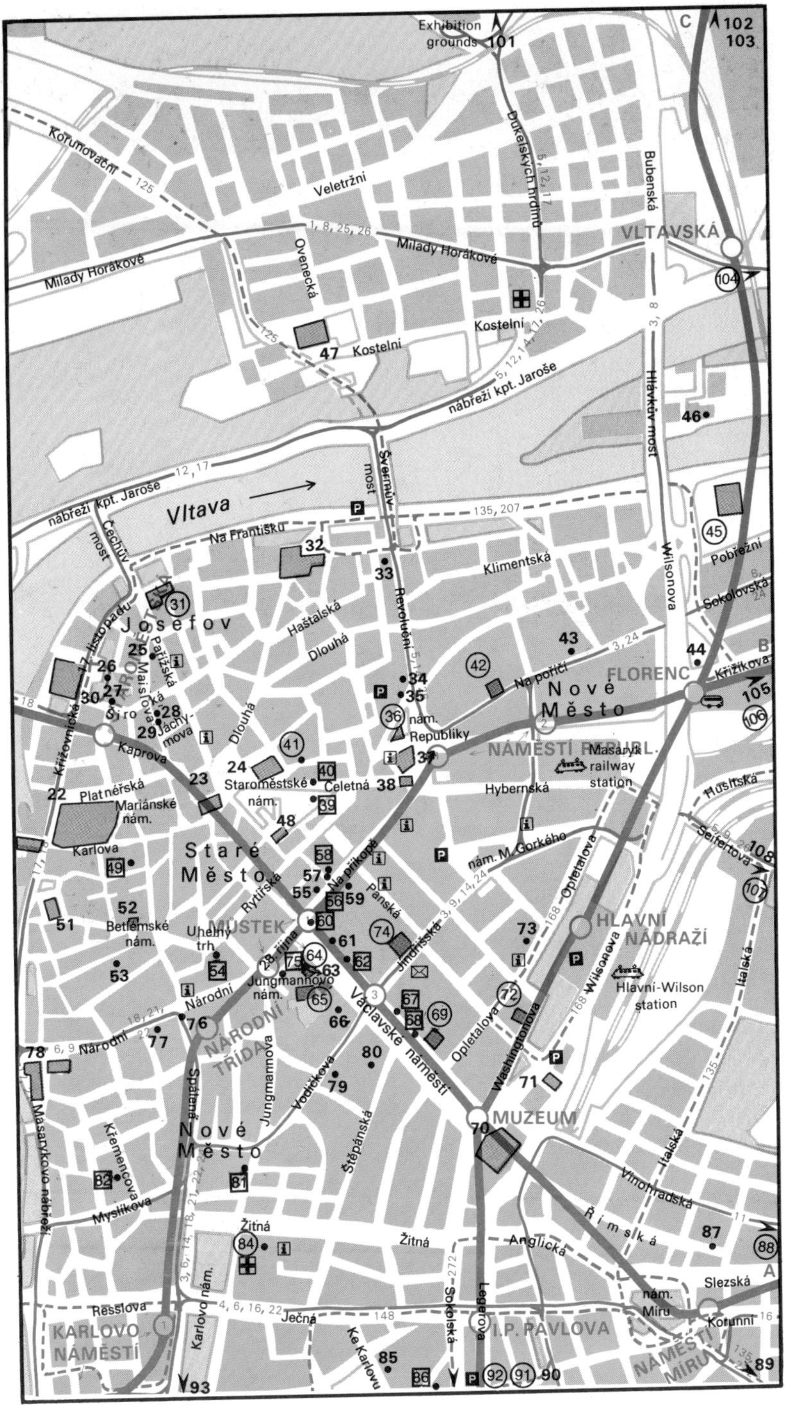

Exhibition grounds
101
C
102
103
Korunovační
Veletržní
Milady Horákové
Ovenecká
Dukelských hrdinů
Bubenská
VLTAVSKÁ
104
Kostelní
47
nábřeží kpt. Jaroše
Hlávkův most
46
Švermův most
Vltava
Čechův most
Na Františku
32
33
45
Pobřežní
Klimentská
Sokolovská
Josefov
31
Revoluční
Haštalská
Dlouhá
43
44
B
Křižíkova
25
26
27
30
28
29
Pařížská
Maiselova
Široká
Jáchymova
42
Na poříčí
Nové Město
FLORENC
105
106
34
35
36
nám. Republiky
37
41
24
40
Staroměstské nám.
Celetná
38
39
NÁMĚSTÍ REPUBL.
Masaryk railway station
Hybernská
Kaprova
23
Křižovnická
17. listopadu
22
Platnéřská
Mariánské nám.
48
Husitská
Seifertova
108
107
Karlova
49
Staré Město
58
57
55
Na příkopě
59
56
Panská
nám. M. Gorkého
Opletalova
51
52
Betlémské nám.
MŮSTEK
60
Rytířská
Uhelný trh
73
HLAVNÍ NÁDRAŽÍ
74
61
62
Jindřišská
64
75
63
53
54
28. října
Jungmannovo nám.
65
Národní
72
Hlavní-Wilson station
Wilsonova
Italská
66
67
68
69
76
77
Národní
78
NÁRODNÍ TŘÍDA
80
79
Václavské náměstí
Washingtonova
71
Jungmannova
Vodičkova
Spálená
Masarykovo nábřeží
Nové Město
70
MUZEUM
Štěpánská
Křemencova
82
81
Vinohradská
Myslíkova
Římská
87
88
Žitná
84
Žitná
Anglická
Legerova
Sokolská
A
Slezská
nám. Míru
Resslova
Karlovo nám.
Ječná
KARLOVO NÁMĚSTÍ
I.P. PAVLOVA
Korunní
NÁMĚSTÍ MÍRU
Ke Karlovu
85
86
92
91
90
89
93

The metro system has three lines – all easy to use, efficient and spotlessly clean

Buses and trams

Buses and trams are usually crowded so avoid travelling with a lot of luggage, especially during the rush hour, or you could make yourself unpopular. Tickets must be bought in advance as there are no conductors. Punch them in the machine after getting on, a fresh ticket for every journey. Anyone without a franked ticket is fined on the spot. Night trams have blue numbers. Express buses carry green badges and go to the suburbs.

Taxis

Taxis are cheap but difficult to find except near the large hotels. There are more during the day than at night. There are 24-hour radio cabs, tel: (02) 20 39 41-5/20 22 95 1-5, but they can take a long time to turn up. If you need one late at night check how much it will cost and don't hesitate to haggle. Beware – as in other capital cities some drivers have been known to 'forget' to turn their meters on for foreigners or to claim they're out of order.

Car rental
Car rental can be arranged through Pragocar. They have offices at Ruzyně airport, tel: (02) 36 78 07; Opletalova St 33, tel: (02) 22 23 24/22 30 94; Inter-Continental Hotel, Curieových Square, tel: (02) 23 19 59 5; Forum Hotel, Kongresová St, tel: (02) 41 02 13.

Parking
Car parking is a headache in the centre where traffic is kept to a minimum. Parking in this area will cost you 2-10 Kčs for 60 minutes, further out it gets cheaper. Only hotel guests with access permits are allowed into Wenceslas Square and neighbouring streets. The permits are obtainable from hotel receptions and allow you to park in spaces reserved by the hotel or in its own garage. If your car is towed away you'll have to go 15km (9 miles) out of the centre to reclaim it. If the streets are full try the multi-storeys.

Taking the tram is one of the best ways of getting around the city quickly

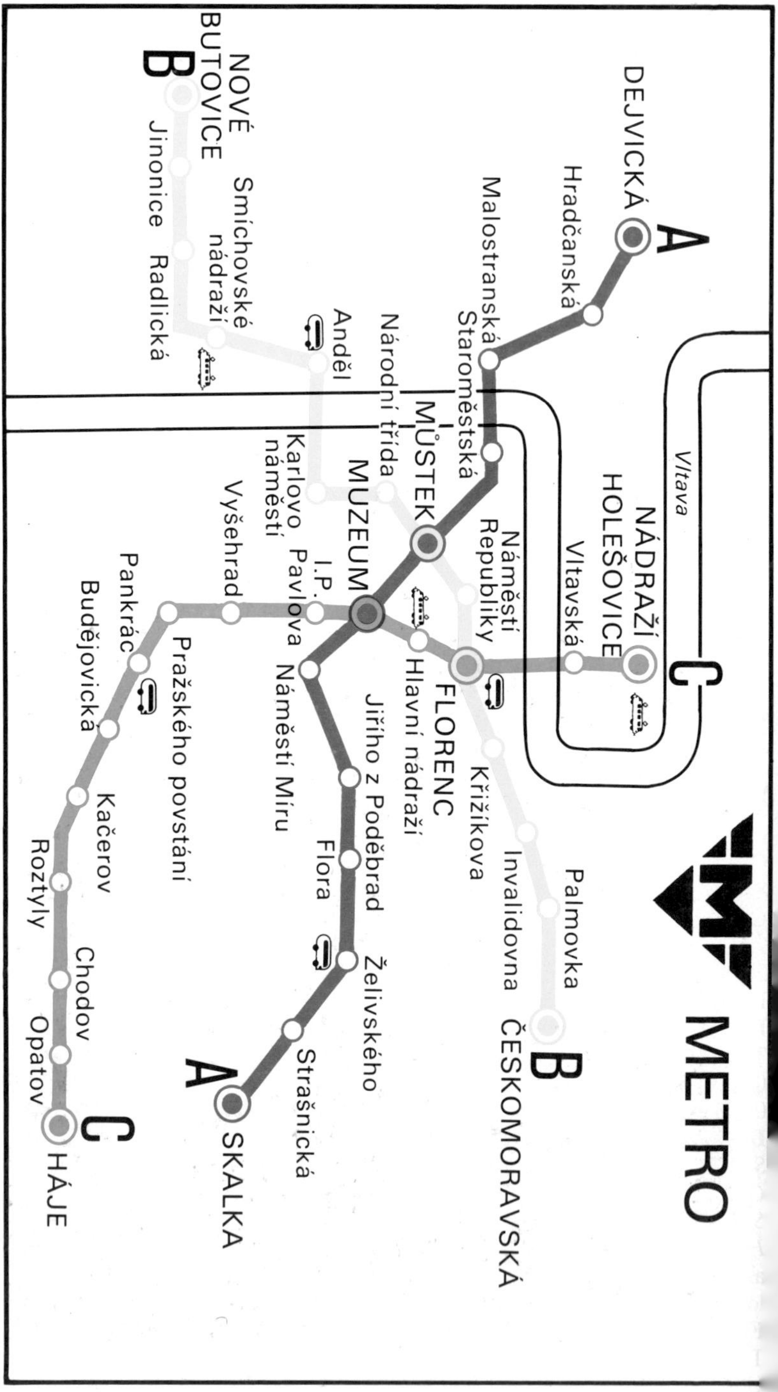
METRO
A
DEJVICKÁ
Hradčanská
Malostranská
Staroměstská
MŮSTEK
MUZEUM
I.P. Pavlova
Náměstí Míru
Jiřího z Poděbrad
Flora
Želivského
Strašnická
A
SKALKA
B
ČESKOMORAVSKÁ
Palmovka
Invalidovna
Křižíkova
FLORENC
Náměstí Republiky
Národní třída
Karlovo náměstí
Anděl
Smíchovské nádraží
Radlická
Jinonice
NOVÉ BUTOVICE
B
C
NÁDRAŽÍ HOLEŠOVICE
Vltavská
Vltava
Hlavní nádraží
Vyšehrad
Pankrác
Pražského povstání
Budějovická
Kačerov
Roztyly
Chodov
Opatov
C
HÁJE

They are convenient at Hlavní nádraží station, the Šverma Bridge, Gorkého Square, Kotva department store, the Palace of Culture and next to the Smetana Theatre.

FACT FILE

Emergency medical aid Dukelských hrdinů St 21, Prague 7. Tel: 155. Health centre for foreigners (including dentist) Fakultní poliklinika (3rd floor), Karlovo náměstí (Charles Square) 32. Tel: (02) 29 93 81. English-speaking doctors 08.00 - 16.00. Payments to be made in foreign currency.
Pharmacy Na příkopě St 7, near Wenceslas Square. Tel: (02) 22 00 81. Open 24 hours.
Police (VB) Konviktská St 14. Tel: (02) 21 49. 24 hours.
Post office Jindřišská St 14. Tel: (02) 26 48 41. 24-hour postal, telephone, telex and fax facilities. Parcels should be taken to the post office at Masaryk railway station.
Banks Československá obchodní banka, Na příkopě St 14. Tel: (02) 22 05 41. Open Mon to Fri 07.30 - 12.00; Státní banka československá, Na příkopě St 28. Tel: (02) 22 53 07. Open Mon to Fri 08.00 - 17.00; Wenceslas Sq 42. Tel: (02) 22 65 62. Open Mon to Fri 08.30 - 13.00; Živnostenská banka, Na příkopě St 20. Tel: (02) 22 43 46. Open Mon to Fri 08.00 - 17.00.
Passport and visas Olšanská St 2. Tel: (02) 21 21. Open Mon to Fri 08.00 - 12.00, 12.30 - 15.30, Wed 08.00 - 12.00 only.
Books and newspapers Štěpánská St 4; Na příkopě St 27. *The Guardian, Financial Times, Wall Street Journal* and *International Herald Tribune* newspapers all arrive daily, others are generally at least a day late.
Embassies British: Thunovská St 14. Tel: (02) 53 33 47/53 33 70/53 67 37. US: Tržiště St 15. Tel: (02) 53 66 41. Canadian: Mickiewiczova 6. Tel: (02) 32 69 41.
Airline offices ČSA, Revoluční St 1. Tel: (02) 21 46. Reservations. Revoluční St 25. Tel: (02) 23 17 39 5. Information about flight schedules and airport bus. British Airways, Štěpánská St 63. Tel: (02) 23 60 35 3. Telephone directories, available in every post office, list the telephone numbers of other airlines.
Travel agencies Čedok, Na příkopě St 18. Tel: (02) 22 42 51. General tourist information and exchange. Čedok, Panská St 5. Tel: (02) 26 18 92. Hotel accommodation. Čedok, Dlážděná St 2. Tel: (02) 23 62 29 2. Sightseeing tours of Prague, accommodation in private homes. Thomas Cook and American Express both have offices in Čedok, Na příkopě St 18. Tel: (02) 22 42 51. Prague Information Service (PIS), Na příkopě St 20. Tel: (02) 54 44 44. Sightseeing tours of Prague, general information on the city.
Rekrea, Pařížská St 26-27. Tel: (02) 23 10 63 3. Sightseeing tours.
CKM, Žitná St 12. Tel: (02) 29 99 41. Youth and student travel.
Pragotour, U obecního domu St 2. Tel: (02) 23 17 20 0. Sightseeing tours, accommodation.
Balnea, Pařížská St 11. Tel: (02) 23 21 93 0. Spa holidays.
Sport-turist, Národní St 33. Tel: (02) 26 33 51. Visits for groups of sportspeople.
Autoturist, Opletalova St 29. Tel: (02) 22 35 44. Motoring information and nationwide breakdown service.

Shopping

The most interesting shops are in the streets leading off the Old Town Square and around Wenceslas Square. Na příkopě St and adjacent streets have the famous Czechoslovak coloured and cut glass and porcelain. If you browse you can buy anything from CDs and records to jewellery and women's clothing. *Dílo* means a shop sells prints and objets d'art; *ÚLUV* or *UVA* local handicrafts. **Department stores** providing a variety of inexpensive goods include Kotva, Republiky Sq; Máj, Národní St; Bílá labuť, Na Poříčí St 23. All are open Mon to Fri 08.00 - 19.00 (20.00 Thur), Sat 08.00 - 18.00. In Na příkopě St there's Dětský Dům, a store devoted to everything for children from clothes to toys. At Wenceslas Sq 6 there's Dům Obuvi with all types of shoes.

Tuzex shops Here you can only buy things with foreign currency or with credit cards. Goods are duty-free and there is generally a good choice including Western brands of cigarettes and alcohol.

WHERE TO STAY

There are over 60 hotels in Prague with plenty of new ones under construction. Even so there's still not enough room for all the visitors from home and abroad. It's advisable to book as far ahead as possible, either

The River Vltava sweeps through Prague spanned by many attractive bridges

Celetná Street and the Old Town Hall as seen from the Powder Tower

by contacting the hotel direct or by going through a travel agent or Čedok office (see Travel agencies on p. 67). If you arrive in Prague without a booking, contact Pragotour (see Travel agencies) for help. They have lists of available accommodation. The hotels selected below are either in the centre or within easy reach of it. The Club Hotel on the outskirts is the exception but is recommended for its excellent sporting facilities.

A* de luxe category hotels

⌂ **Atrium** Pobřežní St. Tel: (02) 28 41 11 1. Grill-restaurant (I), café-patisserie (I), ale-room (I), day-bar (I), night club (I), V.I.P. club (I), health centre.

⌂ **Diplomat** Evropská St 15. Tel: (02) 33 14 11 1. Fax: (02) 34 17 31. Restaurant and bar (I), café (I), night club (I).

⌂ **Esplanade** Washingtonova St 19. Tel: (02) 22 25 52/22 60 57. Fax: (02) 26 58 97. An old town house redecorated in the early eighties but still with a traditional feel. Restaurant (I), café (I), wine bar (I). Not far from the National Museum.

⌂ **Forum** Kongresová St. Tel: (02) 41 01 11/41 02 18/41 02 40. Fax: (02) 49 94 80. Modern high rise building with French restaurant (I), Czech restaurant (I), self-service buffet (I), wine bar (I), café (I), night club (I), casino, bowling alley. Near Vyšehrad.

⌂ **Intercontinental** Curieových Sq. Tel: (02) 28 00 11 1/28 00 11 8-9. Fax: (02) 23 10 50 0. Opened in the mid-seventies and beautifully situated on the riverside in the Old Town. Restaurant (I), restaurant (II), wine bar (I), bar (I), café (I).

⌂ **Jalta** Wenceslas Sq 45. Tel: (02) 26 55 41. Fax: (02) 26 53 47. Worn but comfortable and very central overlooking the square. Restaurant (I), café (I), bar (I), casino.

⌂ **Palace** Panská St 12. Tel: (02) 23 60 00 8. Fax: (02) 23 59 37 3.

Pařížská St, Joseph's Town or the Jewish Quarter, leading to the Old Town

Restored art nouveau building with café-restaurant (I), night club-restaurant (I), delicatessen-buffet (I), piano bar (I), conference room, casino.
⌂ **Club** Průhonice 400. Tel: (02) 72 32 41-9. Fax: (02) 72 32 41. Restaurant (I), 24-hour café (II), 6 indoor tennis courts, squash courts, bowling alley, indoor swimming pool. 15km (9 miles) from the city centre.

A* category hotels
⌂ **Atlantic** Na Poříčí St 9. Tel: (02) 23 18 51 2. Fax: (02) 23 26 07 7. Restaurant (I), day bar (I), night bar (I).
⌂ **Praha** Sušická St 20. Tel: (02) 33 38 11 1. Fax: (02) 31 21 75 7. Restaurant (I), café (I), sauna.
⌂ **U tří pštrosů (The Three Ostriches)** Dražického Sq 12. Tel: (02) 53 61 51. Charming 17th-century period piece very much in demand with restaurant (I). At the Lesser Town end of Charles Bridge.

B* category hotels
⌂ **Družba** Wenceslas Sq 16. Tel: (02) 23 51 23 2-3. Fax: (02) 23 59 27 0. 100-year-old building with restaurant (III), bar (I).
⌂ **Paříž** U Obecního domu St 1. Tel: (02) 23 22 05 1. Turn-of-the-century art nouveau building restored in the mid-eighties with restaurant (I), café (II). Good location in the Old Town.
⌂ **Tatran** Wenceslas Sq 22. Tel: (02) 23 52 88 5. Older hotel with café (II), night bar with cabaret (II).
⌂ **Ungelt** Štupartská St 1. Tel: (02) 23 20 47 0. Central hotel in 500-year-old building, part of the Týn Cathedral complex. *Ungelt* means customs in German and the building was originally a customs hall. Restaurant (II), day bar (II). 10 rooms only.

C category hotels
⌂ **Balkán** Svornosti St 28. Tel: (02) 54 07 77. Restaurant (III). Rooms set aside for young tourists. Take a number 15 tram from Lidická tram station.
⌂ **Moravan** U Uránie St 22. Tel: (02) 80 29 05. Restaurant (II), café (II).
⌂ **Tichý** Seifertova 65. Tel: (02) 27 30 79. Restaurant (II).

Tourist hostels
⌂ **B CKM Juniorhotel** Žitná 12. Tel: (02) 29 99 41. Fax: (02) 23 51 29 7. Restaurant (III), day bar (II), night wine bar (II), Very cheap accommodation but usually full. Contact CKM (address in Travel agencies on p. 67) for other options. In the summer holidays student accommodation can also be used by visitors.
⌂ **C TJ Dolní Měcholupy** Na paloučku 223. Tel: (02) 75 12 62. Buffet (III). Cheap accommodation 30 mins from the centre. Take metro line A to Želivského, then bus number 229 to Měcholupy.
⌂ **C TJ Cěchie** Malého St, Karlín. Tel: (02) 22 20 09. Mixed dormitory accommodation with a welcoming staff. Next to Florenc bus station so it can be noisy.

Private accommodation
Rooms can be rented through Čedok and Pragotour (addresses under Travel agencies on p. 67) who can also arrange for you to stay with a family. Most of the homes are outside the centre but conveniently near to public transport.

Campsites
△ **A Sportcamp Motol** V podhájí St. Tel: (02) 52 18 02/52 47 14. Also has chalet accommodation. Restaurant (II), sauna. Golf course and tennis courts nearby. Open Apr 1 to Oct 31. West of Prague on Highway 5 to Plzeň.

EATING OUT
Have no fears about going hungry or thirsty during your stay in Prague. The Czechoslovaks enjoy their food and drink so there are literally hundreds of restaurants, bars and cafés with prices and menus to suit everyone. However finding a free table in the city centre requires some patience and legwork and you'll probably end up in an expensive hotel. Booking is essential everywhere. Most restaurants are open until 22.00, some to 23.00. After that you'll have to go to a night club, wine cellar or bar which serves food. A typical meal will consist of poached carp (*kapr vařeny*), pork (*vepřové maso*) or goose (*husa*) accompanied by dumplings (*knedlíčky*) and sauerkraut. Fruit dumplings made with plums or cherries are also popular. All restaurants ban smoking at the busiest times (midday to 14.00 and around 19.00) but it's usually allowed at other times. The following places are worth a visit.
🍴 **I Beograd** Vodičkova 5, New Town. Yugoslavian cooking.
🍴 **I Nebozízek** Petřínské sady (Gardens), Prague 1. A restaurant

Eating out in one of the many restaurants on Na příkopě St in the Old Town

Or you may prefer to sample the fare in the Old Town Square. Be sure to book

offering superb views of the city; it can be reached either on foot or by funicular railway leaving regularly from Most Legií.

🍴 **I Pelikán** Na příkopě St 7, Old Town. Popular stylish restaurant.

🍴 **II++ U sv Tomáše (St Thomas')** Letenská 12, Lesser Town. 14th-century brewery selling Braník beer.

🍴 **II++ Vikárka** Vikářská St 6, Hradčany. Pleasant restaurant within the castle complex which first opened in the 16th century and has been popular, especially with writers and artists, ever since. Good value, traditional food. Booking in advance is strongly advised.

🍴 **II+ U kalicha (The Chalice)**, Na bojišti St 12, Prague 2. Excellent food and a good bar selling 12° Pilsner Urquel beer. Mentioned in *The Good Soldier Schweik* and much frequented by its author Jaroslav Hašek.

🍴 II **Hospoda U dvou koček (The Two Cats)**, Uhelný St 10, Old Town. Cosy bar with friendly staff and excellent food; plenty of atmosphere.

🍴 II **Moskva** Na příkopě St 29, Old Town. Good value Russian and Georgian food.

🍴 II **Rybárna** Wenceslas Sq 43, New Town. Restaurant specializing in fish, especially carp.

🍴 II **Staročeská rychta** Wenceslas Sq 7, New Town. Good traditional Czechoslovak food.

🍴 II **Sofia** Wenceslas Sq 3, New Town. Good Bulgarian restaurant.

🍴 II **U Schnellů** Tomášská St 2, Lesser Town. Good food at reasonable prices.

🍴 II **U supa** Celetná St 22, Old

Národní divadlo (National Theatre) where you can see opera, ballet and drama

Town. Well-known bar selling Braník beer.

II U zlatého tygra (The Golden Tiger) Husova St 17, Prague 1. Typical, straightforward bar for beer drinkers. Try the pork fillet in potato pancake with a sauerkraut salad.

III Jihočeské pohostinství (South Bohemian Restaurant), Na příkopě St 17, Prague 1. A popular restaurant offering south Bohemian specialities.

III Koruna Wenceslas Sq. The most popular self-service restaurant and buffet (IV) in the city.

III U Fleků (Flek's) Křemencova St 11, New Town. Dating from 1459 this is the oldest bar in Prague. Excellent atmosphere. Try Flek's 13° dark beer.

III U kocoura (The Cat) Nerudova St 2, Prague 1. Popular beer bar near Malostranské náměstí (Lesser Town Square) which sells 12° Pilsner Urquel.

III U Pinkasů (Pinkas's) Jungmannovo Sq 15, Prague 1. Popular traditional restaurant, selling 12° Pilsner Urquel. Try the speciality, goulash. You can also add your signature to the thousands already on the walls!

III Vegetárka Celetná St 3, Old Town. Good vegetarian restaurant.

NIGHTLIFE

All the more expensive hotels have evening entertainment ranging from dance bands and variety acts to cabaret and video-discos. They're all open to non-residents.

Nightclubs and bars with shows

Cabaret U Fleků Křemencova St 9. Various types of entertainment in this 15th-century brewery, which is still in production. On some evenings there's an amazing German-type 'oompah' band – great fun, but not for the faint-hearted. The taxis outside have been known to fleece weary revellers so be careful. Excellent dark beer.

The Night Club of the Palace of Culture 5. května St 65, Nusle. Dancing and entertainment.

Revue Alhambra Hotel Ambassador, Wenceslas Sq 5. Nightly variety show.

Tabarin bar Wenceslas Sq 16. Nightly cabaret.

Tatran bar Wenceslas Sq 22. Floorshow.

Varieté Praga Vodičkova St 30. Nightly cabaret with international performers.

Theatres

There are more than 30 theatres offering opera, ballet, drama, mime, musicals and even a puppet show. Getting tickets to the most popular venues is a problem so advance booking is advisable, either through a travel agent or Sluna at Černá růže Arcade, Na příkopě St, or Alfa Arcade, Wenceslas Sq 28. All are open Mon to Fri 09.00 - 18.00. Most performances begin at 19.30 except for the National Theatre (19.00) and Laterna Magika (20.00). All theatres are closed July and August. The following are worth a visit.

Laterna Magika Národní St 2. Booking office: Reduta, Národní St 20. Tel: (02) 20 38 25. A unique venue where performances are an enthralling mixture of drama, singing and dancing with films projected onto screens of varying size and shape. Internationally acclaimed, the shows are very popular with visitors as you need no understanding of Czech. Kill to get tickets!

Hudební divadlo v Karlíně (Music Theatre at Karlín), Křižíkova St 10, Karlín. Tel: (02) 22 08 95; 22 70 73 for group bookings. Czechoslovak and international musicals.

Národní divadlo (National Theatre), Národní St 2. Tel: (02) 20 53 64. Opera, ballet and drama performances.

Smetana Theatre Wilsonova St 25. Tel: (02) 26 97 46. Opera and ballet.
Divadlo Spejbl a Hurvínek Rímská St 45. Tel: (02) 25 10 57. Stunning puppetry.
Divadlo Na zábradlí (Theatre on the Balustrade), Anenské Sq 5. Tel: (02) 23 60 44 9. Homebase of the renowned Black Theatre mime group led by Ladislav Fialka. If you're very lucky you might catch them in town.

Concerts
Prague has a rich musical heritage from medieval church music through to the great names of Smetana, Dvořák and Suk. Mozart and Beethoven also lived in Prague for a time. The city continues to be the hub of Czechoslovakia's musical life, the high point being the annual International Music Festival which starts on the anniversary of Smetana's death on May 12 and ends at the beginning of June. Leading personalities from the world of music always attend. In the past these have included Herbert von Karajan, Leonard Bernstein, Rafael Kubelík and Sviatoslav Richter. The popular concert halls are at the Palace of Culture, 5. května St 65, Anežský klášter (St Agnes' Convent), U milosrdných St 17, Smetana Hall, Republiky Sq 5 and Dvořák Hall, Jana Palacha Sq which is currently under renovation until May 1992. Jazz is very popular and you can catch nightly jazz and folk music at Malostranská beseda, Malostranské Sq (Lesser Town Square) beginning at 20.00. It's advisable to book. Tel: (02) 53 04 82. The Reduta Theatre and Jazz Club at Národní St 20 specializes in classical jazz. Tel: (02) 20 38 22.

ALTERNATIVE PRAGUE
There's not such an obvious youth scene as in Western countries but it's there and it's growing. The present rules, the past is forgotten and the future can wait so bars, discos and bands are preferred to earnest political discussions on 'Whither Czechoslovakia?' Video discos are not up to Western standards yet, noise levels are. Current scenes include the Discotheque Zlatá Husa and Video Disco Alfa, both on Wenceslas Square, discos on the boatels Admiral and Albatros on the river, U Holubů at Stefánikova St 7 and Na Chmelnici at Koněvova St 10. Hard rock bands play every Thursday at the Kulturní dům Barikádníků (House of Culture) at Saratovská St 1, Prague 10. Concerts are held in the Palác Kultury (Palace of Culture) and in the open air in the summer at the Holešovice exhibition grounds. Yuppies and beautiful young things are currently congregating in the grill room of the ČKD Dům on Wenceslas Square, next to metro station Můstek.

WHAT TO SEE
Prague Castle
Without doubt this is the major tourist attraction in the city. It's been the seat of 9th-century tribal princes, Czech kings and since 1918 Czechoslovak presidents. President Havel is the exception – he's decided to stay at home. Over the centuries the castle has been rebuilt and extended so that it's now a showcase of several architectural styles, harmoniously blending together without detracting from the building's overall charm. The castle is open Tues to Sun 10.00 - 18.00. Changing of the guards takes place every odd hour 05.00 - 23.00. English-speaking guides are available from the information centre in the Old Deanery, behind St Vitus' Cathedral.

There's much to see within its precincts, but St Vitus' Cathedral, St

Smetana Theatre, a beautiful venue to see great performances of opera and ballet

George's Church and the castle district Hradčany should definitely not be missed.

Katedrála sv Víta (St Vitus' Cathedral)
The cathedral and its lofty spires take pride of place in the Third Courtyard. The main steeple is a lofty 97m (318ft) high. Remains of the first churches on this site, built in the 10th and 11th centuries, can be seen beneath it. Work on the main part started in 1344 during the reign of Charles IV. Fires and wars interrupted progress and the present building wasn't completed until 1929 – hence the blending of Gothic and neo-Gothic styles. Architects of the stature of Matthias of Arras and Petr Parléř were involved along the way. Their faces appear either side of the huge **Rose Window** more than 10m (30ft) across which depicts the creation of the world. The beautiful interior is notable for the stained-glass windows and the triforium, a walkway above the pillars. In the **Royal Crypt** lie the remains of Czech kings, including those of Charles IV, Wenceslas IV and Rudolf II. Of the 21 chapels the most important is the one dedicated to Prince Václav (Wenceslas) I, a popular monarch who encouraged the spread of Christianity during his short reign (920-929). He was murdered by his brother who disapproved of mixing religion and government. Wenceslas was made the patron saint of Bohemia, St Václav, and today he personifies the unification of Czech people against foreign forces. The chapel is decorated with frescoes and semi-precious stones, the work of Petr Parléř in the 14th century. A small door connects the chapel with the **Treasure Chamber** where the crown jewels are kept under lock and key. They are rarely on display but you can see faithful replicas in the museum of the **Lobkowicz Palace** at Jiřská St 1, Hradčany. The main collection is on the history of the Czechs and Slovaks up to 1848. It's open Tues to Sun 10.00 - 18.00.

Bazilika sv Jiří (St George's Church)
This beautiful basilica was built on the orders of Prince Vratislav around 921 and completed early in the 12th century. Along with the adjoining **Benedictine Monastery of St George** it formed the nucleus of the castle complex in the early Middle Ages. After a fire in 1142 two towers were added to the church's eastern side. Further work was carried out at the end of the 19th century and again between 1958 and 1960. The monastery has been superbly restored and possesses an outstanding display of Bohemian art from the 13th century onwards as part of the collection of the **National Gallery**. It's open Tues to Sun 10.00 - 18.00.

Hradčany (The castle district)
Hradčany was founded in about 1320, the third of the Prague towns. It developed around Hradčany Square in the shadows of the castle complex. The buildings around the square date from 1541 when a fire destroyed the originals. The **Schwarzenberg Palace** was restored in 1957 and now contains the **Museum of Military History** with displays of European weaponry, uniforms and militaria up to World War I – it's one of the largest exhibitions in Europe. Medieval jousting tournaments take place in the grounds in the summer months. The museum is open May to Oct Mon to Fri 09.00 - 15.30, Sat and Sun 09.00 - 17.00.

A passage leads from the square to the **Sternberg Palace** where you can see the **National Gallery's** magnificent collection of European

St Vitus' Cathedral, commissioned by Charles IV in 1344 and completed in 1929

art of all the leading schools, including works of El Greco, Rubens, Dürer, Goya, Canaletto and the French Impressionists. A must for art lovers. It's open Tues to Sun 10.00 - 18.00.

From the square it's a short walk along Loretánská St to **Loretánské Square**, one of the most attractive squares in the whole of Prague. Built in the 18th century it's dominated by the **Černín Palace (the Foreign Ministry)**, in whose shadows is the **Loreta** shrine and church. A place of pilgrimage, it takes its name from the Italian town to where, so it is said, the house of the Virgin Mary was miraculously transported by angels in the 13th century to escape plundering by the armies of Islam. This copy of the house was a gift of a Czech noblewoman in the 17th century to help promote the spread of Catholicism. It was enlarged later with the addition of a courtyard, cloisters and the **Church of the Nativity of Our Lord**. The **Loreta Tower** has a lovely carillon of 27 bells which rings out on the hour. The treasury is full of gifts from the wealthy in the hope of eternal absolution and contains a trove of glittering treasures, including the monstrous **Sun of Prague** with its 6,222 dazzling diamonds. Almost 1m (3ft) high, it weighs in at 12kg (26lb).

Nový svět (The New World)

North of Loretánské Square is the area called the New World, once a very poor district. Despite renovations even today the houses bear witness to the simplicity of people with little money to spare for extravagant decoration. From the square, go along Pohořelec and then up some steps beneath the **House at the Golden Tree** to the courtyard of

The magnificant Černín Palace in Loretánské Square, now the Foreign Ministry

Changing of the guard at the castle takes place every odd hour from 05.00 - 23.00

the **Strahov Monastery**. Founded by Prince Vladislav II in 1140 the monastery has been altered many times in different architectural styles. It became renowned throughout Europe for its valuable collection of manuscripts and books, so it is fitting that it is now home to the **Museum of Czech Literature**. It's open Tues to Sun 09.30 - 17.00 and has a replica of a 17th-century printing press and an exhibition of some 50,000 documents, including letters of Jan Hus. The complex also includes the **Church of Our Lady** on Strahovské Square where Mozart once played the organ. It's surrounded by a beautiful garden with good views of the city. From here a path takes you to the slopes of Petřín Hill.

Petřín Hill

The hill is 318m (1043ft) high. A funicular railway to the top operates daily 05.00 - 24.00 from the lower station near Most Legií or if you prefer you can walk up one of the many paths criss-crossing its slopes. On the top you'll find the **Petřín Tower**, a 60m (197ft) replica of Paris' Eiffel Tower built in 1891. Next to it is a building containing a mirror maze and a diorama of Prague students fighting the Swedes on Charles Bridge in 1648. There's also the **Hunger Wall** constructed during a drought under the orders of Charles IV. The starving poor had the job of building it and were paid no money but rewarded with food and clothing. It took two years to extend the wall from the castle over Petřín Hill and down to the river – tough work, but life saving.

Malá Strana (The Lesser Town)
Many members of the nobility and senior clergy used to live in this quarter to be near the castle. A large chunk of it suffered in the fire of 1541 and after the Battle of White Mountain in 1620 whole streets of houses were demolished and grand palaces put up in their place. The district's status declined when the centre of power shifted to Vienna. Even though it's no longer the power-house of Bohemia, it remains 'the' place to live. With its narrow snaking streets, splendid palaces, ornate churches and cosy bars, it's the most picturesque part of the city. Many of the buildings have fallen into disrepair but great efforts are being made to return them to their former glory. Some of the palaces now house embassies, government ministeries and museums. The largest, **Valdštejnský palác (Wallenstein Palace)**, was built between 1624 and 1630 and its Italian architect wanted it to outshine the castle complex. To provide enough space for it 23 houses, a brick factory and three gardens were destroyed. Today you can visit the art gallery in the former riding school and concerts are held in the gardens. It's open May to Sept Tues to Sun 10.00 - 18.00. The entrance is in Letenská St.

The heart of this neighbourhood is **Malostranské náměstí (Lesser Town Square)** which is dominated by **Chrám sv Mikuláše (St Nicholas' Church)**, a masterpiece of baroque architecture and yet another creation of the Kilian Dientzenhofer. The ceiling fresco above the main nave of scenes from St Nicholas' life, the work of Kraker in 1761, is one of the biggest in Europe at 1500 sq m (1800 sq yds). St. Nicholas' Church is open daily 09.00 - 16.00.

One of the prettiest corners of the Lesser Town is **Kampa Island**, separated by a branch of the River Vltava called the **Čertovka (Devil's Stream)**. Since the 16th century it's been famous for its pottery markets.

South of the gardens in the **Smíchov** district you'll find the **Muzeum české hudby (Mozart Museum)** at Mozartova St 2. Mozart composed *Don Giovanni* here during one of his visits to Prague. The harpsichord and piano he used are on view along with period furniture. It's open Mon to Fri 13.00 - 17.00, Sat and Sun 10.00 - 12.00, 13.00 - 16.00.

Karlův most (Charles Bridge)
This magnificent bridge connects the Lesser Town to the Old Town and is the oldest bridge in Prague. It was originally called Stone Bridge or Prague Bridge but the name was changed in the 19th century to Charles Bridge after Charles IV. It was built on the site of the original **Judith Bridge** which had been washed away by flood waters in 1342. At that time Judith Bridge was one of only two stone bridges in Europe. The other was in Regensburg. The construction of Charles Bridge started in 1357 under

An unusual view of Charles Bridge as seen from the Malá Strana (Lesser Town)

the supervision of Petr Parléř and was completed early the next century. Until 1841 it was the only bridge in the city. Built of sandstone it's 10m (32ft) wide and its 16 arches span 520m (1706ft). According to legend eggs and wine were added to the mortar to make the bridge stronger. As there weren't enough eggs in Prague all the towns and villages in Moravia and Bohemia had to contribute too, some even sending curd and cheese for good measure. There are towers at either end. The one on the Old Town side is all that remains of the ill-fated Judith Bridge. The other one was added in the following century. The bridge is decorated with 30 sculptures, mostly from the 18th century, which together form a unique open-air gallery. The bridge is only open to pedestrians and a stroll along it is popular with both visitors and residents, even though there's usually a good-natured mêlée of buskers, artists and hawkers trying to part you from your money

Josefov (Joseph's Town or the Jewish Quarter)

Jews first arrived here in the 10th century and by the 17th they had

St Nicholas' Church in the Malá Strana — the work of Kilian Dientzenhofer

made it a focal point in Europe for the Hebrew culture. In 1896 much of the neighbourhood was knocked down as part of a huge urban renewal programme, leaving only the Jewish town hall, six synagogues and the old Jewish cemetery intact. Together, these now form the **Státní židovské muzeum (Jewish State Museum)** at Jáchymova St 3. It's open April 1 to Oct 30 Sun to Fri 09.00 - 19.00, Nov 1 to Mar 31 Sun to Fri 07.00 - 16.30.

The **Staronová Synagoga (Old-New Synagogue)** on Pařížská St from 1270 is the oldest one still in use in Europe while the **Maisel Synagogue** on Maislova St has a fine collection of sacred artefacts used in worship. The old **Jewish cemetery** was opened in the 15th century after the existing one had reached capacity. It too was soon full, so the graves were covered over and new ones placed on top of them. This process continued until 1787. By then at least 12,000 people had been buried there in 12 layers. The oldest tombstone is dated April 25 1439 and belongs to the poet Avigdor Karo. Also buried here is Rabbi Jehuda Löw, allegedly the creator and master of Golem, a sinister monster made of mud and clay. Bits of paper bearing messages and prayers are still left in a crack in his tombstone, beneath which, rumour has it, many Jews hid their valuables before being transported to concentration camps.

In the **House of Ceremonies** at the entrance to the cemetery there's a poignant exhibition of illustrations by children in the **Terezin (Theresienstadt)** camp. Equally moving is the list of 77,297 names on the walls of the **Pinkas Synagogue**, currently closed for renovation, of the Czechoslovak Jews who were killed by the Nazis throughout World War II. With haunting precision the name, date of birth and deportation date of each individual victim is detailed.

Across the river to the north in the Holešovice district is the **Národní technické muzeum (National Technical Museum)** at Kostelní St 42. It documents the development of rail, road, air and water transport in the country, with separate exhibitions on astronomy and audio-visual technology. It's open Tues to Sun 09.00 - 17.00.

Staré Město (The Old Town)
Life in this area revolves around the **Staroměstské náměstí (Old Town**

National Technical Museum has exhibitions documenting the history of transport

Square), the most popular tourist attraction after the castle and Charles Bridge. In one corner is the 14th-century **Staroměstská radnice (Old Town Hall)** with its late-Gothic (1470 and mostly destroyed in World War II) and neo-Gothic (1838-48) additions. Its 15th-century **astronomical clock** draws huge crowds to witness the Grim Reaper striking the bell every hour. He strikes it and turns an hour-glass upside-down. Then the Twelve Apostles march past two windows while a cock flaps its wings and crows. The hour rings out. By the side of the Grim Reaper, a Turk nods his head to indicate he's not ready for death. Two other figures symbolize human greed and vanity. The upper part of the clock contains a sphere showing the time and the positions of the sun and the moon in the Zodiac. The lower part is a calendar with signs of the Zodiac and scenes from the seasons by 19th-century artist Josef Mánes. The Old Town Hall is open daily 08.00 - 18.00.

The square has had a colourful history. In 1621 the victorious Habsburgs executed 27 Czech noblemen there taken prisoner during the Battle of White Mountain. The square was also a meeting-place for supporters of Jan Hus (John Huss), the religious reformer who denounced the Church's abuse of its power in the 15th century. He was burnt at the stake in 1415, an event which sparked off the Hussite wars in Bohemia and Moravia. A **statue of Jan Hus** in the middle of the square was unveiled in 1915 to mark the 500th anniversary of his death.

The two 70m (230ft) towers of the **Church of Our Lady of Týn** rise defiantly above the Old Town Square. Enter the church through the Týn School or Celetná St 5. Inside is the oldest font in the city, a fascinating Gothic pulpit and altars decorated with paintings by famous Czech artists. The church was built between 1380 and 1511 and to the right of the main altar is the marble tombstone of the famous Danish astronomer, Tycho de Brahe, who died in 1601.

The Old Town is also home to the **Smetana Museum** at Novotného lávka St 1.The exhibition is devoted to the famous composer and includes some of his original manuscripts. It's open Wed to Sun 10.00 - 17.00.

The Klementinum

Well worth a visit is the second largest complex of buildings after the castle, the Klementinum. Originally a Dominican monastery, it was acquired by the Jesuits in 1556 and gradually extended. Consisting of two churches, the former Jesuit college, the Chapel of Mirrors and several other buildings, it now contains the **State Library of the Czechoslovak Republic** and the **State Technical Library**. Both are open Mon to Fri 09.00-18.00. The highest tower is an observatory.

The Karolinum

Želzná St. This is the oldest university in Central Europe, founded by Charles IV in 1348. The present baroque façade was added in 1718 by architect F.M. Kaňka.

Betlémská kaple (Bethlehem Chapel)

Betlémské Sq. The original building was erected in the years 1391-94. Between 1402-13 Jan Hus preached and taught here in the forbidden Czech language. In 1786 the chapel was partially demolished. The remaining walls were restored in the early 1950s. It's open daily Apr to Sept 09.00 - 18.00 (17.00 Oct), closed Nov to Mar.

Once a Dominican monastery, the Klementinum now houses two State Libraries

Anežský klášter (St Agnes' Convent)
U milosrdných St 17. King Václav (Wenceslas) I founded this convent in 1233 and his sister Agnes became the first abbess. She introduced the Order of the Poor Clares – the female branch of the Franciscans – into Bohemia and was proclaimed a saint in 1989. The convent is now a venue for concerts and lectures and is part of the **National Gallery** with an amazing collection of 19th century Czech painting, well worth taking the time to visit. It's open Tues to Sun 10.00 - 18.00.

Prašná brána (The Powder Tower)
Celetná St. A gateway to the Old Town, the tower was built between 1475-78. In the 17th century it became a gunpowder store, hence its name. Its present appearance reflects the reconstruction carried out between 1875-86. The tower is open May to Sept Wed, Sat, Sun and bank holidays 10.00 - 18.00 (17.00 Apr to Oct), closed Nov to Mar.

Nové Město (The New Town)
Passing through the Powder Tower you come to the New Town, the heart of Prague. This is the area for most of the theatres, museums,

hotels and shops – contemporary Prague overshadows historical Prague. It's also the commercial centre of the city. In the early 14th century there was just a handful of small settlements outside the walls of the Old Town. In the 1340s Charles IV united them into a new district of his expanding city. The majority of the buildings date from the present or last centuries but scattered among them are reminders of bygone times.

Václavské náměstí (Wenceslas Square) The hub of the New Town – perhaps even of the whole of Czechoslovakia – has got to be seen to be believed. At over 750m (818 yds) and 60m (55 yds) wide it's more of a bustling boulevard than a square. Charles IV ordered building work to begin in 1348. Horse dealers used to do business here, hence the square was first called Koňský trh (Horse Market). It took on its current name in 1848 and traders

Patron saint of Bohemia St Václav (Wenceslas) in pride of place in Wenceslas Sq

Wenceslas Sq, the hub of the New Town, more a bustling boulevard than a square

have been replaced by mass demonstrations such as those of the Prague Spring of 1968 and the 'velvet revolution' of 1989. Just below the statue of King Wenceslas is an informal shrine in memory of Jan Palach, the student who burned himself to death in protest at the Soviet invasion of 1968. His photograph and those of recent political activists are constantly surrounded with fresh flowers and burning candles.

The old two-storey baroque houses which once enclosed the square have long gone, their place taken by nondescript hotels, banks, department stores, cafés and restaurants. Glowering down on it all is the ugly exterior of the **Národní muzeum (National Museum)** built in the 1880s. The museum was founded in 1818 and houses prehistoric, historic, numismatic, zoological and natural science collections. The minerology section is world-famous. It's open Wed to Mon 09.00 - 16.00, 17.00 Sat and Sun.

Not far south of the National Museum you come to the **Muzeum Antonína Dvořáka (Anton Dvořák Museum)** at Ke Karlovu St 20. It's housed in the beautiful 'Villa Amcrica' built in the late 18th century by Kilian Dientzenhofer and has displays of manuscripts, photographs and letters. It's open Tues to Sun 10.00 - 17.00.

Still in the New Town but a bit further out near the main bus station and Florenc metro station is the **Muzeum hlavního města Prahy**

Relaxing boat trips up the River Vltava give a very different view of the city

(Museum of the City of Prague) on Švermovy sady (gardens) 1552/54. Its comprehensive collection of exhibits charts the fascinating history of Prague from earliest times up to the present. There are many interesting examples of sculpture, painting and handicrafts on display, including the famous model of the city by Antonín Langweil dating from the first half of the 19th century. There are special displays on the work of goldsmiths between the 16th and 19th centuries and on the Loreta treasure which is on view in the Loreta (see the section on Hradčany on p. 78). It's open Tues to Sun 09.00 - 12.00, 13.00 - 17.00.

At the southern edge of the New Town is **Vyšehrad**, the site of the first settlement in Prague. It stands on top of an impressive bluff overlooking the River Vltava and gives a beautiful view of the city.

Vyšehrad was the seat of the early Přemyslid princes and Charles IV built a castle here with walls connecting it to the New Town. Little of these remain but you can see the Church of SS Peter and Paul and the deanery.

The most interesting sight is the **Slavín cemetery** where some 600 artists, writers and musicians are buried, including the famous composers Dvořák and Smetana, and the novelist Čapek.

Prague Zoo
U Trojského mostu 3, Prague 7. Set in beautiful natural surroundings on the banks of the River Vltava the zoo has over 600 different kinds of animals. It's open Feb to Dec daily 07.00 - 17.00, 19.00 in summer. Bus 112 will take you from Nádraží Holešovice metro station (line C) to the zoo in the northern suburb of Troja. In the summer you can also catch a boat up the river. Next door is **Troja Castle**, which is also worth a look.

SPORTS
If the culture all gets too much for you and you feel the need to get physical there are facilities to suit. If you fancy a day on the green there's a 9-hole golf course in Motol but if you prefer a bit more excitement there are trotting races, flat races and steeplechases every weekend Mar to Nov at the horse track in Velká Chuchle, 12km (7 miles) from the centre on the road to Strakonice. The more active might like to go ice skating at the Slavia Praha IPS Stadium in Vršovice or the Štvanice Sport-Areal, Prague 7 or even swimming in the indoor pools at Dům Kultury Klárov, Nábřeží kapit, Jaroše 3 or at the Holšovice exhibition grounds.

For further information on sports facilities, contact the Prague Information Service (see Travel agencies on p. 67).

FURTHER AFIELD
Březové Hory near Příbram. 62km (39 miles) S. There's an interesting museum of ore mining and mineralogy here. It's open Tues to Sun 09.00 - 16.00.

Svatá Hora (The Holy Hill), near Příbram. 53km (33 miles) SW. This is a place of pilgrimage, on a hill overlooking the town of Příbram. The **14th-century church**, originally built in Gothic style, gained baroque additions in 1658-75. A **cloister** and **Jesuit monastery** were added in the 17th century by the Italian architect Carlo Lurago. Its rich baroque decoration is worth seeing.

Karlštejn (Karlstein Castle) 25km (16 miles) SW. A glorious example of medieval architecture built by Charles IV as a safe deposit for the crown jewels and important state documents. It's in a beautiful setting too, surrounded by forests. Although it was besieged several times by the Hussites – once for seven months – and attacked by the Swedes, the castle was never conquered. Part of the original furnishings and decorations can still be seen. Look out for the **Chapel of the Holy Cross** with its walls studded with some 2500 precious and semi-precious stones. Tours are currently only in Czech and German but there's good multi-lingual information on signs and displays. The village itself is also worth a visit and the surrounding countryside is picture-book stuff, ideal for walking tours.

The castle is open daily May to Sept 08.00 - 18.00, Oct to April 09.00 - 16.00, closed Mon in Jan and Feb.

Koněprusy caves 30km (19 miles) SW. In Palaeolithic times – pre-12,000BC – people lived in these caves, the largest in Bohemia. In the 15th century they were put to less reputable use as a centre for making counterfeit coins. There are many stalactites to be seen – they're the ones that hang down. The caves are open daily Apr to Oct 08.00 - 15.00.

Konopiště Palace near Benešov. 45km (28 miles) SE. Originally constructed in the 14th century, the palace was totally altered in the late 19th and early 20th centuries by

Archduke Franz Ferdinand, whose assassination in Sarajevo in 1914 sparked off World War I. It has a large collection of weapons and hunting trophies. The Archduke was an enthusiastic hunter who meticulously logged the 300,000 birds and beasts he shot. The beautiful grounds contain a motel and a stylish restaurant (I) in an old gamekeeper's cottage.

The palace is open May to Aug Tues to Sun 08.00 - 16.00, Apr and Sept 09.00 - 15.00.

Lidice 22km (14 miles) NW. This village was razed to the ground by the Nazis on June 10, 1942 in retaliation for the assassination of Reichsprotektor Reinhard Heydrich by Czechoslovak patriots airlifted from Britain. Lidice's 173 men were shot and its women and children transported to concentration camps. A museum, monument and **Rose Garden of Friendship and Peace** commemorate the tragedy. The museum is open Oct to Mar 08.00 - 16.00,17.00 Apr to Sept.

Průhonice Palace 10km (6 miles) SE. A Renaissance-style palace constructed at the end of the 19th century. In its spacious grounds there's a **12th century church** and an **arboretum** originally planted in the late 19th century and now with one of the largest collections of different tree species in the world.

Slapy Dam 24km (15 miles) S. Here's the place to get away from it all. In the summer you can take a three-hour boat trip down the Vltava from the landing stage near Palacký Bridge to the reservoir created by this dam. Boats leave daily July 1 to Aug 31, Sat and Sun only May 25 to June 30, Sept 1 to Oct 15. Once you're there you might like to try your hand at some of the many watersports available.

Karlštejn was built by Charles IV to protect the crown jewels and state documents

WEST BOHEMIA

THIS IS ONE of the most popular regions in Czechoslovakia, mainly due to its world-famous spa towns of Karlovy Vary, Mariánské Lázně and Františkovy Lázně. Over the years hundreds of thousands of patients from all over the world have come to take the waters and improve their poor health.

West Bohemia is also the home of Plzeň, famous for its Pilsner Urquel beer and Škoda cars, while the area around Karlovy Vary is famous for the liqueur *becherovka*, china and cut glass.

Sightseers will enjoy the beautiful colonnades and historic buildings of the spa towns but there's plenty of countryside too. The Krušné Hory mountains are easily accessible to the north-west, and the Šumava Mountains in the south-west have wonderful forests and plenty of well marked hiking trails.

Vest Bohemia is famous for its lovely spas

KARLOVY VARY

The 60-odd thermal springs of this spa town where the rivers Teplá, Ohře and Rolava meet have attracted many famous visitors, among them Tsar Peter I, Göethe, Schiller, Beethoven, Chopin, Brahms, Bismarck, the Empress Maria Theresa and the more modern hero, Soviet astronaut Yuri Gagarin. Nowadays 61,000 people live here and people from all over the world come to take the waters and soak in the grandeur of the many old buildings throughout the town to which the Bohemian King and Holy Roman Emperor, Charles IV, gave his name in the 14th century.

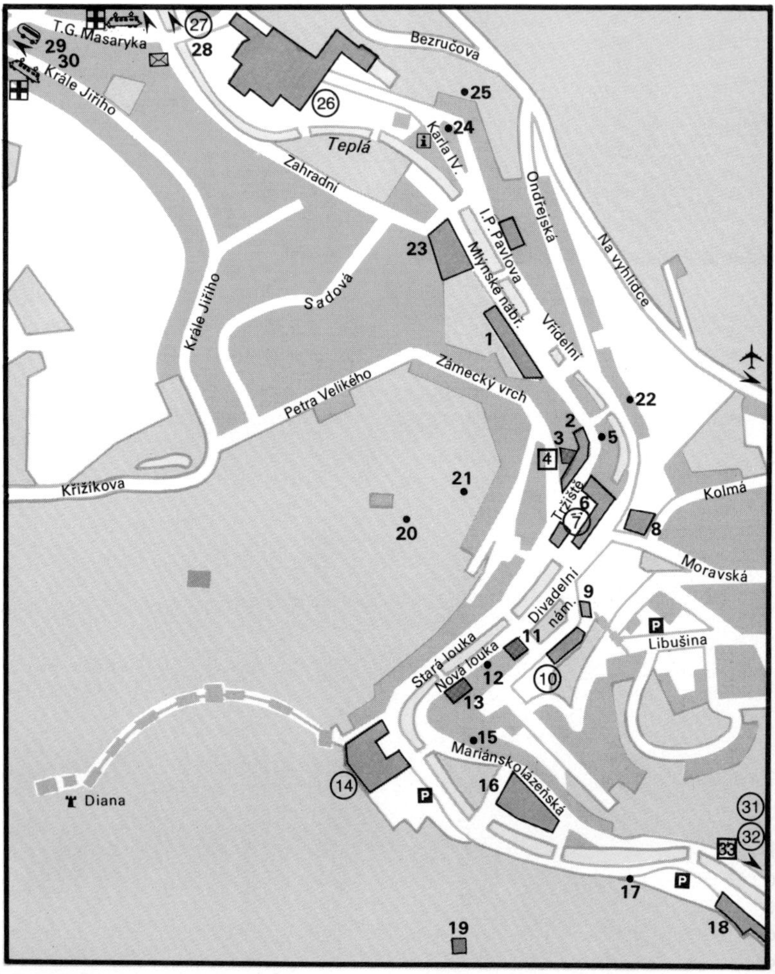

KARLOVY VARY

1 Mill colonnade
2 Market colonnade
3 Château colonnade
4 Castle Tower restaurant
5 Tuzex
6 Spring colonnade
7 Atlantic hotel
8 Church of Mary Magdalene
9 ČSA
10 Central hotel
11 V. Nezvel Theatre
12 Tuzex
13 Dlouhá louka museum
14 Pupp Grandhotel
15 Tuzex
16 Spa House I/Casino
17 Göethe statue
18 Art gallery
19 Observation point
20 Peter the Great statue
21 Stag's Leap
22 Pharmacy
23 Spa House III
24 Library
25 Police
26 Thermal hotel
27 Slavia hotel
28 Tuzex
29 Taxi stand
30 Pragocar
31 Alice Juniorhotel
32 Campsite
33 Post Courtyard café

The castle tower, Karlovy Vary – try the liqueur becherovka in the wine bar

The local thermal springs are rich in dissolved minerals and carbon dioxide and are particularly good for the treatment of diseases of the digestive system and metabolic disorders. The mineral waters are used for drinking cures and baths as well as the extraction of medicinal salts. Today the thermal springs get to the surface through bore holes sometimes 80m (262ft) deep. Water taken from the **Mlýnský pramen (Mill Spring)** is bottled and visitors often buy souvenirs made of sinter, a kind of clay produced by the springs.

SETTING OFF

By air ČSA fly from Prague, Ostrava and Bratislava.

By car E48 from Prague - 122km (76 miles). E49 from Plzeň - 83km (52 miles). E48 or E49 from German border crossing point at Pomezí - 46km (29 miles).

By bus Connections from Prague and other major towns within Czechoslovakia. Coach connections with Vienna in Austria and Weiden in Germany.
By train Express and local trains to main (Upper) railway station from Prague. Express from Berlin, seat reservations essential. From other European cities change at Cheb near the German border. Local trains to Mariánské Lázně from Lower railway station.

ON THE MOVE
Local transport is by bus.
Main bus station Koněvova St 9. Tel: (017) 24 35 9.
Upper railway station Nákladní St 21. Tel: (017) 23 37 7.
Lower railway station Koněvova St 30. Tel: (017) 23 37 7.
Taxi stands Dimitrovova St 24. Tel: (017) 29 44 4/25 03 7/25 48 6.
Car rental Pragocar, Teplárenské St 50. Tel: (017) 22 83 3.

FACT FILE
Emergency medical aid Americká St. Tel: (017) 21 51 11. Hospital. Poliklinicka, Dr Horákové Sq 8. Tel: (017) 24 67 9/26 14 1.
Pharmacy Americká St. Tel: (017) 27 19 4. Vřídelní St 39. Tel: (017) 22 61 9.
Police (VB) I.P. Pavlova St 25. Tel: (017) 23 52 6.
Post office T.G. Masaryka St 1. Tel: (017) 22 67 5.
Airline offices ČSA, Divadelní Sq 1. Tel: (017) 27 85 5/25 76 0/25 33 5.
Travel agencies Čedok, Karla IV St 1. Tel: (017) 27 59 7/26 70 5/26 11 0.
Shopping
There's only one main street so you can take your pick of the shops. Good buys are gold, furs, porcelain and souvenirs made from sinter — a kind of clay produced by hot springs. Tuzex stores are at Vítězná St 18 (textiles and clothes), Nová louka 9 (foodstuffs), Tržiště St 1 (cosmetics and glass), Mariánskolázeňská St 15 (electrical goods) and Mariánskolázeňská St 13 (children's toys).

WHERE TO STAY
Accommodation can be very hard to come by in Karlovy Vary, especially in summer, so you are well advised to book in advance.
⌂ **A* de luxe Pupp Grandhotel** Mírové Sq 2. Tel: (017) 22 12 1/ 22 12 2/22 12 3. Fax: (017) 24 03 2. One of the oldest hotels in the world, built in 1701, with restaurants (I), disco, car rental. Casino opposite.
⌂ **A* Thermal Hotel** I.P. Pavlova St 11. Tel: (017) 28 39 1. Fax: (017) 26 99 2. Spa hotel offering treatments or accommodation only with restaurants (II), wine bar (I), coffee bar (II), snack bar (II), outdoor swimming pool also open to non-residents.
⌂ **B* Central Hotel** Divadelní Sq 17. Tel: (017) 25 25 1/ 25 25 2/25 25 3. Fax: (017) 29 08 6. Restaurant (II), wine bar (II).
⌂ **B Atlantic Hotel** Part of the Central Hotel above. Bed and breakfast only.
⌂ **B Slavia** Lidická St 12. Tel: (017) 27 27 1/27 27 2. Restaurant (II), café (II), bar (II).
Tourist hostels
B Alice Juniorhotel Pětiletky St 1, Karlovy Vary-Břesová. Tel: (017) 24 84 8/24 84 9. Fax: (017) 27 85 6. Dormitory accommodation. Restaurant (II), wine bar (II).
Campsites
△ **A Karlovy Vary-Břesová** Slovenská St 9. Tel: (017) 25 10 1/25 10 2. Fax: (017) 24 03 2. Accommodation in rooms and chalets with pitches for tents. Also A* motel. Restaurant (II + 50%), restaurant (II), bar (II + 50%), garden restaurant (II). Open Mar 21 to Oct 30.

EATING OUT

There are many restaurants where you can eat well but be sure to taste the regional aperitif *becherovka*. It's made from selected herbs to a secret ancient recipe and is exported all over the world.

Many of the restaurants are being privatized so for the moment your best bet is probably to eat in one of the hotels. The wine bar in the Castle Tower (I) is worth a try as is the café (III) in the Post Courtyard where there's dancing to brass music every afternoon.

NIGHTLIFE

Vítězslav Nezvel Theatre Divadelní Sq 19. Opera, drama.
Karlovy Vary Symphony Orchestra Spa House III, Mlýnské nábřeží. Concerts. The orchestra also play at other venues in the town.

Musical festivals such as **The Young Stage** for young musicians in mid-August and **Dvořák's Autumn** Festival take place in the spa buildings, the church and outside in the summer. There's also a festival of magic called **Magiales** in July and an international **film festival** in the same month, as well as an open-air cinema.

WHAT TO SEE

Spring Colonnade This was once named the Yuri Gagarin Colonnade, after the world's first cosmonaut who stayed here in 1961 and 1966. His statue stands outside the impressive steel structure faced with Bulgarian marble. Inside is the main spring Vřídlo, which jets water to a height of 12m (39ft) from a depth of 2000m (6560ft). Other springs can be seen throughout the spa area along

Splendid spa buildings house the 60-odd thermal springs in Karlovy Vary

the River Teplá which is certainly the most interesting part of town. Most have been tapped and spurt out of pipes.

Church of Mary Magdalene Spring Colonnade. The most outstanding monument in the town, this baroque church was designed in 1736 by Kilian Dientzenhofer.

Muzeum Dlouhá louka Dlouhá louka 23. Exhibition on history of Karlovy Vary. Open Wed to Sun 09.00 - 12.00, 14.00 - 17.00.

Art Gallery Puskinova stezka 6. Exhibitions on 20th century Czech and Slovak painting. Open Tues to Sun 9.30 - 12.00, 13.00 - 17.00.

Knihovna Library I.P. Pavlova St 7. Books in foreign languages and reading room. Open Mon, Tues, Thur, Fri 10.00 - 18.00. There is also a music department open Mon, Tues 13.00 - 18.00, Thur 09.00 - 11.00, 13.00 - 16.00.

WALKS AND SPORTS

The town itself is so beautiful you might not want to venture beyond its impressive colonnades although the surrounding countryside offers good walking along well-marked paths. The part of the spa area in the River Teplá valley is the most interesting with the **Spring of Freedom** and the **Park Colonnade**. Up the hill past the turn-of-the-century **Market Colonnade** and **Château Colonnade** is the statue called Stag's Leap and a bust of Peter the Great from 1877. It's a nice walk up to the observation tower on the top of the hill behind the Pupp Grandhotel and you can get great views of the town from here. If you don't feel quite that energetic a cable car will take you all the way to the top.

FURTHER AFIELD

Jáchymov 26km (16 miles) N. Another spa town with mineral springs, Jáchymov was the third largest producer of radium in the world in the 50s. Under Communist rule many political prisoners were put to work in the mines and their health severely suffered.Watch out for the Renaissance and baroque **Church of All Saints**, founded in the 16th century. The museum has paintings from the 16th, 17th and 18th centuries and is open Sun to Fri 09.00 - 12.00, 13.00 - 16.00.

There are good hiking trails and facilities for winter sports in the nearby Krušné Hory mountains. A chairlift takes you to the highest peak **Klínovec** at 1244m (4080ft) where there is a hotel, hostel and observation tower.

Other towns in this range make good starting points for hikes and we recommend **Klášterec nad Ohří, Měděnec, Boží Dar, Pernink**, **Nejdek** and **Kraslice**. Wildlife watchers will enjoy the nature reserve **Boží Dar**, near Boží Dar border crossing point.

Loket 11km (7 miles) SW. The large Gothic castle with a square tower from the 13th century, later rebuilt, now houses a museum of china. It's under reconstruction at the moment and will reopen in 1993.

CHEB

Only a short distance from the German border, Cheb is one of the few towns with a medieval centre which is practically intact and it's worth visiting for this fact alone. Founded in the beginning of the 13th century, much of the town has been restored and there are a great number of Gothic, Renaissance and baroque burgher houses to enjoy. Modern industries include bicycle production and textiles and more than 31,000 people live here.

Typical houses in the immaculately preserved medieval centre of Cheb

SETTING OFF
By car E49 from Karlovy Vary - 46km (29 miles). E49 from Pomezí border crossing - 10km (6 miles).
By bus Connections from Prague and Františkovy Lázně. Regular buses from Karlovy Vary and Mariánské Lázně.
By train Connections with Prague, Františkovy Lázně and Pomezi on the German border. Regular trains from Karlovy Vary and Mariánské Lázně.

ON THE MOVE
Local transport is by bus.
Bus station Žižkova St 10. Tel: (0166) 31 97 8.
Train station Žižkova St 10. Tel: (0166) 30 90 6.
Taxi stands Svobody St 52. Tel: (0166) 33 10 0/33 00 0.
Car rental Pragocar, Smeralova St 52. Tel: (0166) 33 10 0.

FACT FILE
Emergency medical aid Tel: (0166) 30 22 1/30 40 1. Hospital.
Pharmacy Valdštejnská St 22. Tel: (0166) 31 52 8. 24 hour.
Police (VB) Žižkova St 10. Tel: (0166) 36 12 45.
Post office Jiřího z Poděbrad Sq 38. Tel: (0166) 23 01 0/23 00 5.
Travel agencies Čedok, 1. máje St 31. Tel: (0166) 33 95 1/33 95 2.
Shopping
Most shops are concentrated in the town centre. The department store Prior is at Svobody St 6.

WHERE TO STAY
Accommodation is always hard to come by in Cheb so it is essential to book. Čedok can help you find a bed in private houses and appartments but these are limited.
⌂ **B* Hvězda Krále** Jiřího z Poděbrad Sq 4-6. Tel: (0166) 22 54 9. Fax: (0166) 22 54 6. Restaurant (II), self-service restaurant (II), snack bar (II). Fine food.
⌂ **B Slavia** Svobody St 32. Tel: (0166) 33 21 6. Restaurant (II), wine bar (II), snack bar (II), beer cellar (II).

EATING OUT
🍴 **II Fortuna** Jiřího z Podébrad Sq 28. Restaurant, wine bar and confectionery.
🍴 **III Railway station** Žižkova St 10. Restaurant and buffet.

WHAT TO SEE
Cheb Castle Friedrich Barbarossa built this Romanesque castle in 1190 on the Ohře River on the site of an ancient Slav settlement. Baroque fortifications were added by the end of the 17th century. Part of F. Schiller's drama *Wallenstein* was set here. The castle is open April to Oct Tues to Sun 09.00 - 12.00, 13.00 - 16.00.

Jiřího z Poděbrad Square All around this main square are Gothic merchant's houses. Behind is the late Gothic house where the celebrated general of the Thirty Years' War, Albrecht of Wallenstein, was murdered in 1634.

Museum Jiřího z Poděbrad Sq 3. Exhibition on local history, open May to Oct Tues to Sun 09.00 - 12.00, 13.00 - 16.00.

Old Town Hall Jiřího z Poděbrad Sq 16. Built in the baroque style in 1724, the Old Town Hall now houses an art gallery with exhibitions of Czech art in the 20th century. It's open Tues to Sun 09.00 - 21.00.

St Bartholemew's Chapel Křížovnícká St. Worth a visit to see

Entrance hall to Glauber's Springs, one of the many in Františkovy Lázně

the permanent exhibition of Gothic sculptures, open Wed to Sun 09.00 - 17.00.

St Clare's Church Františkénské Sq. Occasional concerts and permanent exhibitions of paintings, art and sculpture, open Wed to Sun 09.00 - 17.00.

SPORTS

If you're at home in or on the water there's plenty to do around Cheb. There are two swimming pools, one indoor, one outdoor and two reservoirs nearby offering a wide variety of watersports. Skalka is towards the Pomezí border crossing and has a campsite while the Jesenická dam lies 7km (4 miles) east and has two campsites. Here you can swim, waterski, sail or fish (permits available at Czech Anglers' Union in Cheb, Plzeň or Mariánské Lázně).

FURTHER AFIELD

Františkovy Lázně 5km (3 miles) NE. The statue of a naked boy **František** stands in Mírové Square and legend has it that if a barren woman touches it she will be cured of her sterility. If this doesn't work the mineral waters of Františkovy Lázně, the third biggest spa resort in Czechoslovakia, are renowned for the treatment of gynaecological disorders as well as cardio-vascular diseases, rheumatism and diseases of the locomotive system. The unique ferro-sulphurous mud is also used in the treatment of ailments. The **Municipal Museum** at Dr. Pohoreckeho 8 houses an exhibition on the history of the town and spa and is open daily 09.00 - 12.00, 14.00 - 17.00.

The town itself was founded in the 18th century and named after the Emperor Franz II. Most of the buildings are in the Empire style and of particular note is the Empire **Parish Church of the Raising of the Holy Rood** on Ruská St, built in 1812 - 1820, and the orthodox **Church of St Olga** from the 19th century in Kollárova St.

Some of the more famous visitors to Františkovy Lázně are now remembered by plaques — there's one of **Beethoven** on the Sevastopol Spa House, Národní St 4-7, and a plaque and statue of celebrated Czech folktale writer **Božena Němcová** is in Mírové Sq.

Soos peat bog 12km (7 miles) N. One of the most interesting and significant nature reserves in Europe for its mineral springs, 'mud volcanoes' and salt marsh flora. Guided tours available, consult Čedok (see p. 100).

Komorní Hůrka 5km (3 miles) NW. The youngest extinct volcano in Central Europe, a mere one million years old. Göethe instigated investigations into its geology.

Aš 62km (39 miles) NW. As far west as you can go in Bohemia, Slav tribes originally settled here in the 9th and 10th centuries. Watch out for the **Catholic Parish Church** from 1820 on Mikulášský Hill and the museum next to it in a former château. With exhibitions on the town's history, the textile industry, workers' movement and arts and crafts, the museum is open Tues to Sun 08.00 - 17.00.

MARIÁNSKÉ LÁZNĚ

You'll also be in good company visiting the second largest spa resort in Czechoslovakia — Kafka, Ibsen, Göethe and Gogel have all taken the waters at Mariánské Lázně. Of the 140 mineral springs in the town 39 are used for treating kidneys, respiratory and urinary disorders.

The town was founded in the last century and many of the buildings are in the Empire style. Sadly a good proportion of them have fallen into poor repair and need extensive reconstruction. Every August or September the town holds a Chopin Music Festival.

SETTING OFF

By air Flight to Karlovy Vary then local bus or train.
By car Roads 20 and 24 from Karlovy Vary - 50km (31 miles). E48 to Cheb from Pomezí border crossing then road 21 - 37km (23 miles).
By bus Daily service from Karlovy Vary, České Budějovice and Domažlice.
By train Express and local trains from Prague, Plzeň, Karlovy Vary and Cheb. Halt on international express line from Frankfurt-am-Main and Nurnberg to Prague.

ON THE MOVE

Local transport is by bus and trolley-bus.
Bus station Nádražní Sq. Tel: (0165) 24 91. Tel: (0165) 33 11 for information.
Train station Nádražní Sq. Tel: (0165) 53 21. Tel: (0165) 48 4 for information.
Taxi stands Hlavní St 100 at Bohemia Hotel. Tel: (0165) 21 24.
Car rental Hlavní St 400. Tel: (0165) 23 18.
Parking Car parks south and north of the town. Bus and trolley-bus connection to centre every 20 minutes or so.

FACT FILE

Emergency medical aid Zeyerova St 8. Tel: (0165) 51 11. Hospital.
Pharmacy W. Píecka St 22. Tel: (0165) 27 64.
Police (VB) Hlavní St. Tel: (0165) 20 97.

Forest Spring, Mariánské Lázně. Kafka, Ibsen and Göethe all visited the town

Post office Posta Mariánské Lázně 1. Tel: (0165) 20 09.
Travel agencies Čedok, Třebízského St 201, in the Evrope Hotel building. Tel: (0165) 22 54/25 00. Three-hour guided tour of the town starts here. Day trips to Karlovy Vary, Cheb and Františkovy Lázně May to Sept.
Shopping
Various shops in the town centre. Tuzex is at Svobody St 8.

WHERE TO STAY
As the town is only small, it's better to book your accommodation in advance, especially in summer.
⌂ **A* de luxe Golf** Zádub 55. Tel: (0165) 26 51/26 52. Fax: (0165) 26 55. Luxury hotel on the outskirts of town with French restaurant (I), café (I), wine bar (I), large golf course, pool, tennis courts, satellite TV.
⌂ **B* Excelsior** Hlavní St 121. Tel: (0165) 27 05/27 06. Fax: (0165) 53 46. Restaurant (II), bar (II), wine bar (II), sauna, solarium.
⌂ **B Corso** Hlavní St 41. Tel: (0165) 30 91/30 92. Restaurant (II), wine bars (I).
Tourist hostels
B Krakonoš Juniorhotel Tel: (0165) 26 24/26 25. For student card holders with restaurant (II), sports facilities, tennis courts.
C Lokomotiva Sports Club Plzeňska St 9. Tel: (0165) 39 17.

Restaurant (IV). Also chalet accommodation.

Campsites

Δ **A Start** Plzeňská St 2062. Tel: (0165) Restaurant (III). Motel, chalets and tents. Open May to Sept.

Δ **B* Luxor** Velká Hlědsebe. Tel: (0165) 35 04. 5km (3 miles) from Mariánské Lázně. Access by trolley-bus. Chalets and tents. Open May to Sept.

EATING OUT

I Lil Club U Sokolova St 336. Restaurant in night club. Open all night.

II Koliba Dusíkova St. Restaurant and wine bar.

III Station restaurant Nádrazní Sq. Cold meals only.

WHAT TO SEE

Göethe Museum Göethovo Sq 11. Oldest building in town where Göethe stayed in 1823. Exhibitions on Göethe, the history of the town and the spa and West Bohemia. Film shows Mon and Wed 13.00 in German, Tues and Thurs 13.00 in English. Open Mon to Fri 09.00 - 12.00, 14.00 - 17.00, Sat and Sun 09.00 - 12.00.

Chopin Museum Hlavní St 47. Exhibition on the great composer who stayed in Mariánské Lázně in 1836. It's open Mon to Fri 10.00 - 12.00, 14.00 - 16.00.

Orthodox Church of St Vladimír Ruská St. Built from contributions by Russian emigrants after 1917. Be sure to see the beautiful icons.

Church of the Assumption of Our Lady Göethovo Sq. Mid-19th century Catholic church.

Great Colonnade Newly reconstructed out of cast iron the colonnade houses the **Singing Fountain,** 18m (59ft) across with

Splendid altar of the Russian Orthodox Church in Mariánské Lázně

hundreds of jets. From 07.00 music is played every odd hour on the hour until 23.00. The fountain looks beautiful at night with all the lights on. In the summer there are open-air concerts at the colonnade or in the spa building Kasino at Rude armády St 95.

In the park below the colonnade you can see the memorial in honour of the US Army troops who liberated the town at the end of the Second World War.

SPORTS

Many visitors enjoy the large golf course at the Golf Hotel while in the summer the open-air swimming pool by the lake is popular. It's easy to get there by bus from the main terminal.

FURTHER AFIELD

Lázně Kynžvart 8km (5 miles) N. Another attractive spa town with mineral springs and even a children's sanatorium. The château was built in the Empire style for the Austrian Chancellor Count Metternich between 1833 - 1839 but is in a very poor state of repair. The château isn't open to the public at the moment but you can see the ruins of the 13th century **Kynžvart castle**.

Slavkovsky les (Slavkov Forest) 15km (9 miles) NW. Nature reserve.

Planá 19km (12 miles) SE. Small town with an attractive early Gothic church.

Teplá 10km (6 miles) E. This small town of 2300 people has a baroque monastery from the 17th and 18th centuries built on a site founded in 1193. For 40 years it was an army base and is now in a terrible condition — the town doesn't have enough money to fund its reconstruction.

Tachov 25km (16 miles) SW. A district town with a baroque château built on the site of a castle. The medieval town walls are well preserved and Tachov boasts a 14th century **Gothic church** and **17th century burgher's houses**. The baroque **monastery** on Míru St has exhibitions on the history of the region, ethnography and zoology. It's open Sept to June Mon to Fri 09.00 - 10.30, 11.30 - 17.00, July and August Tues to Sat 9.00 - 10.30, 11.30 - 17.00, Sun 13.00 - 18.00.

PLZEŇ

Drinkers will raise a toast to Plzeň — as well as being the sixth biggest town in Czechoslovakia and the capital of Bohemia, it is the home to the world-famous Pilsner Urquel (Prazdroj) beer. Pilsner has been brewed in the town since 1295 and the present brewery was founded in 1842.

Thanks to its situation at the point where the rivers Mže, Radbuza, Úhlava and Úslava meet, other industries have developed over the centuries, notably automotive manufacturing — Plzeň is now the base of Škoda Cars. At the end of the Second World War, Plzeň was the target of heavy bombing and many buildings were flattened but there are still some Gothic, Renaissance and baroque buildings.

Plzeň was liberated after the Second World War and there are several memorials to the US Army troops responsible. Parks surround the town on the site of former city walls and today over 170,000 people live here. Every summer the numbers are boosted by visitors to the food exhibition at Ex Plzeň.

SETTING OFF

By air Flight to Karlovy Vary then local bus or train.

By car E50 from Prague - 75km

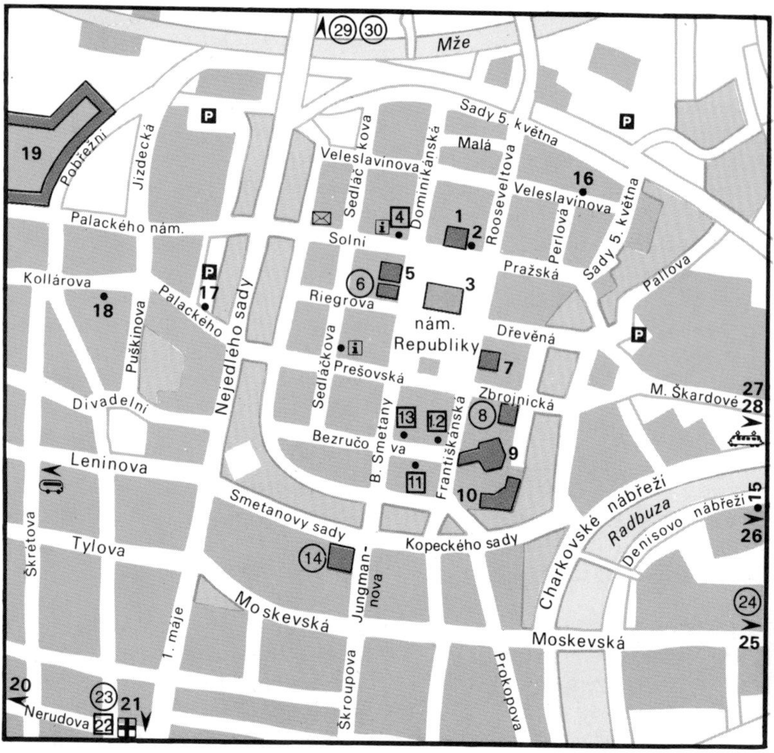

PLZEŇ

1 Town Hall
2 Jiří Trnka Gallery
3 St Bartholomew's Church
4 Dominik café
5 Archdeanery
6 Central hotel
7 Ethnographical museum
8 Continental hotel
9 Franciscan Church
10 West Bohemian museum
11 Jadran wine bar
12 Moravská wine bar
13 U Žumbery bar
14 Slovan hotel
15 Pharmacy
16 Beer museum
17 Taxi stands
18 Tuzex
19 Ex Plzeň exhibition grounds
20 Car rental
21 Police
22 Chodská rychta restaurant
23 Škoda hotel
24 Lokomotiva hostel
25 Prior
26 Indoor swimming pool
27 Plzeň brewery
28 Centrum
29 Ostende campsite
30 Bílá Hora campsite

(47 miles). E50 from Germany crossing at Rozvadov - 73km (45 miles). E53 from Austria crossing at Železná Rudá - 83km (52 miles).

By bus Regular service to Prague, Brno, České Budějovice and major towns in Czechoslovakia. Coaches to Nurnberg and Vienna.

By train Connections to Prague and major towns in Czechoslovakia.

ON THE MOVE

Local transport by trams and buses.

Bus station Leninova St. Tel: (019) 22 37 04/22 40 19.

Train station Nádražní St. Tel: (019) 22 20 79.

Taxi stands Palackého St 6. Tel: (019) 22 22 60.

Car rental Nerudova St 43. Tel: (019) 22 29 50.

FACT FILE

Emergency medical aid Dr. Beneše St 13. Tel: (019) 21 62. Hospital. Denisovo nábřeží 4. Tel: (019) 22 77 77.

Pharmacy Denisovo nábřeží 6. Tel: (019) 21 67. 24 hour.

Police (VB) 1. máje St 45. Tel: (019) 21 72/11 11.

Post office Solní St 20. Tel: (019) 34 00 5.

Travel agencies Čedok, Sedláčkova St 10. Tel: (019) 36 57 8/35 27 7/35 05

9/33 25 1. CKM, Dominikánská St 1. Tel: (019) 37 34 7.

Shopping

Most of the shops are around Republiky Sq. Department stores Prior and Centrium are at Ameriká St 47 and Masarykova St 75. Tuzex is at Kollárova 1.

WHERE TO STAY

⌂ **A* Skoda** Českých bratří Sq 10. Tel: (019) 27 52 52. Restaurant (I), wine bar (I), bar (I).

⌂ **A* Central** Republiky Sq 33. Tel: (019) 22 67 57/22 60 59. Fax: (019) 22 60 64. Restaurant (II), snack bar (II), night bar (I).

⌂ **B* Continental** Zbrojnická St 8. Tel: (019) 33 06 0/36 47 9. Fax: (019) 33 06 0. Restaurant (II), café (II), wine bars (II), bar (I), casino.

⌂ **B Slovan** Smetanovy sady 1. Tel: (019) 33 51 1. Fax: (019) 33 89 0. Restaurant (II), café (II), bar (II).

Tourist hostels

⌂ **A Lokomotiva Plzeň Sports Club** Úslavská St 75. Tel: (019) 48 04 1. Fax: (019) 42 20 1. Dormitory accommodation.

Campsites

Δ **A Ostende** Malý Bolevec. Tel: (019) 52 01 94. Restaurant (II), swimming in lake. Chalets and tents.

Δ **A Bílá Hora Intercamp** Rijna St 28. Tel: (019) 35 61 1. Restaurant (II). Chalets and tents.

EATING OUT

II Dominik Café Dominikanska St 3. Coffee house.

III Moravská vinarná Bezručova St 2. Moravian wine bar with home made wines and local specialities.

II Jadran Bezručova St 9. Wine bar serving Serbian specialities.

III U Žumbery Bezručova St 14. Bar serving Czech specialities and dark beer.

III Chodská rychta Borská St 9. Restaurant serving regional specialities. Book in advance.

WHAT TO SEE

Plzeň Brewery U pivovaru St 1. Unfortunately only groups can take a tour around the brewery and its 9km (5.5miles) of storage cellars.

St Bartholomew's Church Republiky Sq. It's worth risking neckache to appreciate St Bartholomew's steeple, the highest church steeple in Czechoslovakia at 103m (338ft). Inside the 14th and 15th century church, there are lovely high ceilings and a sculpture of the Madonna from the 14th century. On the iron gate there are figures of angels, all black except for one. They say if you touch the white angel and make a wish it should come true.

Town Hall Republiky Sq. Watch out for the superb façade on this 1558 Renaissance building. Many other facades in the square were decorated from designs by Czech painter Mikoláš Aleš.

Archdeacon's residence Republiky Sq. Baroque building dating from 1700.

Franciscan Church Františkánská 13. Gothic church and baroque former monastery, now a **museum** with an exhibition on the Gothic, Renaissance and baroque art of West Bohemia. It's open Tues to Sun 09.00 - 17.00.

West Bohemian Museum Kopeckého sady 2. You'll have to wait until the refurbished museum reopens in 1995 to see the exhibitions on the history of West Bohemia, old weapons, arts and industry. There will also be a rare collection of ancient Roman and Greek ceramics and an oriental collection from the 17th - 20th centuries.

Ethnographical Museum Republiky Sq 13. Occasional exhibitions, open Tues to Sun 09.00 - 17.00.

Beer Museum Veleslavínova St 13. Open Tues 13.00 - 16.00, Wed to Sun 09.00 - 16.30.

Jiří Trnka Gallery Republiky Sq 2. Occasional exhibitions, open Tues to Sun 09.00 - 17.00.

WALKS AND SPORTS
The suburb of Bílá Hora is a nice place to go for walks through woods and around the lakes. There's swimming in the lake by the Ostende campsite and in the Hracholusky dam reservoir north of the town. In Plzeň itself there are three swimming pools, on Denisovo nábřeží (Denisovo Embankment), Koterovska St and Lochotin.

FURTHER AFIELD
Kladruby 35km (22 miles) W. If you fancy a day at the races this is the place to go. Kladruby is known for its racecourse and thoroughbred horses. The Benedictine monastery founded by King Vladislav in 1115 should not be missed.

Stříbro 32km (20 miles) W. Once a royal town with thriving lead and silver mining industries, Stříbro now welcomes tourists to the resorts on the River Mže on the outskirts of town and at the Hracholusky dam reservoir. Buildings worth a visit include the 1590 **Renaissance Town Hall**, the **13th century** monastery and the Gothic **Church of All Saints** reconstructed in the baroque style.

Klatovy 42km (26 miles) S. A good place to go for its architecture, Klatovy was a royal town as far back as the 13th century. Near the Renaissance **Town Hall** stands the 76m (249ft) **Black Tower**. If you've got a head for heights there are great views from its gallery. And if you're not claustrophobic, visit the catacombs under the Baroque **Jesuit Church** from 1679 where they used to bury members of the order. Otherwise a stroll in the town will show you Gothic, Renaissance and baroque houses.

Domažlice 52km (32 miles) SW. A town with remarkable history and traditions, Domažlice is the centre of the Chod region. The Chods were a community of unknown ethnic origin given special privileges in return for their work guarding the border. Their customs, dialect and folklore live on and every August Domažlice hosts the **Dudácký Bagpipe Festival**.

The **Chod Museum** in the 1284 Chod Castle has paintings, arts and crafts and rare documents about the region. It's open April to Oct Tues to Sun 08.00 - 12.00, 13.00 - 16.30.

Another good collection is in the **Jindřich Jindřich Ethnographical Museum** at Dolejší Sq 61. Jindřich Jindřich was a writer and collector of fairy tales and in the museum you can see a reconstructed Chod living room, furniture, clothing, ceramics and glass paintings. It's open April to Oct Tues to Sun 08.00 - 12.00, 12.30 - 14.30.

The round castle tower gives you a good view over Domažlice and the tower of 13th century **Church of Our Lady** is a striking landmark. The main square has attractive arcades and Gothic, Renaissance, baroque and Empire buildings.

Kozel Château 12km (7.5 miles) SE. Only the ground floor remains of this rare Classic château. The park is used for pheasant breeding and has unusual trees.

Klatovy – view of the town square, the Jesuit church and the Black Tower

SOUTH BOHEMIA

IT IS EASY to see why writers are inspired by South Bohemia – it's a region of picturesque villages with typical architecture, good-hearted people and beautiful folk songs. Those looking for a quiet summer holiday will find plenty of peace and plenty to do visiting the many lakes, châteaux and historical towns. South Bohemia is also renowned for its excellent beer.

Those who prefer the mountains will find plenty to do in the unspoiled Šumava range along the border with Austria and Germany. There's good walking in summer and skiing in winter while water babies enjoy the watersports and fishing opportunities offered by the lakes and the rivers Lužnice and Vltava.

ČESKÉ BUDĚJOVICE

An attractive medieval city almost entirely rebuilt after a fire in 1641, České Budějovice is the regional capital of South Bohemia and well worth a visit. Sightseers will love the main square — one of the largest in Europe — with its magnificent 18th century arches, while beer drinkers will prefer its more liquid assets — České Budějovice is the home of Budweiser (Budvar) beer.

The city was founded in 1265 by King Přemysl Otakar II at the point where the rivers Malše and Vltava (Moldau) meet and today boasts a population of 90,000. Through the 16th century it was a centre for crafts and trade, most notably salt and wine from Austria and later the mining of silver. Booming trade demanded better transport links and in 1832 led to the building of a horse-drawn railway connecting České Budějovice with Linz in Austria — a first in Central Europe.

Industry continued to grow and in 1847 the first factory was established manufacturing pencils and pottery. Now České Budějovice has many industries including the Sfinx enamel works and a Škoda factory. The city doesn't ignore its agricultural heritage though — every August it is host to a national exhibition 'Earth the Provider'. It is also the cultural

Beautiful countryside along the Vltava

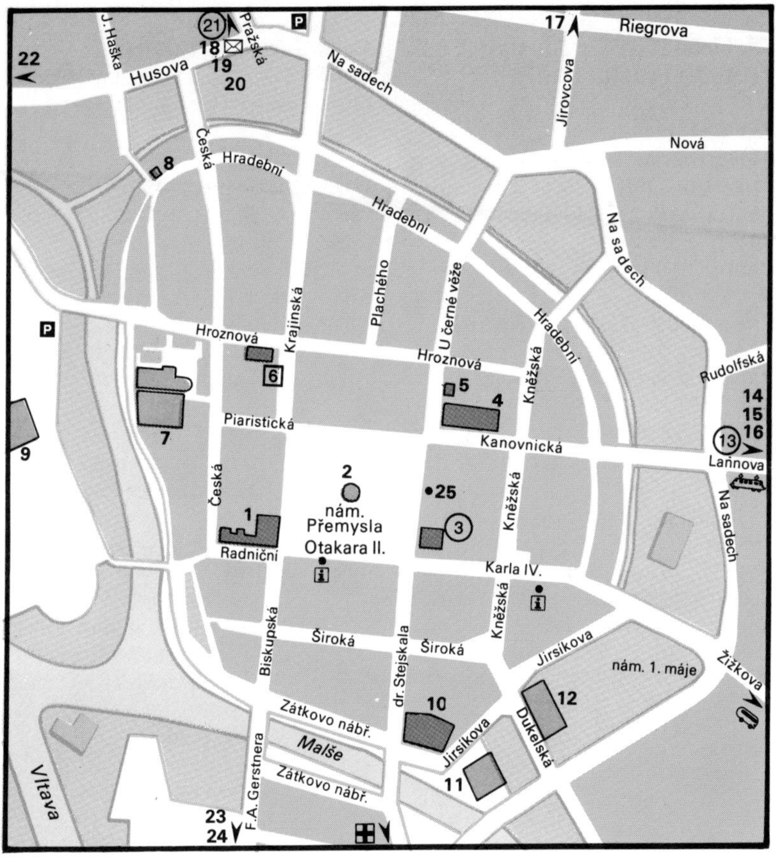

ČESKÉ BUDĚJOVICE 1 Town Hall 2 Samson's Fountain 3 Zvon hotel 4 St Nicholas' Cathedral 5 Black Tower 6 Masné krámy 7 Dominican monastery	and church 8 Rabstejn Tower 9 Sokol swimming pool 10 South Bohemian Theatre 11 Municipal House of Culture 12 Museum of South Bohemian History	13 Grand hotel 14 Taxi stand 15 Prior department store 16 Little Theatre 17 Pragocar 18 Tuzex 19 Police 20 Passports and visa	office 21 Gomel hotel 22 Exhibition 'Earth the Provider' 23 Koh-i-noor pencil factory 24 Terminus of horse-drawn railway 25 Pharmacy

capital of South Bohemia with a developing university centre, museum and theatre.

SETTING OFF

By car Road 23 from Brno - 129km (80 miles). E55 from Austria via the border crossing at Dolní Dvořiště - 38km (24 miles).

By bus Connections with major towns in Czechoslovakia including Prague, Plzeň, Brno, Ostrava. Routes from Linz and Vienna.

By train Express train links with Prague and Vienna.

ON THE MOVE

Local transport is by bus. A trolley-bus network is under construction to be completed in 1992.

Main bus station Žižkova St Tel: (038) 25 55 5.

Train station Nádražní St. Tel: (038) 82 31 11.

Taxi stands Lannova St 1. Tel: (038) 23 31 7.

Car rental Pragocar, J.Š. Baara St 35. Tel: (038) 26 31 0.

FACT FILE

Emergency medical aid B. Němcové St 54. Tel: (038) 82 19 11. Hospital.
Pharmacy Přemysl Otakar II Sq 26. Tel: (038) 37 40 2.
Police (VB) Pražská St 5. Tel: (038) 82 01 11 1.
Post office Pražská St 5. Tel: (038) 82 49 11.
Passports and visas Pražská St 23. Tel: (038) 26 01 7/28 50 6.
Travel agencies Čedok, Přemysl Otakar II Sq 39. Tel: (038) 35 75 3. CKM, Karla IV St 14. Tel: (038) 37 75 1/36 13 8.
Shopping
Most shops are concentrated on Lannova St and Přemysl Otakar II Sq. Prior department store, Leninova St 22. Tuzex, Pražská St 2137.

WHERE TO STAY

⌂ **A* Gomel** Pražská St 14. Tel: (038) 28 94 1/27 94 9. Fax: (038) 28 33 8. Four restaurants (I&II), café (I) with a view of the city (16th floor), bar (I), snack bar (II), night club (I), car park.
⌂ **B Zvon** Přemysl Otakar II Sq. Tel: (038) 35 36 1/36 35 2. Restaurant and café (I), restaurants (II & III), snack bar (III), parking nearby.
⌂ **B Grand** Nádražní St 27. Tel: (038) 36 59 1. Fax: (038) 33 58 2. Restaurant (I), café (I), snack bar (II), wine bar (I), parking.

EATING OUT

🍴 **III Masné krámy** Krajinská St. Restaurant and ale house in 1554 building. The name means Butcher's Shop after the trade that went on there until the mid-19th century.

NIGHTLIFE

Municipal House of Culture 1. máje Sq. Ballet, opera and cultural events.
South Bohemian Theatre Stejskalova St 12. Opera and drama.
Little Theatre Hradební St 18. Programmes for children.

WHAT TO SEE

Přemysl Otakar II Sq Dating from the 15th century, the square is dominated by the 72m (236ft) high **Black Tower**, once a belfry and watchtower and now offering panoramic views over the city. It was built from 1549 to 1578 and reconstructed in 1982. The lower part is Gothic, the upper part Renaissance. It's open April 1 to Oct 30 10.00 - 17.00. Another tower, the **Rabštejn Tower** is all that remains of the original town walls destroyed in the last century.

Next to the Black Tower is **St Nicholas's Cathedral** founded in the 13th century, destroyed by fire, rebuilt 1641 - 1649 and reconstructed several times since, the last time being in 1988. It contains some impressive frescoes by J.A. Schöpfl.

Samson's Fountain (1727) stands in the middle of the square while on one side you'll see the baroque **Town Hall** (1727 - 1730) with its three towers and a splendid cornice with allegorical sculptures of Justice, Courage, Wisdom and Prudence by J. Dietrich in 1731. It also bears the coats of arms of Bohemia, Moravia, Silesia and České Budějovice. If you want to pick up some art, the exhibition hall at the **House of Arts** on the square has works for sale.

Dominican Monastery and Church of the Self-Sacrifice of Our Lady Piaristická St. This is the oldest historical monument in České Budějovice, founded in 1263. The church itself is early Gothic but the interior is predominantly pseudo-Gothic. Look out for the baroque cloister, 17th century organ box and the 1759 rococo pulpit.

Samson's Fountain in the middle of the main square in České Budějovice

Netting carp in Rožmberk Lake, the largest fishing lake in Czechoslovakia

Museum of South Bohemian History Dukelska St 1. Exhibitions on South Bohemian nature, primeval history, 12th to 20th century history, particularly the Hussite movement. Renaissance and baroque halls. Open Tues to Sun 09.00 - 12.00, 13.00 - 17.00.

WALKS AND SPORTS

Although it can be very pleasant to walk through České Budějovice itself there is little in the way of organized sports but there is a swimming pool at the Tatran Sports Centre. Consult Čedok.

FURTHER AFIELD

Třeboň 18km (11 miles) E. Nestling in a sea of fishing lakes in a protected area is this spa town of 5000 people. The lakes were created centuries ago to breed fish and the largest lake in Czechoslovakia is just 3km (2 miles) from Třeboň. Called **Rožmberk** it covers a massive 720 hectares (1778 acres). Next to the town is the smaller 201 hectare (496 acres) **Svět** lake used not only for fishing but for swimming and boating. Try the **Rybárška bašta** restaurant (II) next to the Svět Hotel if you want to savour the fish.

6km (4 miles) to the north is **Velký Tisý** lake and next to it **Malý Tisý**, a rare water bird sanctuary with silver and purple herons.

Třeboň is popular not just for fish and fowl however - its curative muds, iodine, herbal and bubble baths attract many visitors who hope to regain their health.

Trocnov 15km (9 miles) SE. Near the village of Borovany, Trocnov is the birthplace of **Jan Žižka**, military commander of the Hussite troops in the 15th century. The **Žižka Museum** is a National Cultural Monument, open Tues to Sun 09.00 - 16.00.

Týn nad Vltavou 30km (19 miles) N. Popular open–air theatre open June 18 to Aug 31. Performances Tues, Fri and Sat 21.00.

ČESKÝ KRUMLOV

Almost unchanged since the 18th century, this small medieval town is one of the most picturesque in Europe. Its 13th century castle, rebuilt in the 16th century, is the largest in South Bohemia and second only to Prague Castle within Czechoslovakia.

Český Krumlov lies in an S-shaped bend of the River Vltava (Moldau) in the foothills of the **Šumava mountains**, 25km (16 miles) south of České Budějovice. From 1302 the town was owned by the famous noble family Rožmberk, until 1602 the biggest landowners in Bohemia. They built a new castle and supported the development of crafts and trade. In the 15th century silver mines were opened in the area and in 1494 Český Krumlov was granted the status of a royal town. In 1602 the town was sold to Emperor Rudolf II and in the 19th century spinning and paper mills, lime and graphite works began to develop.

Until the Second World War the town was populated mostly by Germans and between 1938 and 1945 it was cut off from Czechoslovakia. When the Germans withdrew after the war, several thousand new settlers moved to Český Krumlov spurring the town's development. It is now the agricultural and fishing centre of the region with a population of 12,000. Industries now include furniture and textiles and there is an extensive network of underground passages and cellars used for cheese-making.

SETTING OFF

By car E55 from Austrian border crossing point at Dolní Dvořiště. After 14km (9 miles) take the road signposted to Český Krumlov - 16km (10 miles).
By bus Regular service from České Budějovice Mon to Fri, sporadic service Sat and Sun. Connection from Lipno and other towns in the Šumava region.
By train Local trains from České Budějovice and other Šumava towns.

ON THE MOVE

Local transport is by bus.
Bus station Hřbitovní St. Tel: (0337) 34 15.
Train station Železniční St 1. Tel: (0337) 32 75.
Taxi stands and car rental FOKR Agency, Přísečná St 8. Tel: (0337) 39 63.

FACT FILE

Emergency medical aid. Hřbitovní St 450. Tel: (0337) 37 41. Hospital
Pharmacy Svornosti Sq 16. Tel: (0337) 33 31.
Police (VB) Na Latráni. Tel: (0337) 27 10. Inside the château.
Post office Na Latráni. Tel: (0337) 22 71.
Travel agencies Čedok, Svornosti Sq 4. Tel: (0337) 21 89/20 62.
Shopping
Most shops are concentrated in Latrán St.

WHERE TO STAY

⌂ **B* Vyšehrad** Tel: (0337) 53 11. Hotel built in 1971 with restaurant (II), wine bar (II), bar (II).
⌂ **B Krumlov** Svornosti Sq 14. Tel: (0337) 22 55. Hotel in 12th century building with restaurant (II), wine bar (II).
⌂ **B Růže** Horní St 153. Tel: (0337) 22 45. Former Jesuit college currently being refurbished until the end of 1991. No restaurant.

EATING OUT

🍴 **II U hroznu** Svornosti Sq.

🍴 **III U města Vídně** Na Latráni.
🍴 **III Kleť** 10km (6 miles) from Český Krumlov towards Lipno. Well signposted from Český Krumlov.

WHAT TO SEE
Krumlov Castle On the banks of the River Vltava (Moldau), this magnificent castle is an absolute must for any visitor to South Bohemia. It is the second largest fortification in Czechoslovakia after Prague Castle and certainly one of the oldest. The most ancient parts are the round tower of the original Hrádek, dating from the second half of the 13th century, and the **Horní Hrad (Upper Castle)** built between

Český Krumlov, its medieval centre barely changed since the 18th century

1320 and 1340. The whole complex was reconstructed in the second half of the 16th century in the Renaissance style. The castle contains many splendid halls. Worth seeing is the **Masquerade Hall** with wall paintings from 1748. Watch out too for the **Lower** or **Guard Courtyard** which contains large guns and the former watch-house, and for the 1730 **mint-house** opposite. Bears were kept in the first moat in the 16th century and the bridge across the second moat goes back to 1574. It's open April 1 - Oct 31 Tues to Sun 09.00 - 12.00, 13.00 - 15.00 (later in the summer if requested).

The **castle park** is beautiful and open all year. The summer pavilion **Belarie**, the riding school and the castle theatre are from the 18th century. More recently a revolving open–air theatre has been built in the castle park and the **South Bohemian Theatre** perform there. Book your tickets at Latrán St 17.

Latrán The outer bailey and Renaissance buildings below the castle are the oldest part of the settlement. The **Českobudějovická Tower** has survived from the original 16th century town fortifications.

The Old Town Crossing the Lazebnický Bridge brings you to the Old Town and a number of important Gothic, Renaissance and baroque houses including the **Zlatokorunní House** from 1309 at Klementa Gottwalda Sq 12 and the **Krčín House** from 1583 at number 54. The Gothic and Renaissance **Town Hall** is on the same square along with a baroque **plague column** from 1716. Worth mentioning too is the late **16th century brewery** on Široká St. The former **Jesuit college** on Horní St is from the same period but is now put to a different use - it houses the Růže Hotel.

Ethnographic Museum Horní St 152. An early baroque building. Open Tues to Sun 09.00 - 12.00, 12.30 - 16.00 (18.00 Wed).

St Vitus' Church Horní St. Impressive Gothic church from 1439 containing the mausoleum of Vilém of Rožmberk and the remains of some Gothic paintings.

FURTHER AFIELD

Mount Kleť 10km (6 miles) NW. High on the hill stands an observatory and hostel with a restaurant (see p. 115). Outdoor types can take the ski tow but for the less energetic there's a chairlift which will take you all of the 1083m (3552ft) to the top. The views are incredible and on a clear day you can see the Alps.

Zlatá Koruna 7km (4 miles) NE. Originally a Gothic monastery belonging to the Cistercian order, it was founded in 1263 by Přemysl Otakar II and rebuilt in the 18th century. It now houses **exhibitions** on South Bohemia and literature. Watch out for the **Kapitulní síň (Chapel of the Guardian Angels)**. It's open April, May, Sept, Oct Tues to Sun 09.00 - 12.00, 13.00 - 16.00, June to Aug Mon to Sat 08.00 - 12.00, 13.00 - 17.00.

Rožmberk 25km (16 miles) S. Built mostly in the Renaissance and Gothic styles, the town of Rožmberk has a **Gothic church** with stellar and reticulated vaulting. Its **Renaissance castle** dates from 1250 when the Rožmberks built it as their family seat. Between 1620 - 1945 the castle belonged to the Buquol family and it is now one of the few castles whose interior still looks much as it did in the last century. The **museum** has a collection of weapons, furniture and paintings, open April, May, Sept,

Oct Sat and Sun 08.00 - 12.00, 13.00 - 17.00, July to Aug Tues to Sun 08.00 - 12.00, 13.00 - 17.00.

Šumava Mountains
Virgin forests, lofty ridge-top walks, rare vegetation and a pleasant climate combine to make the Šumava mountain range a magnet to all serious nature lovers. Otherwise known as the **Bohemian Forest**, the Šumava range stretches 120km (75 miles) from Vyšší Brod in South Bohemia to Všeruby in West Bohemia. It forms part of the natural frontier between Czechoslovakia, Germany and Austria. For 40 years a large part of the Šumava range along the border with Germany was closed, leaving nature a free hand to nurture unspoiled beauty. Now-adays the area is no longer off-limits and marked footpaths are gradually making it accessible to the public.

The highest peak in the range is **Grosser Arber** in Germany at 1457m (4779ft), the highest in Czechoslovakia is **Plechý** near the Lipno dam reservoir at 1378m (4520ft). In the central part of the range lies the **Boubín virgin forest**, virtually untouched by human influence throughout the centuries and one of the largest nature reserves in Czechoslovakia. To the west, glacial activity has created the biggest mountain lakes of Šumava, **Černé (Black Lake)** and **Čertovo (Devil's Lake)**.

Outdoor types are in their element here — walkers can enjoy great trails through the foothills, while the lakes and the Lipno dam reservoir offer watersports while trout and grayling coax anglers from far afield. (For fishing permits see p. 18). Snow covers the slopes until late spring, ideal for cross-country skiing, and pheasant, deer, hare and wild boar please nature watchers.

There are plenty of places to stay in the Šumava range with many hotels, mountain chalets and camp sites. Health centres and modern sports complexes appeal to the body-conscious and there are winter sports resorts at **Špičák**, **Hofmanky**, **Hojsova Stráž**, **Churáňov** and **Kleť**.

Kvilda The highest village in Czechoslovakia at 1049m (3441ft) near the source of the mighty River Vltava (Moldau). **Pseudo-Gothic church** from 1892 - 1894 with shingle facing typical of the area. Starting point for hikes to **Chuŕaňov**, **Horská Kvilda**. Accessible by regular bus.

Horská Kvilda Typical mountain village with rustic houses. Setting for the novel *Bílý Samum (White Simoom)* by local writer Karel Klostermann.

Antigl Typical Šumava farm with timbered houses, now a campsite. Starting point for 7km (4 miles) nature trail through beautiful nature reserve in the **Povydří (Vydra) river valley**. Watch out for the fascinating rock forms, waterfalls and rapids.

Medvědí stezka (Bear Path)
Nature trail beginning at the Lipno dam by Ovesná railway station crossing the forested slopes of **Pernik** and passing bizarre rock formations. Passes **Medvědí kámen (Bear Stone)** where the last bearin Šumava was shot on November 14, 1856. The stuffed beast is now on display at the **Šumava Museum** in **Kašperské Hory** 12km (7 miles) S of Sušice. It's open Tues to Sun 09.00 - 17.00. There are good views of the **Schwarzenberg Canal** linking the Vltava and Danube rivers, built in 1789 - 1822 to transport logs and in use up to 1962.

The River Vydra rushes through the lush forests of the Šumava Mountains

PRACHATICE

Founded in the 14th century as a trading centre for salt, the town prospered and was fortified in the 15th century. The **Písecká Gate** still remains from this period. Prachatice is now an historical town reserve with a population of 10,000 and many rare houses in the centre. **Jan Hus**, the religious reformer whose death by burning at the stake in 1415 sparked off the Hussite wars, was born very near here. Every year on the anniversary of his death on July 5 there are celebrations at Husinec 5km (3 miles) to the south.

SETTING OFF

By car E53 from Plzeň to Klatovy then road 22 to Vodňany and local road to Prachatice - 140km (87 miles). E49 from České Budějovice to Vodňany then local road - 51km (32 miles).

By bus Several local buses daily from České Budějovice.

By train Several local trains daily from České Budějovice.

ON THE MOVE

Local transport is by bus.

Bus station Nádražní St. Tel: (0338) 22 88 1.

Train station Nádražní St. Tel: (0338) 21 03 7.

Taxi stands Rogačevská St 558. Tel: (0338) 22 71 5.

FACT FILE

Emergency medical aid Vodňanská

St 1.Tel: (0338) 22 22 0.
Pharmacy Vodňanská St. Tel: (0338) 21 03 4.
Police (VB) Pivovarská Sq 4. Tel: (0338) 38 32 4.
Post office Husova St 6. Tel: (0338) 22 55 5.
Travel agencies Čedok, Zvolenská 30. Tel: (0338) 21 86 4.
Shopping
Libín department store, Vodňanská St.

WHERE TO STAY
⌂ **B Národní dům** Velké Sq. Tel: (0338) 21 56 1. Set in three historical buildings with restaurant (II), wine bar (II), coffee bar (II).
⌂ **B Zlatá stezka** Hlavní Sq Tel: (0338) 21 84 1. Old two-storey building with restaurant (II).

NIGHTLIFE
Municipal Theatre Horní St 170. Based in Renaissance Town Hall reconstructed in 1981. Drama.
Exhibition Hall Dolní brána. Classical concerts, poetry recitals.

WHAT TO SEE
In the town there are some valuable historical buildings including the former **Prince's Palace** built in 1572 by the Rožmberks and **St Peter and Paul's Church**, a Gothic construction with the remains of a 12th century romanesque church, one of the oldest in Bohemia. **St James' Church** is the oldest preserved building with original towers, one of them unfinished. The **Old Town Hall** from 1571 has biblical carvings.

WALKS AND SPORTS
Many hiking trails and cross-country skiing routes start from Prachatice but one not to be missed is a walk through the **Boubín virgin forest** 18km (11 miles) to the south-west. It's accessible only by marked paths but is well worth the effort. There are no places to hire cross-country skis as yet so you'll have to take your own. If you're a watersports fan there's plenty of opportunity for swimming at the Tatran Sports Stadium on U Stadionu St and the indoor pool at Solarium next door.

FURTHER AFIELD
Husinec 5km (3 miles) N. The birthplace of Jan Hus, founder of the Hussite revolutionary movement in the 15th century (see p. 31). There's a statue in the main square by Karel Lidický and a museum in the house where he is said to have been born, open May to Oct Tues to Sun 08.00 - 11.30, 13.00 - 16.00.

Helfenburk near Husinec. Ruins of Rožmberk Gothic castle from 1355 visible from a considerable distance.

Strakonice 30km (19miles) NE. District centre with a population of 21,000 and the place to go for folklore. **Bagpipe festival** every summer in the gardens of rare 13th century water castle, one of the oldest in Czechoslovakia. Beautiful **Renaissance church** and houses, as well as a lovely **Gothic church**.

Netolice 19km (12 miles) NE. Once the site of a 10th century castle of the Vítkovcik tribe, Netolice has Renaissance and baroque houses and a square with attractive arcades. Gothic **St Wenceslas Church** has a **museum** with a collection of national costumes and folk embroidery. It's open May to Oct Tues to Sat 09.00 - 12.00, 13.00 - 16.00. 3km (2 miles) away lies the Renaissance **Kratochvíle Château** built 1583 - 1589 and now a museum of puppets and animated films, open April Sat to Sun 09.00-12.00, 13.00-15.15, May to Sept Tues to Sun 09.00-12.00, 13.00-16.15. The state stud farm is in the grounds.

Bohemian glass is exquisite – you might be able to pick up some nice pieces

Volary 15km (9 miles) S. Historical town with old Alpine-style wooden houses. Good place to start hikes and go cross-country skiing.

Vimperk 23km (14 miles) NW. Worth visiting for the **glass-making museum** at the château. It's open May to Oct Tues to Sun 09.00 - 12.00, 13.00 - 16.00. There's also the second oldest **printing workshop** in Bohemia (1482) and **glass cutting** and **jewellery workshops** from 1814. Tel: (0339) 21 75 7 to book a visit. You might pick up some bargains.

Mrtvý luh 22km (14 miles) S. Nature reserve where the Teplá and Studená Vltava rivers meet. Typical Šumava swamp with beautiful meadows, forests and wooded peaks.

Lenora 27km (17 miles) SW. Resort at the foot of **Mount Boubín**, good place to buy Bohemian crystal and look at folk architecture.

Lipno 30km (19 miles) S. Largest reservoir in Czechoslovakia at 4970 hectares (12,029 acres) and a great centre for watersports of all kinds including swimming, canoeing, angling, boat hire and water skiing. Remarkably, a dam wall only 25m (82ft) high holds back a reservoir over 42km (26 miles) long and 16km (10 miles) wide. Next to the dam you can see the huge **Čertova Stěna (Devil's Wall)** with a stone sea of granite rocks at the bottom. The reservoir is the only underground hydro-electric plant in Czechoslovakia. Forests rise up on every side and there are plenty of campsites to stay at. Boat trips across the lake will take you to the resorts of **Lipno nad Vltavou**, **Frymburk**, **Černá v Pošumaví** and **Horní Planá**.

TÁBOR

If you want to discover why Bohemia gained its unconventional reputation, a visit to Tábor might go some way to provide you with the answers. Jan Žižka and his Hussite 'Warriors of God' founded the town in 1420 on the principles of collective possession and responsibility. They built Tábor as a fortress on a hill overlooking the Lužnice river.

Double fortification walls are still preserved at Parkány. The streets were made narrow and irregular to slow down the enemy and below ground there are 15km (9 miles) of catacombs built to hide and protect the defenders.

In 1437 Tábor was made a royal town and crafts and trade flourished there until two great fires in 1532 and 1559 when most of the houses were destroyed. The decline continued to 1620 when the town was under siege for a year after the defeat of the Czech estates in the **Battle of White Mountain**. When it fell all property was confiscated, the population decreased and all economic activity was paralyzed. It wasn't until 1750 when the district office was established there that the town began to prosper once more.

A Czech-speaking secondary school was founded in Tábor in 1862 – the first of its kind under the Habsburg monarchy. In 1866 an

The Gothic Old Town Hall in the square has magnificent Renaissance gables

important Agricultural College was also established.

From the mid 19th century Tábor decided to revive its Hussite heritage and regular festivals in the memory of Jan Žižka and the Hussites began. A monument to Žižka was erected in 1877 and in 1878 the municipal museum dedicated to the Hussites was founded.

After the Second World War, new industries sprang up in the town which has now grown to a population of 30,000.

SETTING OFF

By car E55 from Prague - 80km (50 miles). E55 from České Budějovice - 53km (33 miles).

By bus Direct connections to Prague, České Budějovice, Plzeň, Brno, Olomouc.

By train International express trains linking Prague and Vienna stop in Tábor. On main line between České Budějovice and Prague.

ON THE MOVE

Local transport is by bus.

Bus station Chýnovská St 215. Tel: (0361) 23 75 1.

Train station Valdenská St 1. Tel: (0361) 22 43 1.

Taxi stands and car rental Soběslavská 1723. Tel: (0361) 22 27 1.

Shopping

The main shopping street is Květná St where there is a Tuzex store.

FACT FILE

Emergency medical aid Ounz. Tel: (0361) 22 12 1. Hospital.

Pharmacy 9. května St 656. Tel: (0361) 33 25 1.

Police (VB) 39021, Tábor-Sídliště nad Lužnic. Tel: (0361) 22 55 1.

Travel agencies Čedok, 9 května St 1282. Tel: (0361) 22 35.

WHERE TO STAY

⌂ **B Palcát** 9. května St. Tel: (0361) 22 90 1/22 90 3. Modern hotel with restaurant (II), coffee bar (II), night bar (I) (closed Fri and Sat).

⌂ **B Slavia** Valdenská 591. Tel: (0361) 22 82 7/23 57 4. Older hotel with restaurant (II), ale house (III).

⌂ **B Slovan** 9 května St. Tel: (0361) 23 43 5/23 69 2. Hotel with restaurants (II & III), wine bar (II), snack bar (IV), video disco.

Tourist hostels

B Vodní stavby dormitory Krakovská St 2805. Tel: (0361) 42 85 0/42 20 9. Italian restaurant (II). Next door restaurant **Slováč** (III) and wine bar **Centrum** (II).

B Motels Planá nad Lužnicí, 391 11 Tábor. Tel: (0361) 98 31 5. Motel on road to České Budějovice. Open 24 hours.

Campsites

△ **A Zárybničná Lhota** Knížecí rybník. Tel: (0361)22 48 0. Campsite with chalet accommodation, self-service restaurant (III). Open May to Sept.

NIGHTLIFE

Olbrachtovo Theatre Palackého St 1. Drama, opera, musicals.

WHAT TO SEE

Žižka Square An 1884 statue of the town's founder stands in the central square along with a 1567 stone fountain with a sculpture of a Tábor warrior. The Gothic **Old Town Hall** from 1521 has magnificent Renaissance gables and houses the **Museum of the Hussite Revolutionary Movement**, open April 1 to Sept 30 Tues to Sun 08.30 - 16.30. From here you can gain access to the dense network of underground passages below the square. On all sides there are rare Gothic buildings, later reconstructed in Renaissance and baroque styles. The other landmark of the square is the **Dean's Church of**

the Transfiguration of Our Lord on Mount Tábor from 1512 with remarkable reticulated vaulting and a neo-Gothic main altar which shouldn't be missed.

Mikuláš z Husi Square Smaller square north of Žižka Square with early baroque **Church of Our Lady** monastery from 1666.

Kotnov Castle A single round tower remains of this 14th century castle behind the entrance to the old town through **Bechyňská Gate**, also part of the ancient fortifications.

Na parkánech St Walking along the old fortifications here you can see a wonderful panorama of the town and the Lužnice river.

Jordán Lake This is the oldest valley dam in Bohemia and accessible right from the centre of town. The water leaving the lake flows over the 18m (59ft) **Jordán Waterfall** at the far end of the lake called **Malý Jordán**.

SPORTS
In Tábor you'll have plenty of chances to have a go at watersports in the **Jordán Lake** and the **Lužnice** river. There are boats for hire or you can go windsurfing or fish (see p. 18 for permits). Unfortunately not many people brave swimming in the river as it is too polluted. If you want more organised sports there's a stadium across the dam, a 25m (82ft) swimming pool and an ice rink. See Čedok (address on p. 123) for details and opening times.

FURTHER AFIELD
Kozí Hrádek 4km (2.5 miles) S.
A good stretch of the legs will take you to this national cultural monument, the ruins of a 14th century castle where Jan Hus lived from 1412 - 1414.

Bechyně 19km (12 miles) SW.
A town to treat the eyes or the body with its 13th century **Gothic castle**, later rebuilt into a **Renaissance château**, and a celebrated peat spa for the treatment of rheumatism and metabolic disorders. Some of the town fortifications still remain and there's a unique concrete bridge over the Lužnice river from 1928. Bechyně is a famous centre for the ceramics industry and has a **museum of ceramics and ethnography**, open Tues to Sun 09.00 - 12.00, 13.00 - 17.00. An electric narrow-gauge railway from 1903, the first of its kind in Central Europe, links the town with Tábor.

Soběslav 19km (12 miles) S.
Picturesque village in Soběslav moors with many examples of folk baroque architecture. A walk in the deep forest around the village will give you the opportunity to gorge on bilberries and to pick mushrooms, so long as you know your Slippery Jack from your Saffron Parasol.

Mladá Vožice 19km (12 miles) NE.
You can get a beautiful view from the ruins of the castle overlooking this historical town. Gold and silver were mined here and there's a **baroque château**, **museum** and **Gothic church** rebuilt in the baroque style.

Planá nad Lužnicí 9km (6 miles) S.
Resort on the Hejtman Lake.

Chýnov 9km (6 miles) E.
Interesting 1730 baroque château. 3km (2 miles) away is **Pacová Hora**, one of the oldest accessible caves in Bohemia.

'he peaceful River Lužnice provides the opportunity to get away from it all

NORTH AND EAST BOHEMIA

ANY REGION which boasts such magical names as the **Krkonoše (Giant) Mountains** and **Český ráj (Bohemian Paradise)** has got to be worth putting on the visitor's itinerary. The Giant Mountains are the playground of Prague where city-dwellers can escape the bustle to walk and ski through some of the most spectacular mountain scenery in Europe. Sadly many of the trees are dying through the effects of pollution and the future of the area is not looking bright. But no-one can fail to be impressed by the intriguing sandstone formations of the **Bohemian Paradise** where climbers can find some of the most challenging faces in the world.

While you're there you might also care to partake of the excellent beers such as Pilsner Urquel and Budvar (Budweiser) of Bohemia, made from local hops and said to be among the best in the world.

With an alpine/arctic climate the Krkonoše are ideal for walking and skiing

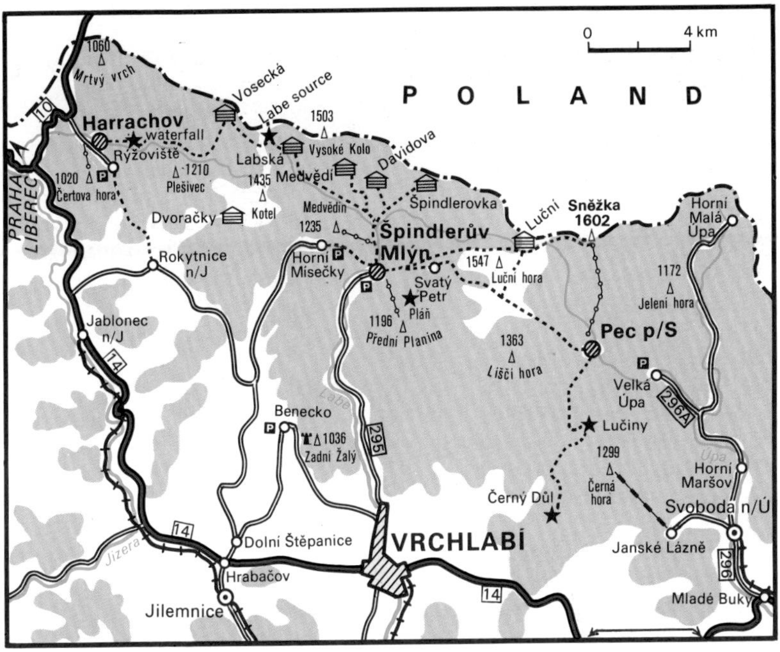

KRKONOŠE (GIANT) MOUNTAINS

North Bohemia does have a less attractive side, notably near the **Krušné Hory** mountains and the towns of **Chomutov, Most** and **Ústí nad Labem** where extensive open-cast coal mining and a concentrated chemical industry have taken their toll on the landscape. These areas are easily avoided though and it would be a shame to miss out on the many good things North and East Bohemia have to offer the visitor.

KRKONOŠE (GIANT) MOUNTAINS

A nature reserve and national park since 1963, the Krkonoše Mountains are the highest in Bohemia and Moravia. With peaks reaching 1500m (4920ft), the Krkonoše stretch over an area of 385 sq km (149 sq miles) and with an alpine/arctic climate, it's an ideal area for walking and skiing. There are a number of resorts with hotels and restaurants to cater for all tastes.

VRCHLABÍ

Buses leave from Vrchlabí to all the resorts in the Krkonoše so it's a good base to start from. It's a typical mountain settlement with beautiful views all around. The town itself is small enough to explore on foot and as you're walking around watch out for the original timber-framed houses from the 18th and 19th centuries and for the 17th century baroque **stone bridge** across the River Labe (Elbe). The **Krkonoše Museum,** with its mineralogy and geology exhibitions, is housed in a **baroque monastery** founded by the Augustinian Pilgrims in 1705. It's open Tues to Sun 08.00 - 16.00.

The **Krkonoše National Park Administration Offices** can be found in the splendid 16th century château. They're open Mon to Fri 08.00 - 16.00.

Čedok is at Hlavní St 148. Tel: (0438) 21 19 1.

WHERE TO STAY
⌂ **B Labuť** Tel: ((0438) 24 12. Restaurant (III).
⌂ **B Krakonoš** Tel: (0438) 25 85. Restaurant (III).
⌂ **C Národní dům** Tel: (0438) 22 28. Restaurant (III).
Campsites
△ **B Vejsplachy**. Tel: (0438) 33 20. Open July 15 to Sept 10.

ŠPINDLERŮV MLÝN

If you want a good base for walking, cross-country or downhill skiing with plenty of places to eat after a long day outdoors and somewhere to sleep in comfort then Špindlerův Mlýn will be the place for you. It's along the upper reaches of the mighty **River Elbe**, at this point little more than a mountain stream. However as it is the largest resort in the Krkonoše Mountains it can tend to get crowded so make sure you book your accommodation well in advance. Cars are not allowed in the town but you can park just off the main road to Vrchlabí and walk ten minutes into the town or leave your car in Vrchlabí and catch a bus.

Hiking tours set off from here to many places including the resorts of **Pec pod Sněžkou** and **Horní Mísečky, Labská bouda Hotel** at the source of the River Elbe and the chalets at **Špindleorvka, Luční, Davidova** and **Medvědí**. Chairlifts for the less energetic take you to the ridges of **Medvědín** at 1235m (4051ft) and **Pláň** at 1196m (3923ft).

Downhill skiers will find slopes of all grades accessible from **St Peter** only 2km (1.25 miles) from Špindlerův Mlýn. It's a venue for top ski competitions with a ski school, chairlifts and ski-tows to 1190m (3903ft). There's another ski-tow at **Hromovka Hill** near the bus station and a chairlift and ski-tow to the intermediate slopes at **Medvědín** 20 minutes' walk away. For Nordic skiers there are many well kept cross country tracks of varying lengths and difficulties. The top station of Pláň chairlift is a starting point for tours along the ridges to resorts at **Pec pod Sněžkou** and **Vrchlabí**. A winter route map is available from hotels Kniha (bookshops) and **Čedok** in the centre of Špindlerův Mlýn.

WHERE TO STAY
⌂ **A* Montana** Tel: (0438) 93 55 1. Restaurant (I).
⌂ **B Savoy** Tel: (0438) 93 52 1. Restaurant (II).
⌂ **B Praha** Tel: (0438) 93 31 5. Restaurant (II).
⌂ **B Alpský** St Peter. Tel: (0438) 93 24 2. Restaurant (II).
△ **B** On the road to Špindleorvka chalet. Tel: (0438) 93 53 4.

PEC POD SNĚŽKOU

With lush meadows, forests and picture-book mountain chalets Pec pod Sněžkou belies its name which means **Furnace Below the Sněžka Mountain**. Iron and copper ore have been mined and smelted here since the 16th century but the community now prospers from its situation at the foot of the highest mountain in Czechoslovakia, **Sněžka** at 1602m (5255ft). It is the second largest resort in the Krkonoše Mountains and a popular centre for winter sports and walking.

Hiking tours lead to **Černý důl**, **Lučiny** and **Špindlerův Mlýn** while a chairlift takes you to the summit of Mount Sněžka where there is a **1681 chapel**. The conditions for downhill skiing are good with a number ofski-tows and slopes of all grades. Cross-country skiing tours set off from here along the tracks on the Krkonoše ridges.The views are terrific. **Čedok** is easy to find near the bus station.

The silent world of cross-country skiing on the magnificent Krkonoše ridges

WHERE TO STAY
⌂ **B* Horizont** Tel: (0439) 96 31 30. Restaurant (I), night bar (I).
⌂ **B Hořec** Tel: (0439) 20 4. Restaurant (II).
⌂ **C Děvín** Tel: (0439) 23 0. Restaurant (III).
⌂ **C Hvězda** Tel: (0439) 242. Restaurant (III).
Chalets
C Lučni bouda mountain chalet No telephone. Restaurant (III).

HARRACHOV

Perhaps the snow and ice inspired the 17th century inhabitants of the small town of Harrachov in the Mumlava river valley to found the glass-making industry which still flourishes today producing painted, etched, cut and pot-metal glass. Near the glass factory there is a **pseudo-Gothic chapel** with a bell from 1916. The 1786 **St Wenceslas Church** was rebuilt in 1830 and has a 19th century altar made partly of glass while the **Museum of Glassmaking** is open Tues to Fri 09.00 - 16.00, Sat and Sun 09.00 - 12.00.

For those who want to see the sculptures of nature Harrachov is an important mountain resort. It's the starting point for walking tours along the mountain ridge of the **Česko-polského přátelství (Czech-Polish Friendship Track)** along the border to **Vosecká bouda chalet**, the **source of the Elbe**, **Čertova Hora Mountain** and the resort of **Rokytnice nad Jizerou**. The nearby **Mumlava Waterfalls** drop 10m (33ft) and are certainly worth a look.

Dare-devil World Championship ski flying competitions take place at **Rýžoviště**, one of the six biggest ski jumps in the world. There is also downhill racing. For the less expert there is a ski school and a chairlift to **Čertova Hora** at 1020m (3346ft) with ski-tows and slopes of all grades, while for cross-country skiers well kept tracks lead along the Krkonoše ridges or to **Čertova Hora** and the chalets at **Dvoračky**.

Every year at the end of the winter skiing season Harrachov hosts a skiing carnival — people dress up and wear masks and even the God of the Krkonoše is said to pay a visit.

Čedok is in the centre.

WHERE TO STAY

⌂ **B Hubertus** Tel: (0432) 92 92 48. Restaurant (II).

⌂ **B Diana** Tel: (0432) 92 92 60. Restaurant (II).

⌂ **C Krakonoš** Tel: (0432) 92 92 53. Restaurant (III).

⌂ **C Lesní zátiší** Tel: (0432) 92 92 37. Restaurant (III).

Tourist hostels

⌂ **C Praha** Tel: (0432) 92 92 63.

Campsites

△ **B Harrachov-Jiskra** No telephone — book through Čedok. On E65 to Prague. Open May 1 to Oct 30.

JIZERSKÉ HORY (JIZERSKE MOUNTAINS)

Dramatic mountain peaks give way to deep gorges flushed with waterfalls in this forested range which is actually a continuation of the Krkonoše. The peat bogs and lakes near **Bedřichov** and **Na Čihadle** are now protected nature reserves while the imposing ridge views, good snow and extensive hiking trails make the southern peaks an attractive sporting destination. Every January one of the biggest international **long-distance ski races** takes place with over 7000 competitors tackling the 50km (31 miles) course starting and finishing in Bedřichov.

Liberec

An important cultural and industrial centre with a flourishing textile industry. Make time to go and see the 16th century **Renaissance château** with an exhibition of the **history of European painting**. It's open Tues to Sun 10.00 - 18.00. There's also an early **17th century chapel**, a **botanical garden** and a **zoo**. **Trade fairs** for consumer goods and clothing are held in Liberec in July and a cable railway runs to the top of **Mt Ještěd** at 1012m (3319ft).

Jablonec nad Nisou

Exquisite crystal and jewellery have been made here since the 16th century. A visit to the **Museum of Glass** is fascinating but prepare to be tempted to buy some of the 'black' jewellery on sale there. It's open Tues to Fri 09.00 - 15.30.

ČESKÝ RÁJ (BOHEMIAN PARADISE)

Not far south of Liberec lies the Český ráj, a region of fantastic scenery with thick forests amid sandstone rocks — this is indeed a paradise for walkers and

Historical Děčín is worth a visit

mountaineers. There are hundreds of marked trails and more than two hundred rock faces to challenge novice and expert climbers alike. Watch out too for the ruins of two Gothic castles, **Valdštejn (Wallenstein)** and **Trosky**. Near the town of **Jičín** you can see the **Prachovské skály** rock formations, 187 hectares (462 acres) of sandstone rock eroded into a host of wierd and wonderful shapes throughout the centuries.

FURTHER AFIELD

Labské pískovce (Elbe Sandstone Rocks)

Nature has carved some other amazing sights out of the sandstone rocks either side of the Elbe river along the border with Germany. **Pravčická brána (Pravčice Gateway)** in **Hřensko** is the biggest natural bridge in Europe, 21m (69ft) high and spanning a massive 30m (98ft). Innumerable paths lead you along the canyons, sheer rock walls and rock towns which characterise the area, also known as **Bohemian-Saxon Switzerland**. Of note are the typical folk architecture houses and the two 'rock towns' of **Malé a Velké Tiské stěny (Lesser and Greater Rocky Walls)**, the dramatic **River Kamenice Canyon** and the highest peak **Děčínský Sněžník** at 723m (2371ft).

Děčín

Walkers often start out from here, an important port on the River Elbe and an historical town. The 16th century château was the domain of the Soviet Army until 1990 when it was returned to the people.Sadly it's in a pretty sore need of repair but the town doesn't have the the money to fund its reconstruction so it is still closed.

However the lovely **rose garden** on the slopes below the château is open while in the town you can enjoy a stroll over the baroque **Ovčí most (Sheep Bridge)** crossing the Jílovský Stream. The **Gothic bridge** over the River Ploučnice has baroque features by K.J. Brokoff from 1714.

And if rivers are of interest there's a good exhibition devoted to **navigation of the Elbe** from the 16th century to 1914 in the **Regional Museum of Děčín,** housed in a 1735 former hunting château. It's open Tues to Sun 08.00 - 17.00.

Rising high above the river is the hill ending in the sheer rock face of **Pastýřská stěna (The Shepherd's Wall)** with a zoo on the nearby plateau.

Terezín (Theresienstadt)

This small town bears a salutary reminder of the grim history of its origins as a military fortress in the **Monument of National Suffering**, the scene of peace demonstrations every May. 14,000 workers were needed to build the 1780 fortress with its 29km (18 miles) of underground passages, making it the biggest fortress in Europe at the time.

The **Small Fortress** was converted into a prison in the 19th century and in June 1940 it was turned into a Nazi concentration camp run by the Gestapo. By the end of the war over 90,000 prisoners had passed through its gates.

In February 1942 the town of **Terezín** itself became a Jewish ghetto and 160,000 Jews from 35 different countries were brought. here. During the course of the war over 35,000 of them died and the monument was erected in their memory after liberation. You can still see the cells and a fascinating and thought-provoking exhibition of the history of the fortress, open daily 08.00 - 16.30.

Bohemian hops are said to be among the best in the world – the beer certainly is!

SOUTH MORAVIA

A TRIP TO the annual folk festival at **Strážnice** would allow you just a glimpse of the spirit of the South Moravians: their love of tradition and relaxed enjoyment of costumes, colour, music and good wines and plum brandy. Distinct from its more industrial northern counterpart, South Moravia has thriving agriculture amid picturesque valleys peppered with castles and fortifications inherited from the days of the Great Moravian Empire. The region along the Dyje River forming the boundary with Austria is ideal for walking tours; while under the ground the Moravian Karst has an amazing array of caves for spectators and potholers. You can even take a boat ride on the underground rivers.

BRNO

As you enter the city the majestic twin spires of the cathedral dominate the skyline, beckoning you onwards to discover Brno's rich architectural and cultural heritage. Earliest evidence show that a settlement was founded here as far back as the 1st century AD and today it's the second largest city in Czechoslovakia with a population of 372,000. Its university, lively restaurants and bustling centre make it an ideal venue for the many international trade fairs and exhibitions and car and motorcycle Grand Prix races it hosts every year.

SETTING OFF

By air No regular airline flies to Brno but some foreign operators do run a service from April to September when the trade fairs are in progress.
By car D1 motorway from Prague - 220km (137 miles). D2 motorway from Bratislava - 130km (81 miles). E461 from Vienna - 140km (87 miles).
By bus Coaches connect Brno with all major towns in Czechoslovakia. There are also coaches from Vienna.
By train Direct connections with Prague, Bratislava, Ostrava, Liberec, Berlin, Budapest and all major towns in Czechoslovakia.

ON THE MOVE

Public transport within the city is by trams, trolley-buses and buses. Tickets are valid for all three and are bought in advance (see p. 25).
Main bus station Zvonařka. Tel: (05) 33 79 26.
Train station Nádražní St 6. Tel: (05) 27 56 2/27 56 4.
Taxi stands Solniční St 4. Tel: (05) 24 50 4/26 61 1/25 60 6. Next to Prior department store, Rovnosti Sq. Tel: (05) 33 94 35. Outside larger hotels.
Car rental Brnocar, Solniční St. Tel: (05) 25 47 5/24 03 9. Fax (05) 27 94 1. International Hotel, Husova St 16. Tel: (05) 21 34 11 1/21 34 81 3.
Parking Unless you are staying at a hotel with its own car park you could have problems parking in the centre. The best bet is to leave your car on the outskirts and take a bus to the

centre. Free car parks are well signposted on main roads into Brno and there's a regular service into the centre for 3 Kčs. Alternatively there is a paying car park in front of the International Hotel in Husova St and another by the Výstavíště exhibition ground.

FACT FILE

Emergency medical aid Bratislavská St 2. Tel: (05) 67 74 48. Žerotínovo Sq 9. Tel: (05) 22 05 9. For children..

Pharmacy Kobližná St 7. Tel: (05) 22 27 5. Open 24 hours.

Police (VB) Kounicova St 46. Tel: (05) 71 61 11

Post office Šilingrovo Sq 3-5. Tel: (05) 23 52.

Passport and visas Kounicova St 24. Tel: (05) 51 54 9.

Airline offices ČSA, Cejl St 4. Tel: (05) 67 12 29.

Travel agencies Čedok, Divadelní St 3. Tel: (05) 23 92 3/23 57 3/23 16 6. Rekrea, Radnická St 11. Tel: (05) 26 05 7. CKM, Česká St 11. Tel: (05) 23 64 1/23 64 2/23 64 3.

Shopping

There are plenty of shops to choose from in the centre, most in Masarykova St, Česká St and Svobody Sq. The biggest department store is Prior, Uhelná St 7. Another branch is at Svobody Sq 8. Tuzex can be found at Křížkovského St, Brno-Pisárky with another branch at E. Beneše St 2-4.

Brno is the second largest city in the country and famous for its trade fairs

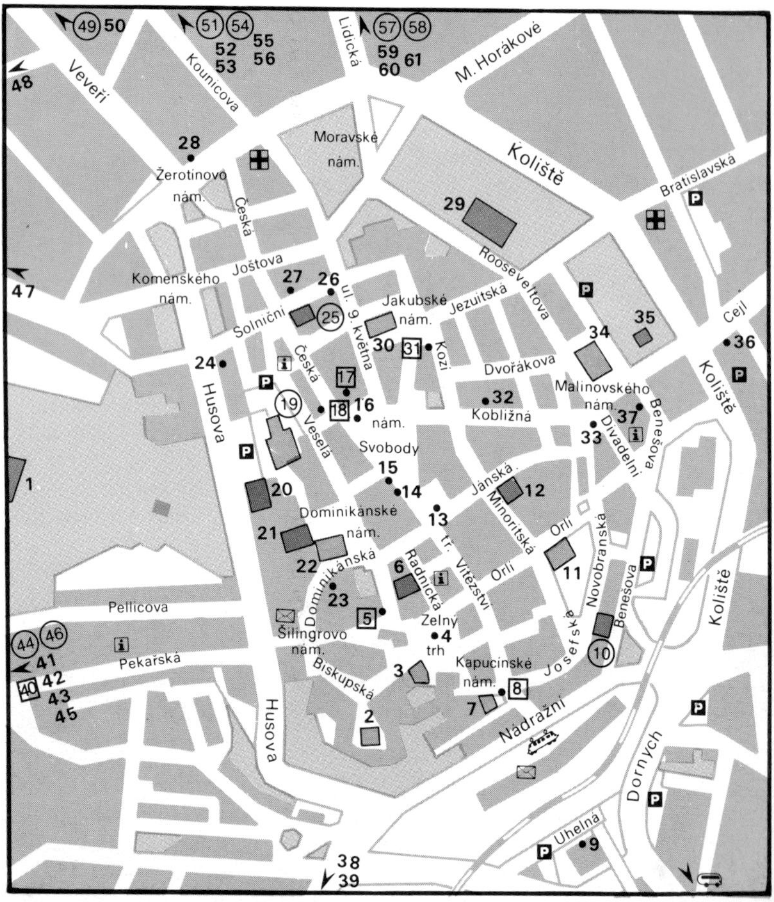

BRNO

1 Špilberk Fortress
2 Cathedral of SS Peter and Paul
3 Moravian Museum
4 Parnassus fountain
5 Špalíček brasserie
6 Old Town Hall
7 Capuchin Monastery
8 Černohorská brasserie
9 Prior
10 Grandhotel
11 Technical Museum
12 Minorite Church of St John
13 Evropa bar
14 Prior
15 House of the Lords of Lipá
16 Column of Our Lady
17 Stopkova brasserie
18 Sputnik restaurant/Bolero bar
19 International hotel
20 Moravian Gallery
21 New Town Hall
22 Dominican Church of St Michael
23 House of the Lords of Kunštát
24 Besední dům
25 Avion hotel
26 Taxi stand
27 Brnocar
28 Rozmarýn Variety Theatre/Bílý krokodýl
29 Janáček Theatre
30 St James' Church
31 Černý medvěd restaurant
32 Pharmacy
33 Taxi stand
34 Mahen Theatre
35 House of Arts
36 ČSA
37 Tuzex
38 Tuzex
39 Rondo
40 U královny Elišky wine bar
41 Convent of Cistercian Nuns
42 Exhibition grounds
43 Anthropos Pavilion
44 Voroněž hotel
45 Race track
46 Myslivna
47 Tennis courts Zlutý kopec
48 'V' Club
49 Obora dam
50 Brno lake/zoo
51 Continental hotel
52 Police
53 Passport and visas
54 Kounicova hostel
55 Janáček Museum
56 Stadion
57 Slovan hotel
58 Královo Pole hostel
59 Tennis courts Lužánky
60 Swimming pool
61 Football and ice stadium

WHERE TO STAY

There should be no problems getting accommodation in Brno in the winter but throughout the summer months there are international trade fairs, exhibitions and car and motorcycle races, so you're advised to book well in advance.

⌂ **A* International** Husova St 16. Tel: (05) 21 34 11 1/21 34 81 3.

Fax: (05) 23 05 1. Modern hotel in the centre with French restaurant (I), Czech restaurant (II), café (I), bar (I), night club (I), casino.
⌂ A* **Grandhotel** Benešova St 18-20. Tel: (05) 26 42 1/23 52 6. Fax: (05) 22 42 6. Rebuilt traditional hotel near to the train station with Asian restaurant (I), restaurant (II), grill bar (I), night club (I), casino.
⌂ A* **Continental** Kounicova St 6. Tel: (05) 75 07 27/75 31 21. Fax: (05) 74 42 32. Modern hotel in the centre with restaurants (I & II), pizza bar (II), night club (I).
⌂ A* **Voroněž I** Křížkovského St 47. Tel: (05) 33 63 43. Fax:

It's a fertile wine-growing region and the local wines are exceptionally good

(05) 33 45 28. Classy hotel with restaurant (I), grill bar (I), bar (I), night bar (I).
⌂ **A* Voronéž II Garni** Křížkovského St 49. Tel: (05) 31 35. Fax: (05) 33 41 60. Bed and breakfast.
⌂ **B* Avion** Česká St 20. Tel: (05) 27 60 6/7. Older hotel in busiest shopping street in Brno with restaurant (II), café (II).
⌂ **B* Slovan** Lidická St 23. Tel: (05) 74 54 55/74 55 05. Fax: (05)74 65 42. Second biggest hotel in Brno 15 minutes' walk from centre with restaurants (II & III), café (II), wine bar (II), night bar (I).
⌂ **B Myslivna** Pisárky 12. Tel: (05) 38 32 45/47 56. Hotel has stylish restaurant (II) with a view over the town (try the venison), snack bar (II), night club.

Tourist hostels
C Kounicova St 88 and 90 20 minutes' walk from centre. Tel: (05) 74 44 04.
C Královo Pole Purkyňova St 93. Tel: (05) 74 08 8. Tram connection to the centre. Accommodation available July and August in student halls of residence. Book through CKM (see p. 135).

Campsites
△ **A Obora** Brněnská přehrada, near Brno dam reservoir. Tel: (05) 79 11 05/79 19 88. 10km (6 miles) from Brno. Driving take D1 from Brno and turn off in direction of Rosice-Tišnov. Bus or tram from city. Restaurant (III). Swimming in reservoir. Open all year.

EATING OUT
I Černý medvěd Jakubské Sq 1. Gourmet restaurant, delicious cuisine, good local wines, pleasant atmosphere.
II Sputnik Česká St 1. Restaurant (II). Also snack bar (III), coffee bar (IV).
II U královny Elišky Mendlovo Sq 1. Wine bar in basement of monastery, fine wines, local specialities and folk music.
III Špalíček Zelný Sq 12. Brasserie.
III Smíchovská pivnice Staroměstská St 7. Brasserie.
III Stopkova pivnice Česká St 2. Brasserie.
III Černohorská pivnice Kapucínské Sq 1. Brasserie serving dark and light beer from the Černá Hora brewery.

NIGHTLIFE
Rozmarýn Variety Theatre Žerotínovo Sq 1. Dancing and variety acts.
Bílý krokodýl Žerotínovo Sq 1. Wine bar with dancing.
Bolero Česká St 1. Bar with cabaret and dancing.
Evropa Svobody Sq 13. Bar with cabaret and dancing.
Janáček Opera Theatre Dvořákova St 11. Opera, drama and ballet.
Mahen Theatre Rooseveltova St 13. Operetta, musicals, drama.
Besední dům Husovo Sq 20. Concert hall.
Stadion Kounicova St 42. Classical and pop concerts, formal dances.
Rondo Křídlovická 34. Pop concerts.

Student clubs
'V' club Gorkého St 43. Open to all. Clubs in student hostels in **Kounicova St 88 & 90, Purkyňova St 93, Králova St 45**. In theory only for students but all young people generally get in. Bar and programme of events, concerts, discos and film shows.

WHAT TO SEE
Špilberk Fortress A grim history surrounds this baroque fortress built between the mid-17th century and the end of the 18th. During the First and Second World Wars POWs

The baroque fortress of Špilberk has a grim history as a prison in the World Wars

were held there. It houses the **Museum of the City of Brno** but is closed for renovation until 1995.

Cathedral of SS. Peter and Paul Petrov Hill. You can be forgiven for being confused at the timekeeping of the bells of this magnificent cathedral. A strange tradition began in 1645 when a Swedish general laying siege to Brno vowed he would retreat if he hadn't captured the city by 12 noon. As the troops attacked the bellkeeper rang the bells for noon an hour early. The general called off the siege and the bells still ring noon at 11.00. The architecture is neo-Gothic built between the 18th and 20th centuries on the site of a Romanesque basilica dating from the 12th century. The interior by sculptor and woodcarver O. Schweigel is worth seeing.

Old Town Hall Radnická St. Dates from the 13th century and boasts a magnificent portal from 1511 behind which you can see the two **symbols of Brno**, a crocodile and a wheel.

House of the Lords of Kunštát Dominikánská St. One of a number of Renaissance and baroque houses and palaces to be seen in the town. Also worth a look is the **House of the Lords of Lipá** in Svobody Sq.

St James' Church Jakubské Sq. Magnificent Gothic church built between the 14th and 16th centuries. The sculptor **Master Pilgram** (1460 - 1515) was influential in its construction.

Dominican Church of St Michael Dominikánská St. Baroque church founded in the 13th century and rebuilt in the late 17th century. There's an **exhibition of sculptures** by Josef Winterhalter from 1736-7. The Court met in the adjacent monastery from the 14th century until the 1580s when the Land House was built. In the 17th and 18th centuries it was expanded and now the complex of buildings forming the **New Town Hall** is the seat of the Office of the City of Brno. The New Town Hall has impressive courtyard and beautiful frescoes.

Minorite Church of St John Minoritská St. Founded in the 13th century, the existing building is a baroque church built in the first half of the 18th century. The interior is exceptional, particularly the fresco by Czech painter J.J. Etgens.

Capuchin Monastery and Church of the Finding of the Holy Rood Kapucínské Sq. The crypt below 1651 monastery houses the mummified remains of members and benefactors of the monastery. Joseph II prohibited mummification in 1780 for reasons of hygiene. The church has a **gallery of sculptures** by J.A. Nessman. It's open Tues to Sat 09.00 - 16.00, Sun 11.00 - 16.00.

Convent of Cistercian Nuns Mendlovo Sq. Nuns still live and worship in the original convent founded in 1322 and the Gothic church adapted in 1795 and 1886. One of its famous residents was geneticist **Johann Gregor Mendel** (1822 - 1884) and there is an **exhibition** of his life and work. It's open Mon to Fri 09.30 - 16.00.

Moravské Muzeum (Moravian Museum) Zelný trh Sq 6. Archaeology, zoology, geology and history of the theatre exhibitions, plus gallery devoted to the Slav missionaries Cyril and Methodius. Information on other exhibitions is available in the main building. It's open Tues to Sun 09.00 - 20.00.

Anthropos Pavilion Hlinký St. Fascinating exhibition on the evolution of the human race, open Tues to Sun 09.00 - 18.00.

Janáček Museum Smetanova St 14. Study of the composer Leoš Janáček who lived in a small house in the garden of this museum, once a school of organ music. It's open Mon to Fri 08.00 - 12.00, 13.00 - 16.00.

Technical Museum Orlí St 20. Open Tues to Sat 09.00 - 18.00, Sun 09.00 - 14.00.

Moravian Gallery Husova St 14. Permanent and visiting exhibitions. Open Tues to Sun 09.30 - 17.30.

Dům umění (House of Arts) Malinovského Sq 2. Occasional exhibitions. Open Tues to Sun 10.00 - 18.00.

Column of Our Lady Svobody Sq. Built in the baroque style by J.K. Ernou in 1680.

Parnassus Fountain Zelný trh Sq. Designed by J.B. Fischer of Erlach 1693 - 1695. There's a **fish market** in the square just before Christmas and until very recently the carp on sale were kept in the fountain.

WALKS AND SPORTS

The forests on the outskirts of the city are ideal for walking, while Brno's biggest recreational facility is the **lake** behind the dam. Both tram and city bus will take you there for swimming, watersports and boat trips in summer. There's also a zoo. A number of tennis courts in the city are open to visitors – in the parks at

Lužánky, and on **Žlutý kopec Hill**. There's an indoor swimming pool at Ponávka 3a. The Brno-Lužánky stadium holds first league football matches and Lužánky also has an ice stadium. Brno's Kohoutovice and Bosonohy districts have an international **Grand Prix racetrack** and the exhibition grounds at Výstaviště hold international **cycling races**.

FURTHER AFIELD

Žuráň Hill 6km (4 miles) N. Napoleon commanded his troops from here on December 2, 1805 in the first part of the Battle of Austerlitz. A memorial stone with a plan of the battlefield commemorates the event. On December 6 the victorious Napoleon made peace in the château at **Slavkov** 3km (2 miles) further north.

Dyje River Valley 60-80km (37-50 miles) SW. Before the November 1989 revolution most of the river valley was closed to the public as it runs along the Austrian border. The river flows from **Vranovská Dam lake** to the point where it meets the Morava. Its network of footpaths through the countryside has great appeal for walkers.

There has been a stronghold on the site of the Lednice chateau for seven centuries

Pálava 60km (37 miles) S. Mighty cliffs of chalky limestone form the core of **Pálava Nature Reserve**. It's now the topic of much controversy as the large artificial lake is threatening the rare flora and fauna, some say even changing the climate. The **Pavlovské vrchy hills** now so popular among climbers were once a settlement of Older Stone Age Man – the Mammoth Hunter – from as far back 24,000BC.

Lednice 60km (37 miles) S. South-east of Pálava lies the community of Lednice and its **baroque château**. There has been a stronghold on the site from the 13th century and in the 15th century it was lent to the Lords of Liechtenstein, later to become their property. The existing château was built at the end of the 17th century. Its neo-Gothic appearance is the work of J. Wingelmüller from the first half of the 19th century. Its interiors are outstanding for their period furniture and richly carved ceilings and the château also has a **hunting museum.** It's open May 1 to Sept 30 Tues to Sun 09.00 - 15.00. Sat and Sun to Oct 31.

An alley established at the beginning of this century links the Lednice château with the **Valtice château**. The château is an outstanding architectural monument, built between 1643 - 1730 under the reign of the Lords of Liechtenstein. It's open daily from May 1 to Sept 30 and on Sat and Sun to Oct 31.

The **English park** surrounding the château is a nature reserve where 130 species of birds are known to nest. The River Dyje and a number of lakes constructed in the 14th century make an ideal habitat and the area is used by the Faculty of Horticulture, part of the College of Agriculture and Forestry in Brno. It's a good wine-growing region with wine cellars offering tastings.

Strážnice has a preserved village with examples of Moravian folk architecture

Mikulov 54km (34 miles) S. Off the E461 from Brno to Vienna the old town of Mikulov is an important wine-growing, crafts, educational, cultural and political centre. It seems to be growing daily with much new building. Between the 14th and 18th centuries it was a Jewish ghetto and the **Jewish cemetery** is still preserved. After the Battle of Austerlitz in 1805 Napoleon I held peace negotiations in the **Mikulov château**. In 1866 it was again the venue for peace negotiations after the **Battle of Hradec Králové** between Bismarck and the Prussian King Wilhelm, later emperor.

Jan Evangelista Purkyně, a natural scientist and physiologist, studied in the **Piarist College of Mikulov** between 1787 - 1869.

Znojmo 65km (40 miles) SW. Dating back to the 11th century Znojmo is the centre of the wine and fruit-growing region along the upper River Dyje. Every September it hosts a **wine-growers' festival**. Its historic centre has a number of preserved baroque and Renaissance buildings with underground passages built between the 15th and 17th centuries open to the public. The **Museum of South Moravia**, Přemyslovců St 6, is open Tues to Sun 09.00 - 16.00.

Vranov Dam lake 20km (12 miles) up the River Dyje has various watersports and a château.

Uherské Hradiště 70km (43 miles) E. Archaeological artefacts link the Great Moravian Empire to the district town of Uherské Hradiště. The history of the town began on nearby Velehrad Hill where a Cistercian monastery was founded in 1205. Today the **basilica of SS. Cyril and Methodius** in Velehrad is a well-known place of pilgrimage. Pope John Paul II paid a visit here in 1990.

Strážnice 80km (50 miles) SE. With a strong tradition of folk culture and ceramics, the town of Strážnice is best known for its annual folk festival which takes place on the last weekend in June and is among the biggest in Europe. The town also has a 19th-century **Gothic château** with an **exhibition of folklore** open May 1 to Oct 31, Tues to Sat 08.00 - 12.00, 13.00 - 17.00, Sunday 09.00 - 12.00, 14.00 - 17.00. Below the château is an **open-air museum** of traditional architecture open Tues to Sat 08.00 - 17.00, Sun 10.00 - 18.00.

Zlín 96km (60 miles) E. In 1894 **Tomáš Baťa** founded his footwear industry in Zlín, 26km (16 miles) north of Uherské Hradiště. His descendants now own the famous Bata firm with factories all over the world. Zlín was the first new town in the Czechoslovak Republic before the Second World War, designed by distinguished Czechoslovak and foreign architects, including Le Corbusier and J. Kotěra. Between 1949 -1989 it was known as **Gottwaldov** after the first communist president of Czechoslovakia. Every May Zlín holds an international **festival of children's films**.

Moravský Kras (Moravian Karst) Just a few kilometres north of Brno lies an area of natural wonderland which simply should not be missed. The Moravian Karst is a 100 sq km (39 sq miles) of unspoiled nature reserve. Its porous limestone has created just about every possible karst (limestone) formation, from yawning chasms amd canyons to caves with deep sink-holes and underground streams. Four cave systems are accessible to the public and significant archaeological finds from the Stone Age have been made in all except the Punkva Cave. Caves are open daily April to Oct

Watch out for the innumerable stalagmites and stalactites of the Moravian Karst

from 07.00 with the last visitor going in at 15.00. In Mar and Oct the latest entry is at 13.00. Group tours can be arranged; contact Reditelství Správy českých a moravských jeskyní, Svitavská St 11, 678 25 Blansko. Tel: (0506) 54 75/05 06. For information contact the Central Information Service next to the Punkva Cave, Skalní Mlýn. Tel: (0506) 35 75.

Kateřinská Cave One of the largest stalagmite and stalactite caves in the Moravian Karst. The main dome is 97m (318ft) long, 44m (144ft) wide and 20m (66ft) high.

Sloupsko-šošůvské Caves Large cave system opened to the public in the 1880s. There is an altitude difference of 70m (230ft) between the two cave floors and the **Sloupsky underground stream** flows along the lower level. Today people go there not only to see the magnificent stalagmites and stalactites but to help treat their breathing problems — the wet and stable temperature and limited bacteria in the cave are considered very beneficial. On important anniversaries choral concerts take place in **Eliščina Cave** at the entrance to the cave system.

Punkva Cave A boat ride along the romantic underground River Punkva will take you through this large system of stalagmite and stalactite caves to the bottom of the 139m (456ft) **Macocha Abyss**, among the deepest of its kind in Central Europe. Not for the faint hearted!

A Moravian wedding is the opportunity for everyone to play their part

NORTH MORAVIA

LUSH FERTILE plains, heavy industry and beautiful soaring mountain ranges make North Moravia a region of contrasts. Agriculture is the major activity in the south-western region of Haná centred around the city of Olomouc while heavy industry occupies the Silesian Basin, flanked to the north and east by the picturesque mountain ranges of Beskydy and Jeseníky.

Culturally North Moravia has rich traditions and many of the great composers — Janáček, Beethoven, Mahler, Dvořák — lived in or visited the region. Galleries have many precious collections, including Titian's *Apollon* and *Marzyaz* in the château at Kroměříž. The people are proud of their traditions and a splendid open-air museum at Rožnov pod Radhoštěm shows how life used to be. The mountains and dams provide plenty of outdoor activity, the castles and monuments many absorbing hours for the historian and the spas a relaxing place to unwind.

Ostrava's main square. The town was originally settled as far back as 1267

OSTRAVA

Originally settled in 1267, it was the discovery of coal in 1763 which put Ostrava on the map. It is now the largest town in North Moravia with a population of 350,000 and lies on the confluence of the Rivers Ostravice and Odra (Oder), one of the biggest rivers in Europe which flows through Poland to the Baltic. In the second half of the 19th century the Rothschilds built **Vítkovice** here, the largest heavy engineering plant in the Austro-Hungarian Empire. Ostrava continues to be a major industrial centre with a huge concentration of iron and steel engineering, mining and chemical industries. Consequently the town itself is not picturesque but it is the gateway to the beautiful mountain regions of **Beskydy** and **Jeseníky**.

SETTING OFF

By air Regular service by ČSA and other companies to Ostrava-Mošnov airport. Connections from Prague, Moscow, Split, Burgas and other major cities. Bus link from airport to the city.
By car E462 to Frýdek-Místek then 17km (11 miles) on Road 56. Road 58 from Bohumín border crossing point with Poland - 13 km (8 miles).
By bus Direct connection with all major cities in Czechoslovakia and Europe.
By train On main lines connecting Prague and Košice, Vienna and Warsaw. All domestic and international trains stop here.

ON THE MOVE

Local transport is by tram, bus and trolleybus.
Main bus station Vítkovická St. Tel: (069) 51 10 0.
Railway station Ostrava-Přívoz. Tel: (069) 23 60 49/23 22 51.
Taxi stands By Hotel Imperial, Tyršova St 6. Tel: (069) 23 51 41/23 48 98.
Car rental Pragocar, Harantova St 25. Tel: (069) 23 66 75/23 64 81.

FACT FILE

Emergency medical aid Nemocniční St 20. Tel: (069) 24 61 11 1.
Pharmacy Nádražní St 26. Tel: (069) 23 56 61. 24 hour service.
Police (VB) 30. dubna St 24. Tel: (069) 22 23 33.
ČSA Airline offices Nádražní St 165. Tel: (069) 23 31 64. Air tickets, reservations, bus terminal for the airport.
Post office Main railway station, Ostrava-Přívoz. 24 hour service.
Passports and visas Milíčova St 20. Tel: (069) 21 44 49.
Travel agencies Čedok, Nádražní St 9. Tel: (069) 23 14 24. Rekrea, Nádražní St 40. Tel: (069) 23 23 01/23 24 27. Autotourist, Husova St 9. Tel: (069) 23 56 42. CKM Hlavní St 102. Tel: (069) 23 45 61.
Shopping
Most shops are concentrated in the centre around Masarykovo Sq, Hlavní St and Nádražní St. Large department store Prior-Laso, Masarykovo Sq 15. Prior-Horník, Zámecká St 18. This store is being refurbished until 1992. There is a choice of Tuzex stores in the city at NF Sq, Nádražní St 162, Tyršova St 14, Zeyerova.

WHERE TO STAY

⌂ **A* Imperial** Tyršova St 6. Tel: (069) 23 66 21. Fax: (069) 35 13 60. City-centre hotel with restaurants (I & II), café (I), bar (I), casino. Excellent cuisine.
⌂ **A* Atom** Ostrava-Zábřeh, Zkrácená St. Tel: (069) 35 38 2. Fax: (069) 351360. Modern hotel outside the city centre near TJ Vítkovice sports ground with restaurant (II), snack bar (I), bar (I). Pool.

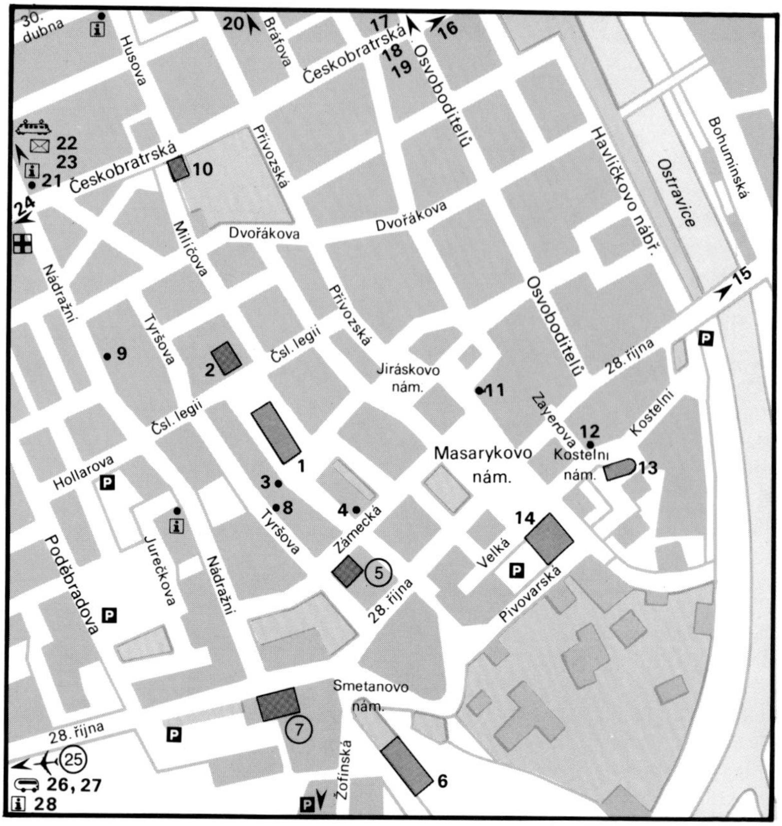

OSTRAVA

1 Basilica of Our Lord Saviour
2 Jiří Myron Theatre
3 Tuzex
4 Prior Horník
5 Imperial hotel
6 Antonín Dvořák Theatre
7 Interhotel Palace
8 Tuzex
9 Pharmacy
10 Passports and visa office
11 Prior-Laso
12 Tuzex
13 St Wenceslas Church
14 Old Town Hall
15 Silesian-Ostrava Castle
16 Football stadium
17 Horseriding
18 Tennis courts
19 Swimming pool
20 Police
21 ČSA office
22 Pragocar
23 Tuzex
24 Hockey stadium
25 Atom hotel
26 Swimming pool
27 Hockey stadium
28 Football stadium

⌂ **B* Interhotel Palace** 28 Ríjna St 54. Tel: (069) 23 21 22. Fax: (069) 23 16 16. Older hotel in the city centre with several restaurants (I), café (I), snack bar (I), wine bar (II), night bar (I) with music and dancing. It includes the Old Czech ale-house.

EATING OUT
There are restaurants in all the hotels above plus plenty of places to choose from in the city centre. The *House of Food* opposite the Imperial Hotel serves good hot and cold meals, while the fish restaurant around the corner is worth a try. You can get a meal in any winebar until 21.00 or 22.00 or even try the street kiosks serving trusty hamburgers and chips.

NIGHTLIFE
Antonín Dvořák Theatre Smetanovo Sq 1. Opera, drama, ballet.
Jiří Myron Theatre Legií St 12. Musical comedy, musicals, drama.

WHAT TO SEE
The Basilica of Our Lord Saviour NF Sq. The three-nave church has

two towers 67m (220ft) high built by H. Meretta 1883 - 1889. It's the second largest church in Moravia after the basilica at Velehrad.

St Wenceslas Church Kostelní Sq. A three-nave late Gothic building erected on Romanesque foundations from the 11th century.

The Old Town Hall Masarykovo Sq. Until 1930 this was the seat of the administration of Ostrava. It was originally built in the 16th century and now houses the **Ostrava Museum** with permanent displays on the history of the region and visiting exhibitions. It's open Tues to Fri 08.30 - 17.00, Sat 10.00 - 12.00, Sun 09.00 - 12.00.

Silesian-Ostrava Castle A 13th-century ruin, the castle has a baroque gateway and part of the fortifications still remaining.

WALKS AND SPORTS

While the nearby **Beskydy** and **Jeseníky** mountains draw walkers away from the town, there are plenty of sporting facilities if you're staying put. Ivan Lendl, one of the world's top tennis players, was born in Ostrava and there are tennis courts at TJ Baník Ostrava on Komenského sady. There are swimming pools at Osvoboditelů 46 and gen. Sochora St 4 in Ostrava-Poruba, Anyone who wants to explore the countryside on horseback can go to Šilhéřovice 10km (6 miles) north of Ostrava.

FURTHER AFIELD

Beskydy Mountains 40km (25 miles) S. You don't have to travel far to get away from the signs of industry. These beautiful mountains form a popular recreational area with several attractive resorts and plenty of walking trails. The highest peak is **Lysá hora** at 1322m (4336ft) which is only accessible on foot. There is a restaurant on the summit.

Pustevny 75km (47miles) S. One of Czechoslovakia's oldest tourist centres with typical folk architecture. The restaurant Libušín dates from 1894. Pustevny has a ski centre and is a crossroads for many footpaths. A track from the town offers a gentle 4km (2.5 miles) pilgrimage walk to the huge statue of Radegast, the ancient Slav pagan god of fertility and hospitality, sculpted in 1930 by Albín Polášek. The same sculptor contributed a group work featuring the missionaries SS Cyril and Methodius on the summit of Mount Radhošť where there is a chapel dating from 1898.

Rožnov pod Radhoštěm 65 km (40 miles) S. A picturesque little town in the foothills of **Mount Radhošť** in the heart of the Valašsko region. The town dates back to 1267 and its major attraction is the open-air museum of folk architecture **Valašské muzeum v přírodě**. The museum is in three places. The **Wooden Town** is the oldest with an original church and houses, open daily May 1 to Nov 15 08.00 - 18.00, Dec 15 to Jan 30 Mon to Weds 09.00 - 16.00, Sat 09.00 - 12.00, Sun 12.00 - 18.00. The second part is a **Wallachian Village** open daily May 15 to Sept 30 08.00 - 18.00 and the third is a **water wheel and saw mill** in the **Mlýnské valley**, open daily April 1 to Oct 30 08.00 - 18.00. The open-air museum is also the venue of an annual folk dance and song festival called **Folklore Summer** with performances every weekend from June to August. On the first Saturday in August the town is home to an enormous market which has pottery and wooden jewellery bargains. Good local food can be

Make time to visit the lovely open-air museum at Rožnov pod Radhoštěm

eaten all year at the restaurant (III) within the museum **U posledního groše (At the Last Penny)**.

Jeseníky Mountains 80km (50 miles) W. Deep forests and unique flora and fauna make this beautiful mountain range a paradise for naturalists: red deer, moufflon (mountain sheep), boar, chamois and pheasant all roam its unspoiled terrain. Walkers can explore the many footpaths and there are excellent conditions for skiing from November to May. The highest peak in Moravia is **Praděd** at 1492m (4894ft) with the popular ski centre of **Petrovy kameny** nearby. In fact skiers are well catered for in the Jeseníky mountains with many centres including **Červenohorské sedlo**, **Ramzovské sedlo** and **Karlov**. Other visitors may prefer the spa resorts of **Jeseník Spa**, **Karlova Studánka** or **Velké Losiny** with its beautiful **Renaissance château** to treat their health and feast their eyes. The château has an extensive **art collection** and an **exhibition** devoted to the witch-hunting trials which took place there in the 17th century. It's open May to Aug Tues to Sun 08.00 - 12.00, 13.00 - 17.00, Sept 09.00 - 12.00, 13.00 - 15.00, April and October Sat to Sun 09.00 - 12.00, 13.00 - 15.00. Other interesting châteaux are to be found at **Javorník** in the most northerly part of Moravia and at **Úsov** in the southern foothills of Jeseníky where collections of weapons and hunting trophies are kept. In the west the 1423m (4667ft) massif of **Kralický Sněžník** links with the Jaseníky range and offers peaceful walks in a beautiful natural environment.

OLOMOUC

This historic centre of the fertile lowland in the River Morava valley has a population of 110,000 and a rich history, as its many important monuments bear testimony. Over the centuries Olomouc has competed with Prague as a centre of the secular and ecclesiastical administration of Moravia. It was the capital of Moravia until 1641 and has been the seat of a bishop since 1063 and of an archbishop since 1777. It has had a university since 1573 but has decreased in importance since the second half of the 18th century. Nonetheless it's a beautiful city and retains all the hallmarks of a cultural centre.

SETTING OFF

By car D1 from Prague to Brno then E462 - 270km (168 miles). E461 from Vienna via Mikulov and Brno.
By bus Connections to all major towns within Czechoslovakia.
By train Express from Prague via Česká Třebová. Train from Vienna via Břeclav, changing at Přerov.

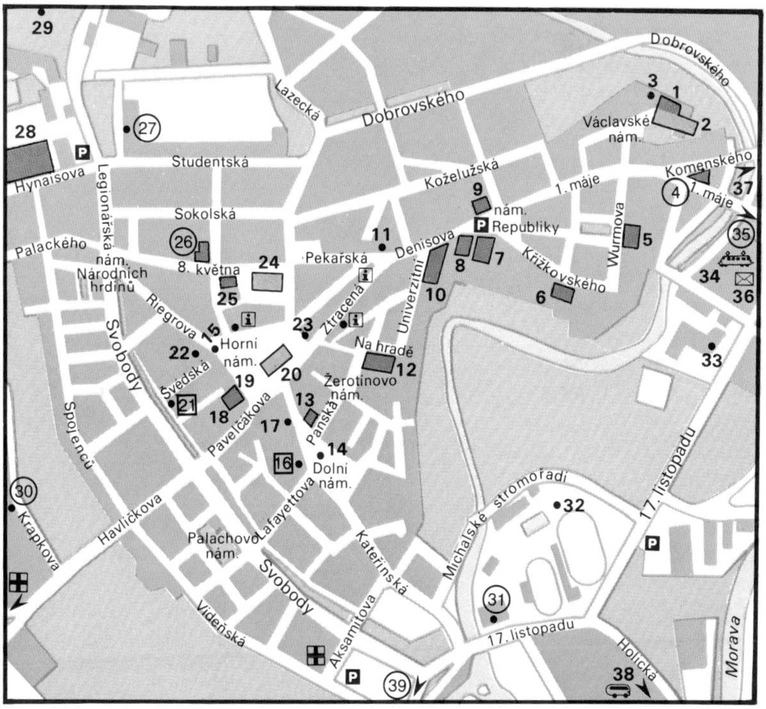

OLOMOUC

1 Přemyslid Palace
2 St Wenceslas Cathedral
3 Chapter Deanery
4 Palac hotel
5 Archbishop's Residence
6 Chapter Provost's Residence
7 Jesuit College
8 Church of Our Lady of the Snows
9 St Clare's Convent
10 Old University
11 Galerie V podloubí
12 St Michael's Church
13 Kabinet grafika
14 Plague column
15 Taxi stand
16 Hanácká restaurant
17 Pharmacy
18 O Stibor Theatre
19 Moravian Philharmonic Olomouc
20 Town Hall
21 Jednota restaurant
22 Petráš Palace
23 Pharmacy
24 St Maurice's Church
25 Prior department store
26 Národní dům
27 Sport hostel
28 Ice rink
29 Velký stadium
30 Flora hotel
31 Lokomotiva hostel
32 Lokomotiva sports grounds
33 'S' Club
34 Police
35 Sigma hotel
36 Passport and visas
37 Car rental
38 Hodolany Music Theatre
39 Sokol-Milo hostel

ON THE MOVE
Trams and buses will get you around the city, with bus connections to suburbs and integrated villages. Fares are collected as you get on.
Main bus station Sladkovského St. Tel: (068) 33 29 1.
Train station Jeremenkova St 60. Tel: (068) 21 75 for information. Trams 1 and 5 take you to the city centre.
Taxi stands Horní Sq 25. Tel: (068) 28 59 1/27 18 1. Near the main railway station.
Car rental Brnocar, Chvalkovická 38. Tel: (068) 32 72 2.

FACT FILE
Emergency medical aid K. Aksamita St 8. Tel: (068) 24 44 4.
Pharmacy U Salvatora, Dolní Sq 51. Tel: (068) 24 38 9. Krajinská lékarna, Horní Sq 10. Tel: (068) 23 08 1.
Police (VB) Masarykova St 4. Tel: (068) 23 33 3.
Post office Jeremenkova St 2. Tel: (068) 29 13 8.
Passport and visas Masarykova St 4. Tel: (068) 23 33 3.
Travel agencies Čedok, Horní Sq 2. Tel: (068) 28 83 1. Rekrea, Ztracená St 9. Tel: (068) 22 73 0/26 32 9. CKM, Denisova St 4. Tel: (068) 29 00 9.
Shopping
Concentrated around Horní Sq and Dolní Sq. Prior department store 8. května St 24.

WHERE TO STAY
⌂ **A* Flora** Krapkova St 34. Tel: (068) 25 44 1/23 14 1/23 24 3. Fax: (068) 25 44 9. Modern well equipped city centre hotel bordering on the park with excellent restaurant (II), café (II), bar (II), night wine bar (II) with dancing.
⌂ **B* Národní dům** 8. května St 21. Tel: (068) 24 80 6/25 17 9. City centre hotel in building which was once the National Theatre. Excellent restaurant (II), café (II), bar (II), night bar (II) with cabaret and dancing Sat and Sun.
⌂ **B* Palac** 1. máje St 27. Tel: (068) 23 28 4/24 09 6. 100-year-old building near city centre with restaurant (II), café (II), night bar (II) with dancing.
⌂ **C* Sigma** Jeremenkova St 36. Tel: (068) 26 94 1. Modern hotel near railway station with restaurant (II), café (II), bar (II).
Tourist hostels
⌂ **C Sport** U Husova sboru 3. Tel: (068) 41 31 81.
⌂ **C Lokomotiva** 17. listopadu St 17. Tel: (068) 26 26 7.
⌂ **C Sokol-Milo** Rooseveltova St 34. Tel: (068) 22 27 8.

EATING OUT
🍴 **I Jednota** Svobody St 31. Tel: (068) 27 93 6. Excellent restaurant, café, Asian bar, night bar with dancing and terrace in the summer.
🍴 **III Hanácká** Dolní Sq 38. Tel: (068) 25 29 6. In the city centre, offers local specialities.

NIGHTLIFE
Moravian Philharmonic Olomouc Horní Sq 22-23. Symphony concerts 3 times a month Thurs 19.30.
Oldřich Stibor State Theatre Horní Sq 22. Opera, ballet and drama, alternating daily 14.00 and 19.00.
Hodolany Music Theatre Ostravská St 1. Regular performances of musical comedies and musicals 14.30 and 19.00.
'S' klub 17. listopadu St 43. Students' club with musical, drama and literary programmes.

WHAT TO SEE
Horní Sq This is the venue of the main city market with a magnificent Renaissance and baroque **Town Hall** and clock in the centre, dating from 1378. There are two fountains of **Hercules** (1688) and **Caesar** (1725) and a sculpture of the Holy Trinity from 1716 - 1754 by F. Sattler, O.

Horní Square, Olomouc, with its plague column and Town Hall dating from 1378

Zahner and J. M. Schehauf. The square is surrounded by palaces and merchants' houses. Particularly worth seeing is the **Petráš Palace** where the oldest educational society in Central Europe — Societas incognitorum eruditorum — was founded in 1746. The **neo-classical theatre** building is the work of J. Kornhaüsel from 1830. Operas and plays are still performed there today.

Dolní Sq The second city market is surrounded by Renaissance and baroque houses. In the centre stands a column with a **statue of the Virgin**

by V. Render, erected in 1723 to commemorate the plague of 1715, and two baroque fountains **Neptune** (1683) and **Jupiter** (1735).

Přemyslid Palace Václavské Sq. This beautiful palace is Czechoslovakia's most important romanesque monument from the mid-12th century, originally the Bishop's Palace. It's open Tues to Fri 09.00 - 17.00.

St Wenceslas Cathedral Václavské Sq. Originally a Romanesque structure from the mid-12th century, the cathedral has been rebuilt several times. The present neo-Gothic building was constructed in the late 19th century. Composer Jacobus Handl Gallus held the seat of organist here in the 16th century.

The Chapter Deanery Wurmova St 9. A baroque building from the 17th and 18th centuries, the Chapter Deanery has memorial plaques to commemorate the assassination in Olomouc of the last Přemyslid ruler Wenceslas III and the period spent here by **Mozart**, then 11 years old. He composed his Symphony No 6 here, known as the *Olomouc Symphony*.

Archbishop's Residence Wurmova St 9. This 1685 building houses collections of ancient art but is closed to the public. Austrian Emperor Franz Joseph I was crowned here in 1848.

The Chapter Provost's Residence Křížkovského St 9. A baroque palace built around 1705, this is now the office of the Chancellor of Palacký University .

St Clare's Convent and Church Republiky Sq. Erected in 1773, the convent is now the **Regional Ethnographic Museum** with extensive collections charting the history of Olomouc and surrounding area and art exhibitions. A tour lasts about two hours. Open Tues to Fri 09.00-17.00.

Jesuit College Republiky Sq. A baroque building from 1722, the college is the work of L. Glöckel and W. Reich. The facade is by Kilian Dientzenhofer.

The Church of Our Lady of the Snows Denisova St. This Jesuit and university church built in 1719 by M. Klein and L. Glöckel has richly decorated interiors and an organ installed by G. Helbig in 1726.

The Old University Universitní St 1-3, Universitní Sq. Founded by the Jesuits in 1573, the complex of baroque buildings forming the Old University was acquired by the state in 1773. During the 19th and early 20th centuries only the theological faculty was based here. Since 1946 it has been the home of Palacký University.

St Michael's Church Na hradě St. A baroque building from 1698 by G.P. Tencalla and D. Martinelli, the church has an interesting exterior and interior with baroque paintings.

St Maurice's Church 8. května St. This late Gothic church has a magnificent baroque interior and an organ by M. Engler from 1745. Annual international organ festivals take place here from Aug 25 - Sept 15.

Kabinet grafika Dolní Sq 7. Here you can see regular exhibitions of painting and graphic art. It's open Tues to Fri 09.00 - 12.00, 13.00 - 17.00 Sat 12.00 - 17.00, Sun 09.00 - 12.00.

The magnificent organ in St Maurice's church, the venue of international festivals

Galerie V podloubí Denisova St. A student gallery with exhibitions of painting and photography, open Mon to Fri 14.00 - 18.00.

SPORTS

Many sporting activities take place near the city centre, notably in the Velký stadium on Legionářská St and the Lokomotiva sports grounds at 17. listopadu St. There's ice skating at the rink at Hynaisova 6.

FURTHER AFIELD

Svatý Kopeček 10km (6 miles) N. The 1679 baroque pilgrimage

church in Svatý Kopeček affords a spectacular view of the Olomouc River Valley. There's also a zoo.

Šternberk 18km (11 miles) N. Well worth a visit, this Gothic castle founded in the 13th century has an exhibition of Gothic and baroque painting and sculpture. There's also a remarkable museum of clocks and watches in the outer bailey of the castle. The castle is open May - Sept Tues to Fri 08.00 - 17.00.

Kroměříž 50km (31 miles) SE. This old town has an impressive Archbishop's Palace and gardens with colonnades and pavillions. It's open May - Sept Tues to Fri 08.00 - 16.00.

Náměšť na Hané 15km (9 miles) W. This neo-classical château has a French park and an exhibition of the finery of Olomouc's high clergy in the 17th and 18th centuries. It's open May 1 - Sept 30 Tues to Fri 08.00 - 16.00.

Olomouc is the setting for a gloriously colourful flower festival twice a year

WEST SLOVAKIA

THIS IS THE region where the massive mountain ranges of the Carpathians give way to the Podunajská lowland, one of the most fertile areas of Czechoslovakia. The mighty Danube creates enormous underground resources of water and the rich land and generous sunshine make the Carpathian slopes a great wine-producing area. Numerous mineral springs in the south have led to the establishment of world-famous spa centres such as Pieštany, many of which are also used for recreation.

The fertile area and pleasant climate has provided a living for the local population from early times — Celts, Romans and Slavs have all settled here throughout the centuries. In the heyday of the Great Moravian Empire, it was West Slovakia which saw the founding of the first university in Slovakia in 1465 and the first texts written in Slav languages which then spread to

.ooking across the mighty Danube to Bratislava with the castle on the left

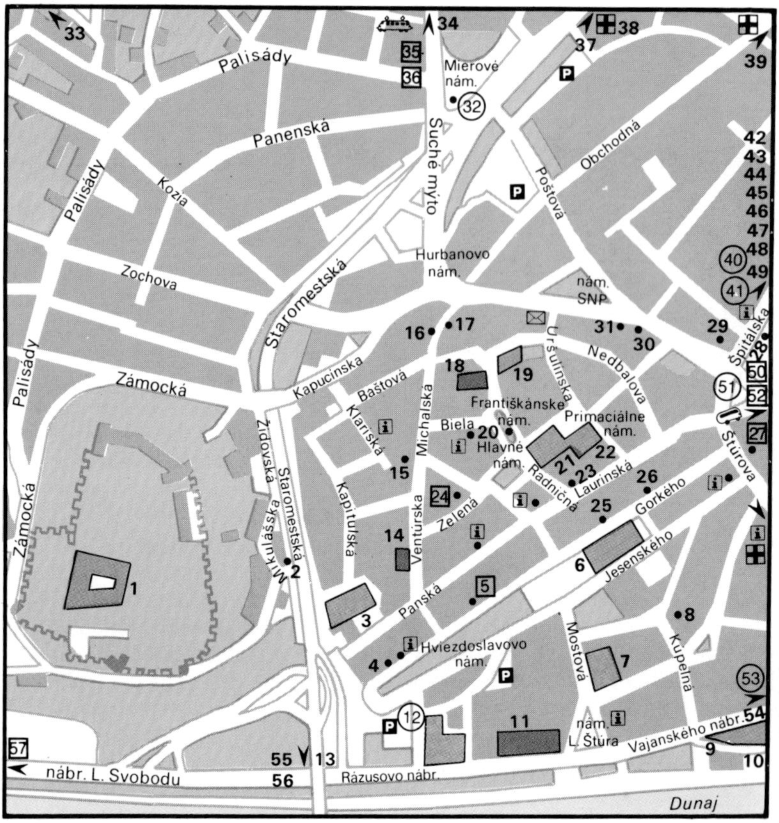

BRATISLAVA			
1 Bratislava Castle	13 SNP Bridge	28 Prior	43 Pasienky stadium
2 Clock Museum	14 Academia Istropolitana	29 Booking agency	44 Sports centre
3 St Martin's Cathedral	15 Palace of the Royal Chamber	30 Dunaj	45 Tuzex
4 Pragocar	16 Michalská Gate	31 Dom Odievania	46 Taxi Stand
5 Maďarská restaurant	17 Museum of Pharmacy	32 Forum hotel	47 Pharmacy
6 Slovak National Museum	18 Mirbach Palace	33 Slavín	48 Passports and visas
7 Slovak Philharmonic	19 Franciscan Church	34 Kamzík TV Tower	49 Bus to airport
8 Tuzex	20 Statue of Roland	35 Vychliadková restaurant	50 Stará sladovňa restaurant
9 Slovak National Museum	21 Old Town Hall	36 Expo Koliba restaurant	51 Sputnik hostel
10 Boat trips	22 Primatial Palace	37 Police	52 Polevnícka restaurant
11 Slovak National Gallery	23 Apponý Palace	38 Pharmacy	53 Bratislava hotel
12 Devín hotel	24 Perugia restaurant	39 Pharmacy	54 Concert Hall of Slovak Radio
	25 ČSA	40 Kyjev hotel	55 Horseriding
	26 Tuzex	41 Zares Zlaté piesky	56 Tuzex
	27 Luxor restaurant	42 Slovan stadium	57 Rybársky cech

the territories settled by other Slav nations. Today West Slovakia is a showcase of history with many fine buildings as well as a region which is sure to charm every visitor.

BRATISLAVA

Called the Beauty of the Danube, Bratislava is a city of contrasts. Ancient buildings and monuments sit a little unhappily with the modern architecture epitomized by the massive SNP bridge across the Danube to the new suburb of Petržalka. It's a bit out of the way at the western end of the Carpathian mountain range, only kilometres from the the Austrian and Hungarian borders, but nonetheless is the capital of Slovakia and the second largest city in the country with a population of 401,000. Industry has sprung up around the city but, thanks to an average temperature of 9.6°C, Bratislava is the biggest wine-growing community in Czechoslovakia.

First settlements in the Bratislava region date to 3000BC and on the site of the present castle from 2500BC. Throughout the centuries **Bratislava Castle Hill** has been an important strategic point — settled by the Celts, fortified by the Romans and adopted by the Slavs as their administrative centre.

For the three centuries of the Turkish occupation of Budapest, Bratislava became the capital of the Hungarian Empire. It was the centre of one of five Hungarian regions from 1850 - 1918 and the founding of the Czechoslovak Republic. It has been known as Bratislava since 1917.

It's not hard to imagine why people call Bratislava the Beauty of the Danube

The first university in Slovakia, the **Academia Istropolitana**, was founded here in 1465.

SETTING OFF

By air Internal flights to Ivanka airport from Prague, Brno, Karlovy Vary, Sliač and the High Tatras. International flights from New York, Montreal, Moscow, Leningrad, Sofia, Bangkok.
By car D2 from Brno - 119km (74 miles). E58 from Vienna - 65km (40 miles).
By bus Connections with most major towns within Czechoslovakia and international links with Budapest and Vienna among others.
By train Good internal rail links within Czechoslovakia and international connections to Budapest, Berlin, Sofia and Warsaw.
By boat Regular service from Budapest and Vienna. Tickets from. Čedok (see below).

ON THE MOVE

Trams, buses and trolley-buses will take you anywhere within the city.
Main bus station Mlynské Nivy. Tel: (07) 21 22 22/63 21 3.
Train station Dimitrovovo Sq. Tel: (07) 68 27 5.
Boat trips Fajnorovo nábrežie (embankment) 2. Tel: (07) 59 51 8/59 52 7. Information and tickets on boats to Vienna and Budapest. As the boats are often fully booked you're better off buying your tickets at Čedok, Jesenského St 5. Tel: (07) 52 72 3/52 74 2.
Taxi stands Rajská St 3. Tel: (07) 50 85 1-4.
Car rental Pragocar, Hviezdoslavovo Sq 14. Tel: (07)33 32 01/33 32 33.

FACT FILE

Emergency medical aid Pionierska St 6. Tel: (07) 44 44 4. Mýtna St 5. Tel: (07) 46 58 0. Bezručova St 3. Tel: (07) 54 81 4. Children's clinic. Mickiewiczova St 13. Tel: (07) 30 6. Hospital.
Pharmacies Mýtna St 5. Tel: (07) 46 58 0. Ružinovská St 10. Tel: (07) 23 11 43. 24 hour. Špitálska St 3. Tel: (07) 51 44 7. Tíhelná St 26. Tel: (07) 67 38 7.
Police (VB) Račianska St. Tel: (07) 20 84 44. Špitálska St 14. Tel: (07) 27 81 11.
Post Office SNP Sq 35. Tel: (07) 33 12 41/33 82 41.
Passports and visas Drieňová St 24. Tel: (07) 20 81 11 1.
Airline offices ČSA, Gorkého St 5. Tel: (07) 33 85 72/33 85 73. Internal flights. Bus to airport. ČSA, Americké Sq. Tel: (07) 64 79 0. International flights.
Travel agencies Čedok, Štúrova St 13. Tel: (07) 55 28 0/54 53 7/55 56 3/52 14 2/52 00 2. General information. Čedok, Jesenského St 5. Tel: (07) 52 72 3/52 74 2. International tickets and boat tickets to Budapest and Vienna.
CKM, Hviezdoslavovo Sq 16. Tel: (07) 33 16 07. CKM, Nálepkovo St 10. Tel: (07) 33 63 77. Slovakoturist, Klariská St 4. Tel: (07) 33 71 46. Tatratour, Františkánske Sq 7. Tel: (07) 33 78 71.
Tourist information BIPS, Uršulínska St 6. Tel: (07) 33 37 15/33 64 41. General information and details of cultural events.
Laurinská St 1. Tel: (07) 33 43 70. General information. Špitálska armády St 7. Tel: (07) 59 76 4. Guides. Booking Agency, SNP Sq 14. Tel: (07) 54 79 2. Theatre tickets.
Shopping
There's plenty of choice in the centre with Tuzex shops at Trnavská St 1, Gorkého St 8 (both foodstuffs), Rožňavská St 24 (auto and electrical goods), Šašovská St 24, Kúpelná St 1 (both textiles), Gorkého St 10 (cosmetics). Department stores Prior, Kamenné Sq 1, Dunaj, SNP Sq 30, Dom Odievania, SNP Sq 30.

Mixing the old and the new Bratislava is certainly a city of powerful contrasts

WHERE TO STAY
⌂ **A* de luxe Forum** Mierové Sq 2. Tel: (07) 34 81 11. Fax: (07) 31 46 45.
⌂ **A* de luxe Devín** Riečna St 4. Tel: (07) 33 36 40/33 08 51.
⌂ **A* Kyjev** Rajská St 2. Tel: (07) 57 08 2/52 65 1-7.
⌂ **B* Bratislava** Urxova St. Tel: (07) 29 56 41/29 59 51.
Tourist hostels
B* CKM Sputnik Juniorhotel Drieňová St 4. Tel: (07) 22 74 42.
Campsites
△ **A Zares Zlaté piesky** Senecká cesta 2. Tel: (07) 66 02 8. Chalets and tents. Restaurant (II), videobar (II). Swimming and watersports at the Zlaté piesky lake. On the Senec road, local bus from town. Open May 15 to Sept 30.

EATING OUT
I Expo Koliba Javorina Kamzík Hill. Folklore restaurant in the TV tower with gypsy music and local specialities,
I Maďarská Hviezdoslavovo Sq 19. Hungarian specialities. Also wine bar Pusta (II).
II+50% Rybársky cech Žižkova St 1. Fish specialities.
II+20% Perugia Zelená St 5. Italian restaurant and wine bar with music laid on.

ЮI **II+20% Vyhliadková** Kamzík TV tower. Look-out restaurant serving Serbian and Slovak specialities.
ЮI **II+10% Stará sladovňa (The Old Malt House)** Cintorínska St 32. Slovak specialities and good beer.
ЮI **II Luxor** Štúrova St 3. Slovak specialities.
ЮI **III Poľovnícka** Duklianska St 2. Slovak specialities.

NIGHTLIFE
Slovak National Theatre Hviezdoslavovo Sq. Opera, ballet.
Slovak National Theatre Laurinská St 24. Drama.
Concert Hall of the Slovak Philharmonic Reduta House, Palackého St 2. Classical concerts.
Concert Hall of Slovak Radio Vajanského nábrežie 12. Chamber, Symphonic and organ music.
Tickets for all events can be bought at SNP Sq 14. Tel: (07) 54 79 2.

WHAT TO SEE
Bratislava Castle Even if you don't want to look at the museum in the castle, it's worth walking up the hill for the view of the Danube and the hills of Czechoslovakia, Austria and Hungary. There's been a castle here since the 9th century but a massive fire in 1811 caused great destruction. The castle has recently undergone much reconstruction and is now used on special occasions by the Slovak National Council. The President has an office here and it also houses part of the **Slovak National Museum** with exhibitions on the history of Slovakia. The castle is open Tues to Sun 09.00 - 16.00.

Staré Město (The Old Town) Walk down the hill from the castle and you come to the Old Town, the historical core of Bratislava contrasting sharply with the ugly modern high rise and prefabs of **Petržalka. Hlavné Square** used to be the main square. After a fire in 1733 it was completely rebuilt in a baroque style. The neo-Renaissance fountain in the centre has a **statue of Roland**, a famous knight and defender of the city. The 1762 rococo **Palace of Count Esterházy** is worth a look but the most interesting building on the square is the **Old Town Hall**, built in the 14th century and reconstructed in the 15th and 19th centuries. Today it's home to the **City Museum** and a **museum** dedicated to the outstanding composer and pianist **Jan Nepomuk Hummel** who was born in Bratislava. Both open Tues to Sun 10.00 - 17.00.

Primatial Palace Primaciálne Sq 1. In this splendid 1781 baroque building you can see the excellent exhibitions of the **Bratislava Art Gallery**. There's a collection of 17th, 18th and 19th century European art but make a point of seeing the six 17th century tapestries telling the love story of mythical figures Hero and Leander. The gallery is open Tues to Sat 10.00 - 17.00, Sun 09.00 - 16.00. The **Hall of Mirrors** in the palace was once a seat of the Hungarian parliament and is where Napoleon signed a peace treaty with Austrian Emperor Franz I in 1805. Now it's used as a splendid venue for celebrations and weddings.

Mirbach Palace Frankiškánske Sq. This 1770 rococo palace is probably the most beautiful historical building in the city. Inside it has an impressive exhibition of arts from the baroque and rococo periods.

Franciscan Church Frankiškánske Sq. The oldest preserved building in the Old Town, consecrated in 1297. King Ondrej III took part in the ceremony. The adjoining monastery was built in the 14th and 15th centuries.

The Slovaks enjoy colour and folklore and the traditional ways still live on

Heralding the modern, the Most SNP

Michalská Gate Michalská St. Dating from the 14th century this is the only preserved gate in Bratislava. Its Gothic tower houses a collection of medieval arms and an exhibition on the building of fortifications. It's open Tues to Sun 10.00 - 17.00.

Palace of the Royal Chamber Michalská 1. Now the University Library, this was once the seat of the Hungarian Parliament. In 1847, Slovakia's political and spiritual leader and member of the Hungarian Parliament, **Ĺudovít Štúr**, delivered his speech calling for the abolishment of serfdom in Slovakia from here. Serfdom was finally abolished by Parliament in Bratislava the following year.

Museum of Pharmacy Michalská St 26. Bratislava's oldest pharmacy dating from the 19th century. Open Tues to Sun 10.00 - 17.00. This street also boasts the narrowest house in the city at number 10.

St Martin's Cathedral Dobšinského Sq. Nine Hungarian kings and eight queens were crowned in this magnificent Gothic cathedral dating from the 14th century. Its **steeple** is 85m (279ft) high. The interior is decorated with a great number of valuable woodcarvings and paintings. Of particular note is the lovely **Gothic bronze font** from 1403 and the 1734 lead statue sculpted by Danner of **St Martin** sharing his meal with a beggar.

Slovak National Gallery Rázusova nábrežie 2. Varied exhibitions of European art, Gothic art in Slovakia, 16th, 17th and 18th century Slovak art. Open Tues to Sun 10.00 - 17.00.

Slovak National Museum Vajanského nábrežie 2. Permanent exhibitions on Slovak natural history, a collection of musical instruments and mineralogy. Open Tues to Fri 08.00 - 18.00, Sat and Sun 09.00 - 17.00.

Apponý Palace Radničná St 1. Museum of Wine-Making, open Tues to Sun 10.00 - 17.00.

Clock Museum Staromestská St 1. Small but interesting exhibition of assorted timepieces. It's open Tues to Sun 10.00 - 17.00.

Slovak National Theatre Hviezdoslavovo Sq. Even if you don't want to catch an opera or ballet this neo-Renaissance theatre is worth a visit. The square has other significant monuments, notably Ganymede's 1888 Fountain, the 18th century **Monastery of Notre Dame**, the neo-baroque palace of the Pálfy family from 1885 and the statue of the Czech poet P.O. Hviezdoslav.

SNP Square The main square of the city, with statues erected in 1974 to commemorate the 30th anniversary of the Slovak National Uprising.

Most SNP (Bridge of the Slovak National Uprising) Love it or hate it, this modern bridge spanning the Danube certainly makes an impression. Much of the oldest part of the city as well as the **Jewish ghetto**, including the **Jewish Synagogue**, was in poor repair and was demolished to make way for the access road. During building work the remains of the walls of the **Old Town** were discovered and preserved. You can get impressive views of the city from the **Bystrica Café**, (II), 80m (262ft) up one of the columns on the bridge.

TV Tower Kamzík Hill. Another elevated café (II), revolving 70m (230ft) above the ground. The tower itself is 200m (656ft) high on top of the 440m (1443ft) hill. There is a monument on the hill to commemorate the defeat of the Turkish troops in Hungary from 1683. A chairlift from Železná studnička takes you to the top.

Slavín On a hill overlooking Bratislava this is a poignant memorial to the 6845 Soviet Army soldiers who lost their lives in the liberation of Bratislava in 1945. It was built in 1960 and covers an area of 10,000 sq m (12,000 sq yds). It's dominated by a column 42m (138ft) high built on the graves of the dead soldiers.

WALKS AND SPORTS

The foothills of the **Malé Karpaty (Little Carpathian)** range rise up from the outskirts of the city so there are plenty of tranquil walks away from the bustle. To the west **Bratislava Park** alone has more than 80km (50 miles) of marked hiking trails through the mountains. Organised sports facilities are plentiful with a swimming pool and sauna in Vajnorská St in Pasienky district and tennis courts, a cycling stadium and two ice rinks in Odbojárov St. There are two football stadiums. At the Zlaté piesky lake there are plenty of facilities for watersports. In winter, Kamzík Hill is a good place for tobogganing and skiing.

FURTHER AFIELD

Devín 10km (6 miles) W. Impressive ruins of a Gothic castle where archaeological research is uncovering evidence of neolithic settlements and Roman occupation as early as the 2nd century up to the 5th. From the ruins there's a magnificent view of the meeting of the Morava and Danube rivers. It's open Tues to Sun 10.00 - 17.00.

Devínska Kobyla 11km (7 miles) W. Nature reserve with 22 rare species of warmth-loving flora protected by law. There's a popular walking route through the reserve along red-marked paths from Devín to Bratislava taking about four hours.

Železná studnička 10km (6 miles) N. A popular resort with people from the city, it has four natural lakes with boating and fishing.

PIEŠTANY

Every year more than 42,000 people — 12,000 from abroad — come to Czechoslovakia's most famous spa resort to take the waters and bathe in the therapeutic mud. Indeed the favourable climate and thermal mineral springs attracted Celts, Romans and Slavs throughout history. The town is first mentioned in historical records in 1113, while the first documents on the spa date back to the 16th century.

Piešťany lies on the River Váh and the centre of the spa area is **Váh Island**, accessible by **Colonnade Bridge**. Near the bridge stands the symbol of Piešťany, a statue of a man breaking his crutches.

The hot gypsum sulphurous springs are best known for their treatment of rheumatic and sciatic diseases and problems with the locomotive system. Seven springs produce 3 million litres (660,000 gallons) of curative water at 67°C each day. Treatment also involves the application of the local sulphurous mud, perhaps a little on the messy side, but said to be one of the most effective natural remedies for rheumatism in the world.

Apart from the health centres, the parks, attractive buildings and excellent recreational, sporting and cultural facilities all combine to make Piešťany a honeypot for visitors from all over the world.

Nature at her glorious best in the wonderful countryside of West Slovakia

SETTING OFF
By air Regular flights from Prague and Bratislava.
By car D61 from Bratislava - 63km (39 miles).
By bus Regular service from major towns in Moravia and Slovakia connections to Bohemia.
By train Connections with Bratislava, Žilina and Vienna.

ON THE MOVE
Local transport is by bus.
Main bus station Dopravná 7.Tel: (0838) 23 00 0.
Train station Dopravná 7.Tel: (0838) 21 21 3.
Taxi stands Pavlovova St 54. Tel: (0838) 26 06 0.
Car rental Pragocar, Winterova St 32. Tel: (0838) 24 64 6-7.

FACT FILE
Emergency medical aid Pavlovova St 66. Tel: (0838) 24 24 1. Hospital.
Pharmacy Pavlovova St 29. Tel: (0838) 21 00 6.
Police (VB) Zahradná St 21. Tel: (0838) 23 33 3/21 30 6/25 45 8.
Post office Postová St 1. Tel: (0838) 22 00 4.
Airline offices ČSA, Nálepku St. Tel: (0838) 26 18 4.
Travel agencies Čedok, Pavlovova St 38. Tel: (0838) 22 21 5. Tatratour, Pavlovova St 28. Tel: (0838) 26 21 2.
Shopping
Main shopping centres are concentrated around Andrej Hlinka St, Sloboda Sq and Winterova St.There are branches of Tuzex at Pavlovova St (food). Obrancov Mieru St (clothing, cosmetics). and Kúpeĺný ostrov 13 (food, spirits, crystal souvenirs).

WHERE TO STAY
⌂ **A* Magnolia** kpt Nálepku St 1. Tel: (0838) 26 25 1. Restaurant (I), café (I), bar (I).

The symbol of hope for Piešťany

⌂ **B* Eden** Pavlovova St 60. Tel: (0838) 23 88 1. International restaurant (II), night bar (II)

Campsites

△ **A Slňava II** Janka Alexyhuz, 92101, Piešťany. Tel: (0838) 23 56 3. Open May 1 to Sept 30.

△ **A Lodenica** 92101, Piešťany. Tel: (0838) 38 03. In Slňava I recreation resort. Open June 1 to Sept 31.

Spa houses It would be a great shame and not stay in one of the beautiful spa houses on Spa Island. **Thermia Palace** Tel: (0838) 51 61 11. **Pro Patria** Tel: (0838) 51 62 11. **Balnea Esplanade** and **Balnea Palace** Tel (0838) 51 52 11. **Balnea Grand Splendid** Tel: (0838) 51 41 11.

NIGHTLIFE

House of Arts Ivana Krasku St. Music Hall, theatre, exhibitions.

WHAT TO SEE

Colonnade Bridge Built in 1932 the bridge carries the inscription 'Get up and walk'. Next to it is the statue of **Man Breaking Crutches** from 1933.

Napoleon Baths Spa Island. Classic architecture, built in 1822.

Memorial to Beethoven Next to Slovan Spa House. Created in memory of the composer's stay in Piešťany in 1801.

Museum of Balneology Spa Court, Central Park. Exhibitions of balneology, archaeology, ethnography and history. Open Tues to Sun 08.00 - 12.00, 13.00 - 17.00.

WALKS AND SPORTS

The relaxed atmosphere of Piešťany makes walking through the town very enjoyable but if you want to go further afield the nearby **Slňava** and **Striebornica** reservoirs are good places to hike. Alternatively there are pleasant routes along the banks of the River Váh. Swimmers might like to try the thermal waters of the indoor and outdoor pools of Eva at Kúpeľný ostrov on Váh Island or the two pools in the Slňava II resort 1.5 km (1 mile) out of town.

Watersports enthusiasts will enjoy **Lodenica** which has canoeing, rowing, yachting, windsurfing and waterskiing. The less energetic can try their hand at minigolf on either of the two courses - one next to the Balnea Grand Splendid spa house and one at Slňava II resort. In winter there are skiing facilities at **Bezovec**, 20 km (12 miles) NW.

FURTHER AFIELD

Čachtice Castle 14km (9 miles) N. The morbid might like to ruminate on the ruins of this Gothic-Renaissance castle whose former woman owner **Alžběta Báthory** was a notorious sadist who reputedly enjoyed bathing in the blood of young girls. In 1611 she was sentenced to life imprisonment in the castle but she eventually went mad and died in 1614.

CENTRAL SLOVAKIA

Vrátna dolina, a beautiful valley

A REGION OF glorious mountains, superb valleys, intriguing caves and therapeutic mineral springs, Central Slovakia captures the imagination of any visitor. From the Malá Fatra (Little Fatra) in the north-west to the Nízke Tatry (Low Tatras) in the centre, there's something for every lover of the outdoors.

Walkers and naturalists will love the Little Fatra which are covered in wild flowers and boast what is arguably the most beautiful valley in Slovakia, the Vrátna dolina with rocky crags and lush forests. And long- distance walkers will enjoy the challenge of the Low Tatras — you can walk the 80km (50 miles) of the main ridge and soak up the spectacular views without ever having to come down to the valley. Skiers are also likely to gravitate to these majestic mountains where you can find luxurious resorts and excellent snow conditions.

One word of warning if you're going to visit the mountains — they might not be the highest in the world but the weather is very changeable. If you're going walking it's best to tell someone your route and not to

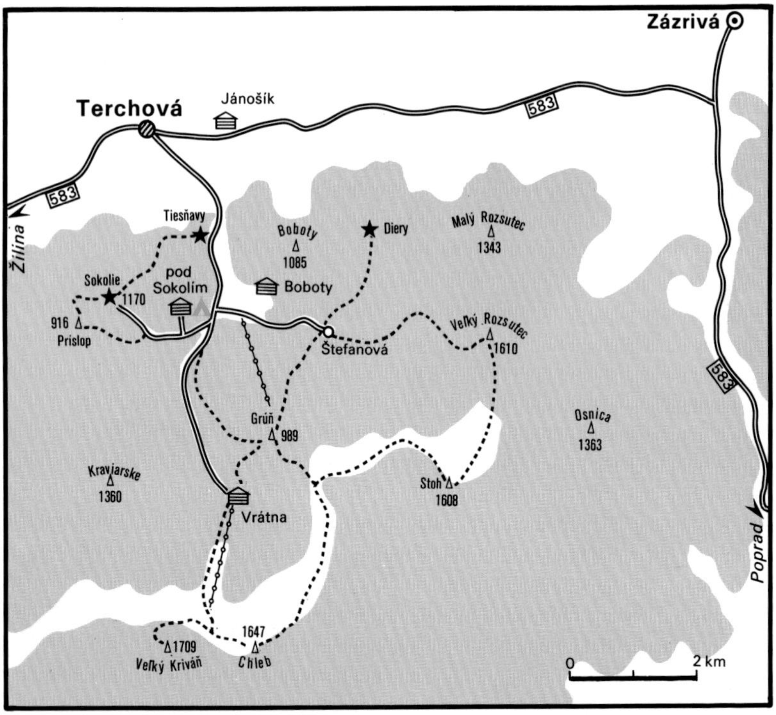

MALÁ FATRA (LITTLE FATRA) — VRÁTNA DOLINA

walk alone. Even if it's sunny when you set off it's wise to carry waterproofs. If the weather turns nasty, get down as soon as possible. There is a mountain rescue service (see p. 173) but it's advisable not to keep them busy!

MALÁ FATRA (LITTLE FATRA)

Little in name only, the Little Fatra have much to recommend them. With splendid crags and beautiful valleys the mountains are good walking country and a great habitat for rare flora. Bizarre rock formations and gushing waterfalls offer a dramatic backdrop to the picturesque villages with their folk architecture and traditions.

Žilina

The centre of the Považie region along the River Váh, Žilina makes a good base for trips into the beautiful surroundings of the river valley and the Little Fatra.

There were settlements at Žilina as early as the Stone and Bronze Ages but the first Slovak settlement was established here at the end of the 12th century. It was subsequently destroyed during Tartar invasions but began to flourish after being granted the status of a town in 1312.

Today 91,000 people live here and it's an important railway junction. **Dukla Square** is the historical centre with burgher houses from the 14th century, reconstructed in the 19th. The late Romanesque church of St Stephen has wall paintings dating back to the 14th century and if you're into folk art, the **Považské Museum and Gallery** is well worth a visit. It's housed in the Romanesque **Budatín Castle**, later reconstructed in the Renaissance and baroque styles on the outskirts of Žilina. There's an exhibition on the history of Slovakia and Žilina and one on tinker arts and crafts, the only one of its type in the world. The museum is open Tues to Sun 08.00 - 16.00. A wide range of cultural activities also take place in the Považské Museum and Gallery.

Žilina is also a cultural centre and has its own music ensemble, the State Chamber Orchestra, who give concerts in the **Fatra House of Arts**. Tickets can be booked at Dolný Váh St 47. Tel: (089) 20 95 2/20 00 7.

Rajecká dolina (valley)
This beautiful valley in the **Žilinská kotlina (Žilina Valley)** is 30km (18 miles) long and leads to the small spa town of **Rajecké Teplice**. The mineral springs here come out at 39°C and are used in the treatment of locomotive disorders. Watch out for the protected rock formation near **Slnečné skaly (Sun Rocks)**.

Čičmianska dolina (valley)
This is the upper part of the Rajecká valley and is equally picturesque with wooded hills on both sides. The quiet village of **Čičmany** is a gem of folk architecture with decorated wooden houses. There's a museum in **Raden House** with ethnographic and folklore exhibitions including examples of traditional embroidered costumes and tools. It's open Tues to Sun 08.00 - 16.00.

Súlovské skály (Sulov Rocks)
Well worth visiting is this amazing nature reserve south-west of Žilina. The bizarre rock formations here have wonderful names such as **Obrovská brána (Giant Gate), Gotická brána (Gothic Gate)** and the cave **Dračí díra (Dragon's Lair)**. One part is called a rock town because narrow paths lead under high rock faces, not unlike streets leading under high-rise buildings in cities. It's a wierd feeling to walk through here. You can see the ruins of **Sulov Castle**, dating from 1470.

Terchová
This small mountain resort is best known as the birthplace of Czechoslovakia's own Robin Hood, the 17th century Slovak hero **Juro Jánošík**. He was a leader of the anti-feudal resistance, a highwayman who stole only from the rich to give to the poor. He was eventually hung by the ribs but his memory lives on in folk songs, ballads and poems. His statue overlooks the village and there is an exhibition devoted to the resistance movement, open Tues to Sun 08.00 - 16.00. A colouful folk festival called **Jánošík Days** is held in Terchová in August every year.

On the road from Terchová to Vrátna you can pick up the **'Highwayman's Trail'**, a blue-marked hiking path leading to the yellow path to **Sokolie** among some pretty bizarre rock formations.

Vrátna dolina (valley)
Said to be one of the most beautiful valleys in Czechoslovakia, Vrátna dolina is criss-crossed with marked hiking trails. A chairlift takes you up to **Snilovské sedlo (saddle)**, the main Malá Fatra ridge. It's a great starting point for hikes to **Mount Chleb** at 1647m (5402ft) and **Mount Velký Kriváň** at 1709m (5606ft). The views from the top are most impressive. The valley is a popular ski centre with slopes for all levels of ability. Ski-tows and cable cars connect Vrátna dolina with the popular resorts of **Gruň, Príslop, Chlebjih** and **Cleb-sever**.

Velký Fatranský Kriváň 1709m (5606ft). It's worth the hike to the top of this, the highest peak in the Malá Fatra. The walk takes about 45

Near Terchová in the Little Fatra. Be sure to take a good camera with you!

minutes along the red-marked trail from the Snilovské sedlo chair lift. The views are magnificent.

Velký Rozsutec 1610m (5281ft). There's a good walking route from the picturesque settlement of **Štefanová** on the slopes of **Mount Velký Rozsutec** along the green marked path to **Medziholie**, then on the red path to the top. A longer but even more stunning route is along the yellow-marked path to **Pddžiar**, through the wild canyon of **Horné diery** with its dramatic waterfalls and then onto the blue path to **Medzirosutce**. This section of the route has metal ladders to get over some of the trickier bits but do wear boots or shoes with a good grip.

SETTING OFF

By car D1 motorway from Prague to Brno then E50 to Žilina - 404km (251 miles). E75 from Bratislava - 247km (153 miles). E50 from Poprad - 143km (89 miles).

By bus Direct bus lines to all major cities in Slovakia and Moravia. International links to Budapest in Hungary and Lwow in the USSR.

By train Direct links to Prague, Košice, Ostrava, Banská Bystrica, Bratislava and other major cities. International connections to Vienna, Warsaw and Moscow.

ON THE MOVE

Taking the bus is the best way to travel around the Malá Fatra region. Check in Žilina for details of times

and prices. Čedok should be able to help you out (see below).
Bus station Rauchova St. Tel: (089) 20 95 0.
Train station Olomoucká St. Tel: (089) 30 63 3.

FACT FILE
Health centre Terchová. Tel: (089) 95 18 2/95 192.
Mountain rescue Centre in Vrátna. Tel: (089) 95 23 2. Seven rescue bases in the mountains.
Post office Terchová. Tel: (089) 95 18 0/95 18 1. In centre.
Travel agencies Žilina. Čedok, L. Štúra Sq 3. Tel: (089) 22 08 7/47 12 0/46 51 3. Slovakotour, Hodžova St 5. Tel: (089) 20 78 9. Slovakoturist, L. Štúra Sq. Tel: (089) 47 86 0. Tatratour, Dukla Sq 21. Tel: (089) 20 07 1/20 07 2. CKM, Dukla Sq 10. Tel: (089) 23 51 8.

WHERE TO STAY
Žilina
⌂ **B* Slovakia Hotel** Tel: (089) 46 88 1. Restaurant (I), bar (I), café (I). Indoor pool and sauna.
Vrátna dolina
⌂ **B* Boboty Hotel** Štefanová Tel: (089) 95 22 7. Modern hotel with restaurant (I), night bar (I), day bar (II), sauna and indoor pool.
⌂ **A Chata Vrátna** Tel: (089) 95 22 3. Below Velký Fatranský Kriváň.
△ **B Autocamping Vrátna** Tel: (089) 95 22 0. Restaurant (III). Tents and timber cabins. Open May 15 to Sept 30.
Terchová
⌂ **B Jánošík Hotel** Tel: (089) 95 18 5. Restaurant (III), bar (IV). Accommodation in private homes can be arranged here and in Štefanová through Slovakotour and Tatratour in Žilina. Alternatively you can ask Čedok for details.
⌂ **A Chata pod Sokolím** Tel: (089) 95 32 6. Chalets and campsite with traditional timber cabins.

NÍZKE TATRY (LOW TATRAS)

You can walk the whole length of the main ridge of this magnificent mountain range stretching 80km (50 miles) from east to west like a giant whalebone. Because of its immense natural, ecological and scenic value, the 810 sq km (313 sq miles) area was declared a National Park in 1978. It has many fine forests which provide a good habitat for wildlife. As well as precious botanical and zoological species — bears and lynx still roam here — the region has many historical monuments and examples of folk architecture.

In their depths, the Low Tatras hide many minerals including gold, tungsten and other iron ores. Mining and iron ore processing became the traditional industries as far back as 1263 when King Belo IV granted Saxon colonialists the right to mine gold in the Magurky area and the surrounding mountains.

Walkers and skiers come here from all over the world to enjoy unparalled views of peaks and forests. There are plenty of well-marked trails but the most scenic part is the middle of the mountain range where the highest summit **Ďumbier** rises to 2043m (6701ft). To the north of Ďumbier the **Demänovská valley** stretches off to **Jasná pod Chopok**, the most popular tourist resort connected by cablecar to the southern slope of **Chopok** and the resorts of **Kosodrevina** and **Srdiečko**. Other popular resorts include **Donovaly** in the west and **Čertovica** in the east.

There are plenty of places to stay in the mountains, with most resorts having the choice of hotels, chalets and campsites. The travel agency Slovrast, based in the resort of **Liptovský Hrádok**, specializes in trips and accommodation in the Low Tatras. Tel: (844) 63 33 8.

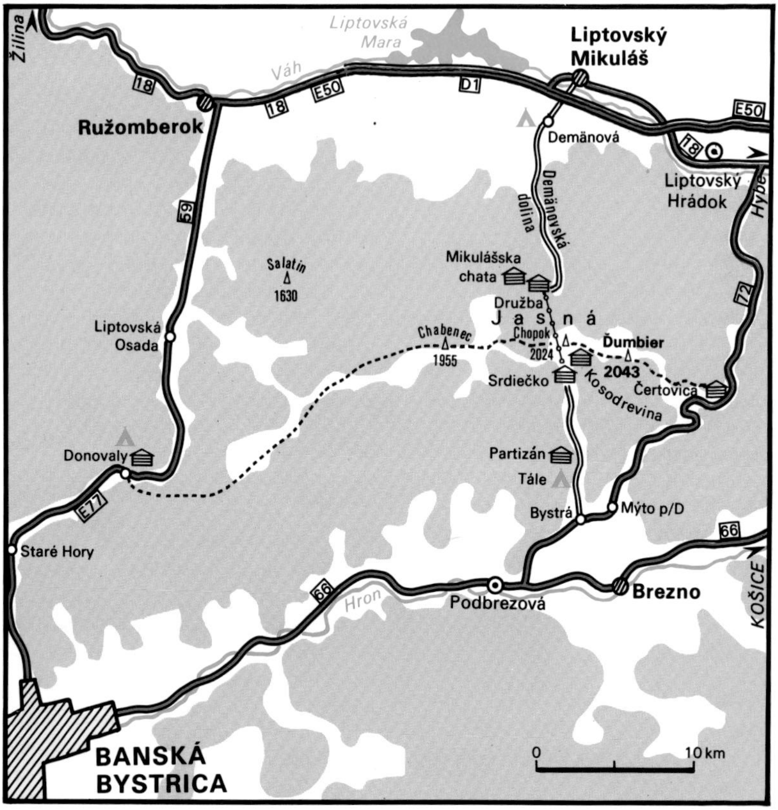

NÍZKE TATRY (LOW TATRAS)

BANSKÁ BYSTRICA

Ringed by picturesque mountains right in the middle of Central Slovakia, Banská Bystrica is one of Czechoslovakia's most important tourist resorts. Whether it's for walking, climbing or skiing in the nearby Low Tatras or simply to take in the beautiful scenery and rich history of the old town, people come here from all over Europe.

The earliest mentions of the town were in the 13th century when precious ores, particularly copper, were discovered here. The industries today have changed but the 90,000-strong town continues to prosper, processing timber and producing cement, matches, knitted garments and electrical goods.

During the Second World War Banská Bystrica became the centre of the anti-fascist movement. On August 29, 1944 the local radio station called for an overt struggle against the German troops stationed in Slovakia. This marked the beginning of the **Slovak National Uprising** in which nationals from more than 20 countries took part. When the town was occupied by the German army, the partisans retreated to the mountains where they continued their resistance until the arrival of the liberating Soviet and Romanian armies in 1945.

Banská Bystrica has an attractive historical centre with numerous attractive buildings from the Gothic, Renaissance, baroque and neo-Classical periods. There's plenty to see so don't be in too much of a rush to get to the mountains.

SETTING OFF

By air Regular flights from Prague to Sliač airport 20km (12 miles) to the south with stopover at Bratislava.
By car E571 from Bratislava - 204km (127 miles). Road 67 then 66 from Poprad - 124km (77 miles).
By bus Direct links to major towns in Slovakia, connections to Bohemia and Moravia. Buses from Budapest.
By train Direct connections to Prague, Košice, Bratislava and other major towns.

ON THE MOVE

Local transport in the area is by bus and trolley-bus.
Main bus station Cesta k smrečine St 1. Tel: (088) 25 34 8. Information. Tel: (088) 53 86 0. Booking office and seat reservations.
Main train station Augusta St 29. Tel: (088) 42 13 2-9.
Taxi stands SNP Sq 27. Tel: (088) 44 64 4/25 55 1/42 69 4.
Car rental Pragocar, Mičínská cesta St 19. Tel: (088) 54 23 1.

FACT FILE

Emergency medical aid L. Svobody Sq 1. Tel: (088) 35 24 1-9. Hospital.
Pharmacy SNP Sq 14. Tel: (088) 24 67 1. Partizánska St 12. Tel: (088) 41 47 1. 24 hour service.
Police (VB) Čs. armády St 16. Tel: (088) 24 44 5-6.
Post office Horní St 1. Tel: (088) 23 16 2.

Snow conditions are excellent in the Low Tatras and there are plenty of resorts

Passports and visas Timravina 12. Tel: (088) 25 38 0.
Airline offices ČSA, Partizánska cesta, blok C-40. Tel: (088) 41 97 5/41 97 6.
Travel agencies Čedok, M.R. Štefánika Sq 4. Tel: (088) 25 75 5. Slovakoturist, Dolná St 6. Tel: (088) 23 02 5. Tatratour, Dolná St 31. Tel: (088) 54 88 0/25 24 8. CKM, Horná St 65. Tel: (088) 24 31 7.

WHERE TO STAY
⌂ **B* Lux** Čs. armády St. Tel: (088) 24 14 1-6. Restaurant (II), bar (II), café (II).
⌂ **B* Národní Dom** Národní St. Tel: (088) 23 73 7. Restaurant (II).
⌂ **B* Urpín** Nejediého 5. Tel: (088) 24 55 6. Buffet (II).
Tourist hostels
⌂ **B Juniorhotel** Národní St 12. Tel: (088) 23 36 7.
Mountain chalets
⌂ **A Chata na Suchom Vrchu** Tel: (088) 97 04.West of Banská Bystrica.
⌂ **A Chata nad Tajovom** Tel: (088) 97 25. Near Tajov, west of Banská Bystrica.
Campsites
△ **A Tajov** Tel: (088) 97 55. 6km (4 miles) from Banská Bystrica. Open all year.
△ **B Banská Bystrica** Tel: (088) 33 01 2. Open all year.

EATING OUT
Most of the hotels in Banská Bystrica have restaurants but there are a few other places to try.
II Gastrocentrum SNP Sq 23. Tel: (088) 24 26 1-5.
II Park Tajovského St 10. Tel: (088) 34 44 3. Italian specialities.
II Wine Bar '6' SNP Sq 6. Tel: (088) 53 70 6/23 52 5.

People come to the historical town of Banská Bystrica from all over Europe

The fine forests and mountains of the Low Tatras are now a National Park

NIGHTLIFE
J.G. Tajovský Theatre Národní St 1. Opera.
Kultúrny dom (Community Centre) M.R. Štefánik Sq 3. Drama, concerts, variety shows.

WHAT TO SEE
Štěpán Moyzes Sq This attractive square is the historical core of Banská Bystrica and a national cultural monument. It's dominated by the castle complex including the **Palace of King Matthias**, the medieval **Town Hall**, the **Church of the Holy Rood** and the **Church of the Assumption of Our Lady**. The latter was built in about 1255 and the lower windows are Romanesque while the interior of the nave is baroque. The side chapels are Gothic and the **Chapel of St Barbara** has an altar made by the famous woodcarver **Master Pavol of Levoča** in the 16th century. On the outer wall of the church you can see a relief of Mount Olivet, dating back to about 500AD.

Dolná St 8 Transylvanian Prince Gabriel Bethlen was crowned King of Hungary here in 1620.

Kapitulská St This street is on the site of the original town fortification walls which can still be seen near the **Monument of the Slovak National Uprising**. At the SNP Sq end of the street you can see the **Capitular Church** and **Jesuit College** dating from 1695.

Monument and Museum of the Slovak National Uprising Kapitulská St 23. Opened in 1969 to commemorate the 25th anniversary

Climbers have long enjoyed the choice and challenge of the many rockfaces

of the anti-fascist resistance movement in Slovakia, this modern building has the grave of an unknown soldier at the entrance and exhibitions on the history of the resistance. Next to the monument is an open air **museum of arms and military equipment**. A tour takes about 90 minutes and the museum is open Tues to Sun 09.00 - 16.00.

Streslovenské muzeum (Museum of Central Slovakia) SNP Sq 4. Ethnographic, historical and scientific exhibitions. Open Tues to Sun 09.00 - 17.00.

Stredoslovenská galeria (Gallery of Central Slovakia) Moyzesovo Sq 25. Paintings and works of art by local artists and occasional exhibitions. Open Tues to Fri 09.00 - 17.00, Sat and Sun 10.00 - 16.00.

Dům umění (House of Arts) SNP Sq 7. Art gallery with occasional exhibitions. Open daily 10.00 - 17.00.

WALKS AND SPORTS

Many resorts are excellent bases for walking in the summer and skiing in the winter. Banská Bystrica is at the 'crossroads' of major mountain ranges — the **Low Tatras, Velká Fatra, Kremnické vrchy, Slovenské rudohorie** and the **Polana** — so walkers setting off from here are spoiled for choice. The mountain resorts of **Ružomberok, Liptovský Mikuláš, Liptovský Hrádok, Brezno** and **Podbrezová** are all good departure points for the Low Tatras.

There are cross-country tracks, ski-tows and chairlifts at **Panský diel-Šachtičky, Turecká-Krížna, Donovaly, Králíky, Tajov** and **Suchý vrch. Štiavničky** has an indoor pool and sauna and a lake where you can go swimming or boating.

FURTHER AFIELD

Špania dolina 10km (6 miles) N. Archaeological finds around this community date back as far as the Bronze Age. The first mentions of the village itself are from 1263 and throughout the Middle Ages it was a major mining centre. The old miners' houses now form part of an **open–air museum** of folk architecture. The **Church of the Transformation of Our Lord** is also worth a look for the valuable paintings inside and the 140 steps leading up to it, making a unique wooden sheltered staircase. Špania dolina is also the starting point for walks to **Panský diel-Šachtičky** at 1104m (3621ft).

Badinsky prales (Badín Forest) 8km (5 miles) SW. This 20-hectare (49-acre) nature reserve is only part of a vast forest area on the eastern slopes of the **Kremnické mountains**. It is virgin forest characterized by huge oak and fir trees but walkers are not allowed into the interior.

Brusno 21km (13 miles) NE. A popular spa resort where you can take the waters of the five mineral springs. Contact Propa, Skutečského St 19, Banská Bystrica, tel: (088) 23 86 0 for details of treatments.

Staré Hory 14km (9 miles) N. Originally a mining town in the Starohorská valley, Staré Hory is now made up of several settlements all with interesting folk architecture. One is **Turecká-Krížna,** a romantic tourist and ski resort with a chairlift to the top of **Mount Krížna** at 1574m (5163ft). Alpine flowers are everywhere, particularly from June to August when the *anemone narcissiflora* is in bloom.

Tajov 6km (4 miles) E. Worth a quick visit for its 18th century folk architecture and the Gothic church with a wooden bust of St John the Baptist from the 16th century. Slovak writer **J.G. Tajovský** and inventor of the wireless telegraph **Josef Murgaš** were both born here and there are permanent **exhibitions** of their work. A campsite, hotel and ski area make it a good starting point for trips to the Kremnicé mountains.

EAST SLOVAKIA

THIS IS TRUE border country which stretches from the main ridge of the Carpathian Mountains on the Polish border across to the Hungarian frontier in the south and the Soviet border to the east. The majority of towns in East Slovakia were founded in the Middle Ages and are showcases of Gothic and Renaissance architectural monuments and art.

East Slovakia is perhaps best known for the magnificent peaks of the **VysokéTatry (High Tatras),** and they are indeed remarkable, but East Slovakia has many other attractions. The **Spiš region** around Levoča is well worth a trip and the natural wonders of the **Slovenský Raj (Slovak Paradise)** and the **Slovenský Kras (Slovak Karst)** should not be missed.

LEVOČA

All those arriving in this medieval walled town are impressed by its silhouette. Levoča is built on a high hill surrounded by other forested hills within easy reach of the High

Levoča Town Hall, home of the Spiš Museum devoted to the town's history

Tatras and the Slovak Paradise. Its ideal location in the centre of the Spiš region and its historical centre make it an excellent stopover on your way through Slovakia.

Levoča was founded in the 13th century and in 1271 Stephen V made it the administrative centre of the Province of Spiš Saxons. The town flourished on the trade routes from the Baltic region to the Balkans and from Turkey to Silesia, Germany, Austria and Italy.

The town prospered and expanded but because it was bypassed by the main railway line, it escaped the major industrialisation of other towns. Levoča still looks much as it did at the turn of the 16th century with a lovely town square with Gothic courtyards and arcades, Renaissance burgher houses and old town walls.

SETTING OFF

By air Flights to Poprad from Bratislava and Prague, then bus or train.

By car E50 from Poprad - 26km (16 miles).

By bus Regular service from Banská Bystrica, Poprad, Košice, Žilina, Bratislava and other major towns.

By train Local train from Spišská Nová Ves, which is on the main line from Prague to Košice.

ON THE MOVE

Local transport is by bus but Levoča is small enough to explore on foot.

Bus station Slobody Sq. Tel: (0966) 22 78.

Train station Slobody Sq. Tel: (0966) 24 64.

FACT FILE

Emergency medical aid Cesta Slobody 6. Tel: (0966) 26 51-4. Hospital.

Pharmacy Majstra Pavla Sq 12. Tel: (0966) 24 56.

Police (VB) Železničný riadok 39. Tel: (0966) 23 33.

Post office Majstra Pavla Sq 42. Tel: (0966) 24 81/33 04.

Passports and visas Železničný riadok St 30. Tel: (0966) 23 33.

Travel agencies Čedok, Majstra Pavla Sq 46. Tel: (0966) 24 12/38 40. Slovakotour, Mierové Sq 17. Tel: (0966) 27 60.

Shopping

All the shops are concentrated around Majstra Pavla Sq.

WHERE TO STAY

⌂ **B Družba** Cesta Slobody 22. Tel: (0966) 23 35. Restaurant (III), café (II).

⌂ **B Biela paní** Majstra Pavla Sq 36. Tel: (0966) 25 59.

Campsites

△ **A Levočská dolina** 054 01 Levoča. Tel: (0966) 27 01. 5km (3 miles) from Levoča towards Prešov-Košice. Open June 1 to Sept 30.

Also **A* Bungalows** open all year.

△ **B Dravce** Tel: (0966) 36 51. Tents and bungalows. Open all year.

EATING OUT

🍴 **II Spišsky dom** Majstra Pavla Sq 35. Restaurant.

🍴 **II Biela paní** Majstra Pavla Sq 36. Wine bar.

WHAT TO SEE

St James' Cathedral Majstra Pavla Sq. A unique treasury of late Gothic art with a remarkable altar from 1507-1517 by famous woodcarver **Master Pavol of Levoča**. Made of linden wood, it's the tallest Gothic winged altar in the world at 17.62m (58ft). The carvings of St James and the apostles at the **Last Supper** are extraordinary while the sculptures of the High Altar are larger than life — the **Madonna** is 2.5m (8ft) tall. Beside the main altar is a number of other Gothic altars, a font and a fine Renaissance pulpit. The wall paintings are of great value, the oldest behind the altar of '**The Man of Pain**' dating from the mid-14th century. On the northern wall you can see paintings of the Seven Christian Virtues and the Seven Deadly Sins. The cathedral itself dates from 1370.

Town Hall Majstra Pavla Sq 2. Today this attractive Renaissance building houses the **Spiš museum** with exhibits documenting the town's history. Frescoes on the façade depict civic virtues and the 16th century 'cage of shame' was used as a pillory for fallen women. It's open Tues to Sun 09.00 - 17.00.

Another branch of the museum is at **The Hain House**, Majstra Pavla Sq 40, and has displays of fine art from the Spiš region. It's open daily 09.00 - 17.00.

Minorite monastery Bernolákova St. Next to this baroque monastery from 1750 stands an unnamed early 14th century Gothic church. Inside you can see examples of beautiful baroque furniture made by Swedish woodcarver Olaf Engelheim in 1700. Nearby is one of the towers that formed part of the town's fortifications in the 14th and 15th centuries. Five of the 16 original towers of the ancient town wall have been preserved.

Master Pavol's House Majstra Pavla Sq 20. A museum dedicated to the famous medieval woodcarver. It's open Tues to Sun 09.00 - 17.00.

Museum of Specialized Education Majstra Pavla Sq 28. Museum dedicated to the blind. Open Tues to Sun 09.00 - 16.00.

FURTHER AFIELD
Spišský Hrad (Spiš Castle) 16km (10 miles) E. Dominating the Spiš valley on the top of a hill stands this National Monument of Culture, one of the largest castle ruins in Central Europe. The site was settled as early as the neolithic period of the Stone Age and the round tower was built in the 11th century.

Master Pavol's remarkable carvings of the Last Supper in St James' Cathedral

The Romanesque Palace and parts of the Upper Castle were built in the 13th century. It was destroyed by fire in 1780 and the ruins are now being restored. From the courtyard you get a splendid view of the countryside. The reconstructed sections of the castle are open to the public with an **archaeological and historical exhibition**, open May to Oct 08.00 - 16.00.

Below the castle lie the **Dreveník** and **Sivá Brada nature reserves**. The rustic sheep farmer's cottage **Koliba (III)** offers Slovak specialities including pork dishes, a special kind of pasta with sheep's cheese called *halušky* and Spiš meat pies.

SLOVENSKÝ RAJ (SLOVAK PARADISE)
Narrow gorges, thundering waterfalls, murmuring streams and quiet mountain ridges with panoramic views earned this protected landscape its name of Slovak Paradise. It covers 210 sq km (61 sq miles) and although its ridges only rise to 1100m (3608ft), there is such a variety of terrain that walkers will find plenty to challenge them.

The villages of **Čingov**, **Kláštorisko**, **Podlesok**, **Dedinky** and **Mlynky** are good starting points for walks in the region along well-marked paths. Dedinky is also a **watersports centre** with an artificial lake while Mlynky is the largest **winter sports centre** with ski tows and a number of well-kept cross country skiing trails.

Kláštorisko During Tartar invasions in the early 13th century, villagers from the region sought refuge in Kláštorisko which, surrounded on three sides by deep canyons, was virtually impregnable. A **Carthusian monastery** was built in 1305, occupied by Hussite armies in the 15th century and then demolished in 1543 to prevent highwaymen from using it as a refuge. Only the walls and parts of the foundations remain.

Hornád Canyon Only 10 - 15m (33 - 49ft) wide in places, the walls of this magnificent canyon reach 150m (492ft). The wild River Hornád thunders through the gorge, popular with walkers and canoeists alike.

Velký and Malý Kysel Two arms of the upper Kysel river, typical of the gorges of the Slovak Paradise. The **Giant Waterfall** and the **Gorge**, in places only 1m (3ft) wide but 150m (492ft) high, are very impressive.

Velký and Malý Sokol Two gorges, the first with walls up to 300m (984ft) high, the second rich in flora.

Suchá Belá One of the most attractive gorges with dramatic cascading waterfalls.

Dobšinská ladová jaskyňa (Dobsinšká Ice Cave) An amazing but chilly geological rarity and the only cave in the area open to the public. The cave complex was discovered in 1870 and the temperature never rises above freezing. There are many bizarre and fantastic ice formations. The caves are open daily 09.00 - 15.00 in summer, closed in winter.

Občasný pramen (Irregular Spring) A unique natural phenomenon. The water in the spring gushes at different pressures and at irregular intervals from under **Havrania skala (Raven Rock)**.

Hradisko A hill not far from Čingov where archaeologists have unearthed remains of a prehistoric settlement.

Medveďia jaskyňa (Bear's Cave) This cave of stalagmites and

It's easy to see how the Slovenský Raj (Slovak Paradise) came by its name

stalactites got its name when the bones of a cave bear were found in 1952. It's not yet open to the public.

Zavojový vodopád (Veil Waterfall)
The highest in the Slovak Paradise at 65m (213ft) in the deepest gorge Sokolia dolina (Falcon Valley).

WHERE TO STAY
Čingov
⌂ **B Flora Hotel** Tel: (0965) 91 13 0. Restaurant (III), wine restaurant (II).
⌂ **B Chalets Čingov-Džurkovec** Smižany. Tel: (0965) 91 10 9.
Kláštorisko
⌂ **B Kláštorisko chalet camp** Tel: (0965) 91 83 07. Restaurant (III). Accessible only on foot. Luggage transportation.
Podlesok
△ **A* Motor camp Podlesok** Tel: (0965) 91 62 81. Restaurant Spišská koliba (III) at Lide nearby. Open May 15 to Sept 30.
Dedinky
⌂ **B Priehrada Hotel** Tel: (0942) 94 36 9. Restaurant (II), bar (II). Also campsite A.
Mlynky
⌂ **B Slalom Hotel** Tel: (0965) 97 20 3. Restaurant (III).
Spišská Nová Ves
⌂ **B* Metropol Hotel** Tel: (0965) 22 24 1-3. Restaurant (I), wine bar (I), café (I), snack bar (I).

FURTHER AFIELD
Spišská Nová Ves 5km (3 miles) NE of Čingov. The nearest large town to the Slovak Paradise, Spišská Nová Ves is an important mining community of 40,000 in the River Hornád valley. The town was founded in 1268 and evidence shows there was a settlement here during the time of the Great Moravian Empire. Its bell-casting workshops were well-known in the 14th and 15th centuries.

There are plenty of interesting historical buildings to see in the town including the 14th century **Gothic Roman Catholic Church**, richly decorated with sculptures. The **Slovak Church** of 1731 and the **Reduta Theatre** built in 1905 are also worth visiting.

Markušovce 12km (7 miles) E of Čingov. Founded in the 13th century this village boasts a château from 1643 built by the Mariassy family which is currently being restored. The French park has the rococo **Dardanelles** summerhouse from the second half of the 18th century. It was renovated in 1983 and now houses a unique collection of rare historic keyboard instruments, including a piano from the mid 18th century. There is an English- speaking guide and the **museum** is open May 1 - Sept 30 Tues to Sun 08.00 - 16.00, Oct 1 - April 30 Mon to Fri 08.00 - 16.30.

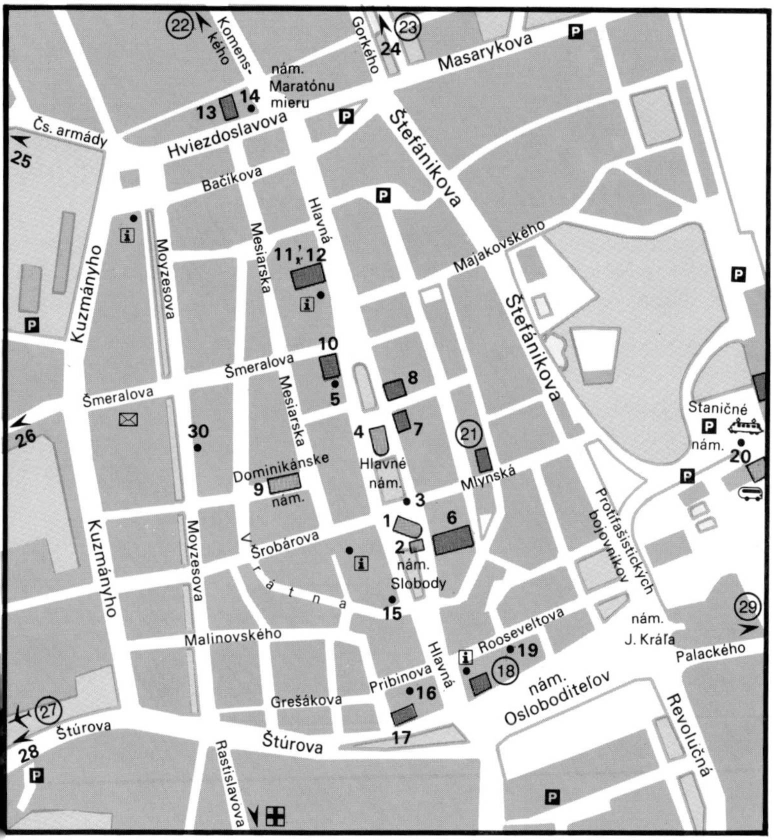

KOŠICE

. St Elizabeth's Cathedral
: St Michael's Chapel
Urban Tower
State Theatre
Spiš Chamber Palace
House of the Košice Government Programme
7 Levoča House
8 University Church
9 Dominican Church
10 East Slovak Art Gallery
11 Technical Museum
12 Planetarium
13 Museum of East Slovakia
14 International Peace Marathon Monument
15 Car rental
16 ČSA
17 Dargov department store
18 Interhotel Slovan
19 Taxi stand
20 Taxi stand
21 Interhotel Imperial
22 Jahodná chalets
23 Hutník hotel
24 Zoo
25 Botanical gardens
26 Passport and visa office
27 Campsite
28 Pharmacy
29 Zelený dvor chalets
30 Police

KOŠICE

The Hungarian influence on this capital of Eastern Slovakia is very strong and its historic core with over 500 protected buildings and monuments is an attraction in itself.

Earliest records of the town date to 1230 and over the centuries it has grown to be the fifth largest town in Czechoslovakia and the second largest in Slovakia. It has a population of 260,000 and important metallurgical, engineering, food production and building industries. It's also a major cultural and educational centre with 12,000 students studying at the four institutions of higher education.

Thousands of visitors come each year to absorb the historical atmosphere and visit the spectacular **Slovak Karst** nearby where you can see dramatic canyons with sheer rock faces and cave systems. It's also a good stopping-off point for travellers on their way to Hungary, only 21km (13 miles) away.

SETTING OFF

By air Regular flights from Prague and Bratislava.
By car E50 from Brno - 480km (298 miles). E50 from Poprad - 120km (75 miles).
By bus Regular connections to Banská Bystrica and most major towns in Slovakia.
By train Connections to most major towns in Czechoslovakia. On main line from Prague to Moscow.

ON THE MOVE

Local transport is by bus and tram.
Bus station Staničné Sq. Tel: (095) 51 61 9.
Train station Staničné Sq 1. Tel: (095) 23 70 0/32 51 1.
Taxi stands Rooseveltova St 3. Tel: (095) 22 24 4/22 24 5/20 04 4.
Car rental Pragocar, Vrátna St 1. Tel: (095) 20 53 5/26 32 7.

FACT FILE

Emergency medical aid. Rastislavova St 43. Tel: (095) 25 25 1/25 55 1.
Pharmacy Toryská 1. Tel: (095) 42 94 91. 24 hour.
Police (VB) Meyzesova St 19. Tel: (095) 21 25 1.
Post office Šmeralova 18. (095) 27 72 5.
Passport and visa office SNP St 35. Tel: (095) 42 78 48.
Airline offices ČSA, Pribínova 4. Tel: (095) 26 87 1.
Travel agencies Čedok, Rooseveltova St 1. Tel: (095) 20 76 4/23 12 1/26 23 5/23 84 7. CKM, Hlavná St 88. Tel: (095) 27 45 8/22 90 3. Tatratour, Šrobárova 5. Tel: (095) 21 33 4. Slovakoturist, J. Bačíka St 11. Tel: (095) 27 74 0.
Shopping
Most of the shops are concentrated around Hlavná St. Prior department store is at Hlavná St 111, Dargov department store is in Sturova St. Tuzex is at Hlavná St 21.

WHERE TO STAY

⌂ **A* Interhotel Slovan** Hlavná St 1. Tel: (095) 27 37 8/27 38 0. Restaurant (I), night bar (I).
⌂ **B* Interhotel Imperial** Gen. Petrova St 16. Tel: (095) 22 14 6. Restaurant (I), night bar (I).
⌂ **B Hutník** Tyršovo nábrežie (embankment) 6. Tel: (095) 37 51 1/37 78 0. Restaurant (II).
Chalets
⌂ **C Zelený dvor**, Prešovská cesta. Tel: (095) 36 25 0. Restaurant (III).
⌂ **C Javorina** Jahodná. Tel:(095) 96 11 72. Restaurant (III).

EATING OUT

🍴 **II Levočský dom** Hlavná St 61. Hungarian specialities.
🍴 **II Zlatý dukat** Hlavná St 16. Restaurant, also wine bars (II & III)
🍴 **III Gastrodom** Gen. Petrova St 27. Restaurant.

St Elizabeth's Cathedral, Košice - a must

NIGHTLIFE
State Philharmonic Moyzesóva 66.
State Theatre Škrobákova 14. Drama, opera, ballets.

WHAT TO SEE
St Elizabeth's Cathedral Hlavná St. Said to be one of the most beautiful Gothic churches in Europe, put this to the top of your list. Side chapels were added to the original five-nave basilica from 1446 - 1453 and it was completed in 1508. Ferenc Rákoczy, leader of the Hungarian nobility in their struggle against the Habsburgs, is buried in the crypt.

St Michael's Chapel Hlavná St. Second oldest church in Košice built in 1330. There are 17 gravestones in the walls of the chapel, the oldest dating to 1375.

Urbanova veža (Urban Tower) Hlavná St 2. Originally a belfry dedicated to St Urban, the patron of vineyards and wine-making which brought prosperity to the town. The tower was built in 1628 and its bell was the largest in Slovakia but was sadly destroyed in a fire in 1966. It now houses an **exhibition of artistic iron-casting**, open Tues to Fri 09.00 - 17.00, Sat and Sun 10.00 - 16.00. On the hour you can hear electronic folk songs.

Spiš Chamber Palace Hlavná St 68. This 1632 palace, adapted in the baroque style in the 17th century, turned out to be a genuine treasure trove. During restoration work in 1935 a collection of 2920 gold coins was discovered. They came from 24 different countries and dated from the 4th century BC to 1679. The coins are now on display in the **Museum of East Slovakia** at Mieru St 2. Open Mon to Fri 09.00 - 17.00, Sat and Sun 10.00 - 16.00.

House of the Košice Government Programme Hlavná St. A baroque and classical building from 1779, originally built as a district administration office. The Košice Government Programme on the co-existence of the Czechs and Slovaks was announced here after the Second World War.

Levočský dom (Levoča House) Hlavná St 65. Originally from the 15th century, re-built in the Renaissance style in the 17th and with baroque additions from the 18th century.

University Church Hlavná St. Belonged to the Jesuits and originally part of Kosiče University, founded in 1657. The interior is a fine example of typical baroque architecture.

Dominican Church Dominikánské Sq. A huge one-nave building from the 13th century and the oldest church in Kosiče. Next to it is the Dominican Monastery from 1761.

International Peace Marathon Monument Maratonu míru Sq. This statue of a runner was erected to commemorate the traditional sporting event held in the town since 1924. The pedestal bears the Greek inscription *Neni khamen (We Have Won)* and the names of the individual winners.

State Theatre Škrobákova 14. Neo-baroque building from 1899, replacing the original 1790 building.

East Slovak Art Gallery Hlavná St 72. Exhibitions of medieval East Slovak art, open Mon to Fri 09.00 - 17.00, Sat and Sun 10.00 - 16.00.

Technical Museum and Planetarium Hlavná St 88. In the 17th century palace, open Mon to Fri 09.00 - 17.00, Sat and Sun 10.00 - 16.00.

Botanical Gardens Mánesova 17. Scientific branch of the university — a visit makes a refreshing walk.

Zoo Kavečany. 5km (3 miles) north, open daily 09.00 - 17.00.

WALKS AND SPORTS
Residents of Kosiče are lucky to have **Čermeĺské Valley** nearby - it's a great place for hiking. The **Kosiče Urban Forest** covering 72 sq km (28 sq miles) isn't far away either and there are organized sports facilities at **Bankov**, **Jahodná** and **Alpínka**.

FURTHER AFIELD
Slovenský Kras (Slovak Karst) 25km (16 miles) W. Over 850 varieties of plants and flowers grow in the Slovak Karst, at 440 sq km (170 sq miles) the largest karst (limestone) region in Central Europe. It's a brilliant place for walking with spectacular canyons, rock faces and caves. The deep canyons of the **Slaná** and **Štítnik rivers** divide it into three separate plateaux – **Silická**, **Plešivecká** and **Koniar**. **Silická** is the largest and is peppered with sink-holes, some up to 500m (1640ft) wide and 50m (164ft) deep. There is a network of cave systems and those at **Gombasecká** and **Domica** have interesting guided tours.

If you get a chance visit the **Zádíelska valley** on the Plešivecká plateau — it's one of the most beautiful canyons in Czechoslovakia. There's a nature trail along its 4km (2.5 miles) which takes about four hours. In places the furrowed limestone rock faces rise up to heights of 350m (1148ft). You can't miss the **Cukrová homola (Sugar Cone)** rock – its huge pyramid stands 108m (354ft) high.

Fertile meadows with the romantic castle at Krásna hórka in the distance

Ruins of castles can be seen at **Plešivecký**, **Brzotínsky** and **Turniansky**. The romantic castle at **Krásna hórka** has been preserved and now houses an historical exhibition, open Tues to Sat 09.00 - 17.00, Sun 09.00 - 16.00. The **Betliar château** adapted in the classical style in 1880 - 1885 is currently under reconstruction and remains closed to the public.

Rožňava 69km (43 miles) W. This royal town is the centre of the Slovak Karst and has a number of historical buildings. The old network of streets has been preserved and the main square is dominated by a **watchtower** from the 17th century while 17th and 18th century burgher houses line the square.

Bardejov 77km (48 miles) N. It was not for nothing that UNESCO awarded this medieval town the European prize for exemplary care of historical buildings. It's one of the best preserved towns in Slovakia with many buildings and fortifications from the 14th and 15th centuries and a Gothic-Renaissance **Town Hall** from 1509. The Gothic church of **St Egidius** from 1415 is a national cultural monument.

Around Bardejov there are 27 other national cultural monuments, all rare wooden churches built mostly in the 18th century in the style of Ukranian orthodox buildings. The best examples are at **Hunkovce**, **Krajná Polana**, **Nižný Komárník**, **Medvedzie**, **Mirola**, **Krajná Bystrá**, **Korejovce**, **Dobroslava** and **Krajná Porúbka**.

Bardejovske kupele 73km (45 miles) N. Not far from Bardejov is this spa whose mineral springs are known for the treatment of diseases of the digestive and nervous systems. It has a modern **open-air museum** that is worth going to see for its examples of folk architecture, open Tues to Sun 09.00 - 17.00.

Kavečany 5km (3 miles) N.New winter sports resort and zoological garden both under construction.

Herlany 27km (17 miles) E. During searches for springs in 1870, an amazing natural geyser sprang up. It comes from 351m (1151ft) underground to burst forth to a height of 20 - 30m (66 - 99ft) every 32 - 34 hours, lasting for 30 minutes each time.

Čaňa Lakes 17km (11 miles) S. The lakes have a gravel bottom and are popular for swimming, various watersports and fishing.

Izra Lake 32km (20 miles) SE. A natural lake of volcanic origin covering 5 hectares (12 acres). The surrounding deep forests are good for hiking and the lake is used for swimming, canoeing and fishing.

Jasov 22km (14 miles) W. A small town with many interesting historical buildings, the most remarkable being the **18th century monastery** on the site of a monastery founded in the 12th century. It is now a national cultural monument and the wall paintings of its baroque church are really worth seeing. Surrounding it is a beautiful **French garden** with exotic trees. The **Jasov cave system** has impressive stalactites and stalagmites.

Medzev 37km (23 miles) W. This medieval town was once colonized by German settlers. A mining village was founded here in 1272 which became known for tool-making. The hammer mills on the Bodva river started in 1356 and some have been preserved.

Štós 53km (33 miles) W. A small spa town not far from Medzev which is known for its treatment of respiratory diseases.

Bardejov won a UNESCO prize for its exemplary care of historic buildings

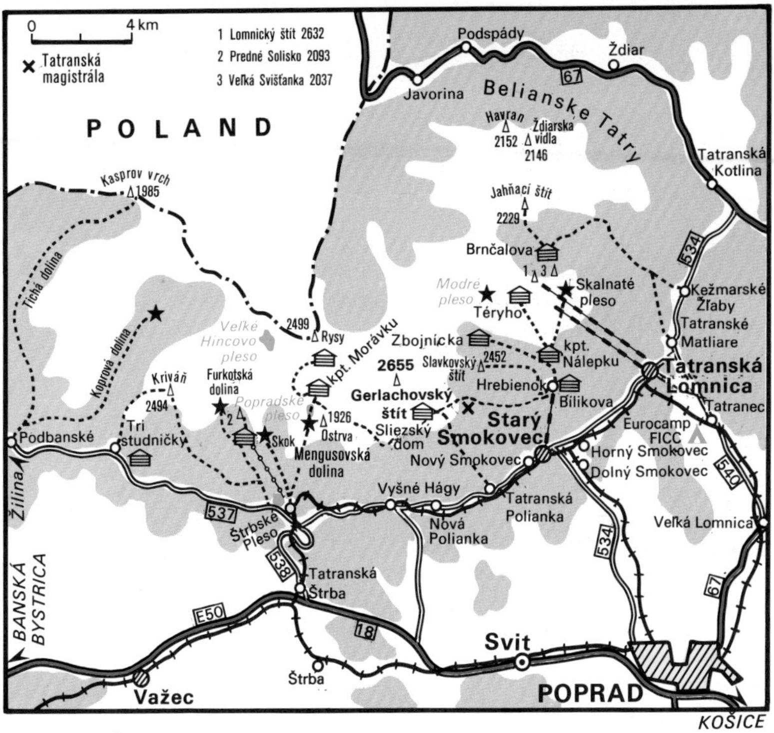

VYSOKÉ TATRY (HIGH TATRAS)

VYSOKÉ TATRY (HIGH TATRAS)

Poachers, chamois hunters, herb pickers and gold diggers were the first people to come to these magnificent peaks, the highest and most northerly of the 1200km (745 miles) Carpathian mountain range that stretches across the border and into Poland. Later, scholars and researchers came and, as early as the beginning of the 17th century, hikers discovered its natural wonders. Nowadays some three or four million visitors come each year to take in the scenery and explore, climb, unwind and enjoy the healthy mountain climate.

The High Tatras cover an area of only 260 sq km (100 sq miles) but boast over 300 proud peaks, 30 above 2500m (8200ft). The main ridge is a massive 26km (16 miles) long and 26km (16 miles) wide.

The present appearance of the High Tatras is due to glacial activity in the Ice Age over 20,000 years ago. Glaciers chiselled out valleys causing waterfalls and beautiful lakes called 'pleso'. There are 126 lakes, the largest and deepest being **Velké Hincovo pleso** covering an area of 20 hectares (49 acres) and up to 54m (177ft) deep. The highest at 2192m (7190ft) is **Modré pleso — The Blue Lake** — and it certainly lives up to its name.

The range is mostly granite while the **Belianske Tatras** in the east are dolomite limestone. Together with the **Western Tatras** they form the most important nature reserve in Czechoslovakia — the **Tatras National Park.** The whole area of some 500 sq km (193 sq miles) is protected and unique flora and fauna thrive here. Over 1200 plant species grow here and

Walkers come for the open landscapes of the mountain valleys and ridges

mountain deer, boars, brown bears, lynx, wolves, chamois, marmots and eagles roam free. For walkers there are innumerable trails through the natural wonderland ranging from easy-going to heart-thumping. The Belianske Tatras are currently off-limits to visitors because of the possible threat to the rare flora which thrives there.

There are many communities, tourist and spa resorts, mostly among the vast spruce and fir forests of the sunny southern slopes.

Poprad is considered to be the gateway to the High Tatras but it's worth trying to get to see **Podbanské, Štrbské Pleso, Starý Smokovec, Tatranská Lomnica** and **Ždiar**. All have accommodation, restaurants and sports facilities. Čedok in Poprad will be able to give you details and arrange bookings (see p. 196).

Štrbské Pleso, the highest and one of the most popular resorts in the High Tatras

SETTING OFF

By air Direct flights to Poprad-Tatry airport from Bratislava and Prague. At 710m (2329ft), it's the highest international airport operating all year in Europe.

By car E50 from Košice to Poprad - 120km (75 miles). Road 66 from Banská Bystrica to Poprad - 214km (133 miles). E50 from Žilina to Poprad - 263km (163 miles). If you've time en route from Žilina, turn off to Podbanské in Liptovský Hrádok and take the long way round - the scenery is fantastic.

By bus Regular connections to Poprad from most major towns in Slovakia and Moravia. International links with Budapest, Vienna and the Polish mountain resort of Zakopane.

By train Direct links to Poprad from Prague and most major towns in Slovakia and Moravia. International connections to Moscow.

ON THE MOVE

Many of the smaller communities in the High Tatras are connected by electric railway. Probably the most popular form of travel is shanks's pony — the High Tatras attract walkers from all over the world.

Poprad 672m (2204ft). With a splendid view of the peaks only 13km (8 miles) away, Poprad has benefitted from its strategic location in the southern foothills. It's the administrative centre of the region and an important junction for airlines, roads and railways. Poprad is the starting point for forays not only into the High Tatras but also into the **Slovak Paradise** (see p. 183).

First mentions of the town date from 1256 and there are several historic monuments worth seeing including the 1655 **Renaissance belfry**, the 14th century early-**Gothic church** and the 18th and 19th century restored burgher houses around the main square. The **Podtatranské Museum** has exhibitions of crafts, ethnography and zoology, open Tues to Sun 09.00 - 16.00, while the **Tatranská Gallery** has changing exhibitions and is open Tues to Sun 10.30 - 16.30.

Podbanské 940m (3083ft). This picturesque spa resort is dominated by **Kriváň**, the national peak of the Slovaks at 2494m (8180ft). In times of subjugation it became the symbol of unity and freedom of the Slovak nation. Every June people come from all over Slovakia to climb to its lofty summit but it can be tackled at any time. The first ascent was in 1841 when the national revivalist **Ludovít Štúr** took part. The best setting-off point is **Tri studničky** by the **Captain Raš chalets** and the climb takes four to five hours. It's easy going in good weather and the views are incredible.

Štrbské Pleso 1350m (4428ft). This is the highest resort in the High Tatras and, thanks to its ski course laid out for the 1970 World Championship, the place has really taken off as one of the best mountain resorts in the world. It's on the southern banks of the picturesque **Štrbské Lake** and has incredible views of the peaks.

There are many good hiking routes starting here. For a relatively easy walk follow the yellow-marked paths along the **Furkotská** and **Mlynická** valleys to the **Skok (Jump) Waterfall.** There's another easy route marked in red through the **Mengusovská valley** to **Popradské Lake** and the **Captain Morávku chalets**. An easy one-hour stroll will take you around the beautiful **Štrbské Lake**. For a reminder of the less hospitable side of the mountains, take the yellow-marked path from Popradské Lake to the symbolic **Cemetery of the Victims of the Mountains** below Mount Ostrava.

Plenty of well marked trails lead through the valleys and along the lofty ridges

Starý Smokovec 1010m (3313ft). This pleasant mountain town at the foot of **Slavkovský štít (Mount Slavkovský)** is the oldest community in the High Tatras and the centre of their administration. It's also the base for the mountain rescue service (tel: (0969) 28 20) but hopefully this is one bit of information you won't be needing.

The local electric railway connects **Starý Smokovec** to **Poprad**, **Štrbské Pleso** and **Tatranská Lomnica** while a funicular railway will take you to the skiing area of **Hrebienok** at 1262m (4139ft). From here there are many interesting yet not too demanding hiking routes. The green-marked paths will take you to **Malá Studená dolina (valley)** and the **Téryho chalet** while the blue-marked path leads to **Velká Studená dolina** and welcome refreshment at the **Zbojnická chalet**. For long distance walkers the most picturesque is probably the red-marked route of the **Tatranská Magistrála (arterial route)** which runs the 80km (50 miles) of the main ridge of the High Tatras.

Tatranská Lomnica 850m (2788ft). This large resort is the seat of the administration of the **Tatras National Park (TANAP)** and there's an excellent **museum** with exhibitions on the history of the High Tatras, mineralogy, zoology and botany. It's open Mon to Fri 09.00 - 17.00, Sat and Sun 08.00 - 13.00. There are many hotels and chalets to accommodate visitors who come to ride in the cable car to the beautiful **Skalnaté pleso** and on to the summit of **Lomnický štít (Mount Lomnický)**, the second highest peak in the High Tatras at 2632m (8633ft). The astrological observatory and meteorological office here are the highest Czechoslovak workplaces.

There's another observatory next to the Encián Hotel by the **Skalnaté pleso** and a chairlift from here runs to **Lomnické sedlo (saddle)** skiing area. Two downhill runs from here take you back to **Tatranská Lomnica** and offer some of the best skiing in the country. In the town, there are two ski jumps, a bob sleigh run and good cross-country tracks.

Walkers can set off from **Kežmarské Žlaby** 5km (3 miles) away towards **Ždiar** along yellow-marked paths to the valley of the **Zelene pleso** and along the blue-marked paths from **Tatranské Matliare,** 2km (1.2 miles) away towards **Ždiar** along the valley of **Kežmarská Biela voda**.

Ždiar 895m (2936ft). This resort has a little extra — a sense of folk tradition and an exhibition of national costumes and furniture to prove it. You'll find it in **Ždiarsky House** where visitors stay in traditional wooden farmhouses and chalets with panoramic views of the **Ždiarska vidla** and **Havran hills**. There are excellent skiing facilities and plenty of good hiking routes, from easy to demanding.

FACT FILE

Emergency medical aid
Poprad Tel: (0969) 23 25 6/24 76 4/23 25 8.
Štrbské Pleso Tel: (0969) 92 35 5.
Tatranská Lomnica Tel: (0969) 96 73 49.
Ždiar Tel: (0969) 98 42.

Pharmacies
Štrbské Pleso Tel: (0969) 92 20 6.
Tatranská Lomnica Tel: (0969) 96 73 95.

Post offices
Štrbské Pleso Tel: (0969) 92 21 1.
Starý Smokovec Tel: (0969) 25 52.
Tatranská Lomnicna. Tel: (0969) 96 79 77.

Travel agencies
Poprad Čedok. Tel: (0969) 23 65 1. Information and flight tickets. Tatratour. Tel: (0969) 36 71 2. ČSA. Tel: (0969) 26 50 5/22 26 9. Slovakotour. Tel: (0969) 36 46 5.
Starý Smokovec Čedok. Tel: (0969) 27 10. Accommodation. Tel: (0969) 24 16. Flight tickets.
Tatranská Lomnica Čedok. Tel: (0969) 96 74 28/46 74 51. Information and flight tickets. Tatratour. Tel: (0969) 96 72 04. In Slovan Hotel.
Ždiar Slovakotour. Tel: (0969) 98 40.

Shopping
Štrbské Pleso Prior department store.
Starý Smokovec Mladost department store (most goods except food). Slovakia (arts and crafts).
Tatranská Lomnica Prior department store. ÚĽUV (arts and crafts).

WHERE TO STAY

From luxury hotels to simple tourist chalets, there are plenty of places to stay in the High Tatras. For most you'd be wise to book ahead, particularly in the skiing season and in the summer months. Here are just a few ideas.

Hotels and campsites

Poprad

⌂ **A* Permon** Tel: (0969) 90 10 2.
⌂ **B* Gerlach** Tel: (0969) 23 45 6.

Podbanské

⌂ **B* Kriváň** Tel: (0969) 90 12 1-2.
⌂ **C Captain Raš chalets** Tel: (0969) 90 11 5.
△ **B Pribylina campsite** Račkova dolina. Tel: (0969) 93 23 5. 9km (6 miles) from Podbanské on Highway 537 to Liptovský Hrádok.

Štrbské Pleso

⌂ **A* Patria** Tel: (0969) 92 59 0-5.
⌂ **B* Panorama** Tel: (0969) 92 11 1-5.
⌂ **B* FIS Hotel and bungalows** Tel: (0969) 92 22 9.

Starý Smokovec

⌂ **A* Grand** Tel: (0969) 21 54-6.

Glacial action some 20,000 years ago created the valleys of the High Tatras

△ **A* Praha Grandhotel** Tel: (0969) 96 79 41. Reception (0969) 96 76 07.
⛺ **A FICC Eurocamp** Tel: (0969) 96 77 41-5. Open all year.
117 bungalows with 3-4 person rooms. Plenty of pitches for tents and caravans. Best equipped camp site in the High Tatras.

Ždiar

We recommend staying in the typical wooden houses to get a real feel for the mountains. Book through Slovakotour. Tel: (0969) 98 82/98 40.

High mountain chalets

All the following offer modest accommodation with the exception of the Sliezky dom which is a hotel. All have basic bars or self-service buffets and are open all year.

△ **B Sliezky dom Mountain Hotel** Tel: (0969) 62 55 90.
B Captain Morávku chalets. Tel: (0969) 92 17 7. By Popradské pleso.
C Bílíkova chalets. Tel: (0969) 24 39.
C Captain Nálepku chalets Tel: (0969) 26 36.
C Téryho chalets Tel: (0969) 92 49 00.

EATING OUT

Štrbské Pleso

I Horizont Restaurant.
II Patria Hotel Restaurant.
II Panorama Hotel Restaurant, wine bar, snack bar.
II Slovenka Restaurant.
II Javorina Snack bar.

Wonderful waterfalls cascade over the rocky heights in a glittering display

Starý Smokovec
🍴 **I Grand Hotel** Restaurant.
🍴 **III Taverna** Restaurant.
🍴 **III Hortex** Day bar.
🍴 **III Pipi Gril** Self-service restaurant.

WALKS AND SPORTS
All communities in the High Tatras are well served with skiing facilities but some have a few more added attractions for the keep-fit fanatic.
Poprad
Indoor and outdoor pools, football and hockey stadium, shooting gallery.
Starý Smokovec
Fitness centre in Grand Hotel.
Tatranská Lomnica
Indoor pool and sauna in Odborar Holiday home. Sauna in Slovan Hotel. Sauna in FICC Eurocamp. Tennis courts. Jogging tracks/cross-country ski tracks near Praha Grandhotel.

RECOMMENDED HIKING TRAILS
Everyone will find their own favourite walking route in the High Tatras — there are certainly plenty to choose from. Below are a few of the more demanding marked trails to whet your appetite. They're listed from west to east and times are obviously approximate.

Kasprov vrch (Kasprov Hill) 1985m (6511ft). 5 hour trip beginning from Podbanské leading through the **Tichá dolina (valley)**. Follow the yellow markers.

Mount Kriváň 2942m (9650ft) 3 hours from Tri studničky. Green markers. 3 - 4 hours from Štrbské pleso. Red markers to Jamské pleso then blue markers to the summit.

Mount Predné Solisko 2093m (6865ft). 1 hour from top of chairlift at chalet below Mt Solisko. Red markers. 20 minutes from Štrbské pleso to the chairlift yellow markers.

Mount Rysy 2499m (8197ft). 1 hour from chalet below Mt Rysy. Red markers. 3 - 4 hours to chalet from Popradské pleso along **Mengusovská dolina (valley)** blue markers, then red markers.

Mount Slavkovský 2452m (8043ft). 4 hours from Hrebienok, red markers then blue. Funicular from Starý Smokovec to Hrebienok.

Mount Velká Svišťanka 2037m (6681ft). 1 hour from Brnčalova chalet. Red markers. 3 - 4 hours from Tatranské Matliare to Brnčalova chalet. Blue then red markers.

Mount Jahňací 2220m (7282ft). 2 hours from Brnčalova chalet. Yellow markers. 3-4 hours from Tatranské Matliare to Brnčalova chalet. Follow the blue markers, then the red.

CLASSIC CLIMBS
Unless you're a really experienced climber we recommend you hire a mountain guide if you want to attempt these popular routes. The guides tend to speak only Czech, Slovak or German but they'll have no trouble showing you the ropes.

Grade III Volia veža. Ošarpance, western ridge. Gerlachovský štít, northern ridge. Ostrý štít, southern face.

Grade IV Žabí kôň, southern face. Batizovský štít, southern face. Vidlové veže, western ridge. Čierný štít, southern face.

Grade V Malý Ĺadový štít, southern face. Mt Ganek from Rumanova dolina (valley).

USEFUL VOCABULARY

Czech is spoken in Bohemia and Moravia and Slovak in Slovakia. The languages are similar and both are understood throughout the country. Some people speak English and this is becoming more widespread, but if you make the effort to say a few words in Czech or Slovak, it will be much appreciated. A smattering of German might help too.

The accents on Czech and Slovak words look daunting, but pronunciation is not difficult when you've learnt the basic sounds.

Czech and Slovak have only five vowel sounds, but each has a short and a long version. Most long vowels carry an acute accent (´). Long **u** is written **ů** except at the beginning of a word, when it is **ú** like the other long vowels. The letters **i** and **y** are pronounced the same.

VOWELS

Pronounce a as in sh**u**t
á as in f**a**ther
e as in m**et**
é as in **air**
i, y as in p**i**t
í, ý as in s**ee**
o as in p**o**t
ó as in p**oo**r
u as in r**oo**k
ú, ů as in d**oo**m

Note that **ě** affects the preceding consonant, not the vowel sound, putting an English **y** sound between the consonant and the **ě**. eg. dě = d**yay**, ně = n**yay**

CONSONANTS

Only those different from English are listed below.

Pronounce c as in **s**its
č as in **ch**ew
ch as in lo**ch**
j as in **y**ellow
n as in **n**ot
ň as in o**ni**on
r has no English equivalent – try rolling your **r** a little
ř has no English equivalent – try **rz**
s as in hi**ss**
š as in po**sh**
z as in ad**z**e
ž as in plea**s**ure

STRESS

The stress on any word falls on the first syllable. Long vowels are only stressed if they fall in the first syllable.

ENGLISH	**CZECH**	**SLOVAK**
good morning/ afternoon	dobrý den (dobree denn)	dobrý deň (dobree dyenj)
good evening	dobrý večer (dobree vetcher)	dobrý večer (dobree vetcher)
goodnight	dobrou noc (dobrou nots)	dobrú noc (dobroo nots)
goodbye	nashledanou (nashledanou)	dovidenia (dovidyenia)
hello/hi	ahoj (ahoy)	
please/you're welcome	prosím (prosseem)	nech sa páči (nyech sa paatchi)
thank you	děkuji (dyekuyi)	d'akujem (dyakuiem)
yes	ano (ano)	áno/hej (aano/hey)
no	ne (ne)	nie (nyieh)
sorry	promiňte, prosím (prominjte, prosseem)	prepáčtě, prosím (prepaatchtye, prosseem)
never mind	nevadí (nevadyee)	nevadí (nyevadee)
do you understand?	rozumíte? (rozumeete?)	rozumíete? (rozumyetye?)
I don't understand	nerozumím (nerozumeem)	nerozumiem (nerozoomiem)
do you speak English?/French?/ German?	mluvíte anglicky?/německy?/ francouzsky? (mluveete anglitsky?/nyemetsky?/ frantsouski?)	hovoríte anglicky?/ nemecki?/francúski? (hovoreetye anglitski?/ nyemetski?/frantsooski?
how far is it to...?	jak dalecko je do...? (yak daleko ye do...?)	ako dúleko je do...? (ako dyaleko ye do...?)
where is the...?	kde je...? (gde ye...?	kde je...? (gdye ye...?)
toilet	záchod (zaachott)	záchod (zaachott)
women's toilet	ženy, dámy (dzennee,	ženy, dámy (dzenny,

	daamy)	daami)
men's toilet	muži, páni (mudzi, paani)	muži, páni (mudzi, paanyi)
how are you?	jak se máte? (jak se maate?)	ako sa máte? (ako sa maatye?)
well, thank you	dobře, děkuji (dobrze, dyekuee)	dobre, ďakujem (dobre, dyakuiem)
one	jeden (jedenn)	jeden (yedain)
two	dva (dva)	dva (dva)
three	tři (trzi)	tri (tri)
four	čtyři (tztirzi)	štyrí (shtiri)
five	pět (pyet)	päť (paitj)
six	šest (shest)	šesť (shestj)
seven	sedm (sedum)	sedem (sedyem)
eight	osm (ossum)	osem (osem)
nine	devět (devyett)	deväť (dyevaitj)
ten	deset (dessett)	desať (dyesatj)
twenty	dvacet (dvatsett)	dvadsať (dvasatj)
one hundred	sto (sto)	sto (sto)
3 o'clock	tři hodny (trzi hodiny)	tri hodiny (tri hodiny)
3.10	tři deset (trzi dessett)	tri desať (tri dyesatj)
restaurant	restaurace (restauratse)	reštaurácia (reshtauraatsya)
menu	jídelní lístek (jeedelnyee leestek)	jédaľny lístok (jedaalny leestock)
the bill	platím (platyeem)	platím (platjeem)
coffee	káva (kaava)	káva (kaava)
tea	čaj (tchai)	čaj (tchai)
beer	pivo (pivo)	pivo (pivo)
soup	polevka (polaivka)	polievka (polievka)
meat	maso (masso)	mäso (maiso)
potatoes	brambory (brambori)	zemiaky (zemiak)
vegetables	zelenina (zelenyina)	zelenina (zelenyina)
fruit	ovoce (ovotse)	ovocie (ovotsie)
dessert	moučník (moutchneek)	múčnik (mootchnik)
airport	letiště (letishtye)	letisko (letyisko)
railway station	nádraží (naadrajee)	železníčná stanica (dzeleznitchnaa stanitsa)
ticket desk	pokladna (pokladna)	pokladňa (pokladnya)
information	informace (informatse)	informácie (informaatsie)
customs office	celnice (celnyicee)	colnica (tsolnyitsa)
passport control	pasová kontrola (passovaa kontrola)	pasová kontrola (passovaa kontrola)
shop	obchod (obchott)	obchod (obchott)
open	otevřeno (otevrzeno)	otvorené (otvorainai)
closed	zavřeno (zavrzeno)	zatvorené (zatvorainai)
I'd like	chtě l bych koupit (chtyel bich koupit)	choel bysom kúpiť? (choel bysom koopitj?)
how much is it?	kolik to stojí? (kolik to stoyee?)	koľko to stojí? (koljko to stoyee?)
bread	chleba (chleba)	chleba (chleba)
butter	máslo (maasslo)	máslo (maasslo)
milk	mléko (mlaiko)	mlieko (mlaiko)
white/red wine	bílé/červené víno (beelai/chervenai vino)	biele/červené vino (biele tchervenai vino)
chocolate	čokoláda (tchocolaada)	čokoláda (tchokolaada)
cheap	laciný (latsinee)	lacný (latsnee)
expensive	drahý (drahee)	drahý (drahee)
reception	recepce (retseptse)	recepcia (retseptsia)
a cheap room for one/two	laciný pokoy pro jednoho/dva (latsinee pokoi pro jednoho/dva)	lacná izba pre jedného/dvoch (latsnaa izba pre yednaiho/dvoch)
bathroom	koupelna (koupelna)	kúpeľňa (koopeljnya)

INDEX

References to illustrations appear in italic, main entries in bold type.

PICTURE CREDITS

Bohumil Landisch pp ii/iii, 1, 7, 15, 23, 35, 36, 39, 40, 41, 45, 54, 59, 65, 68, 69, 70, 72, 74, 79, 84, 85, 87, 89, 90, 93, 95, 101, 103, 110, 110, 113, 114, 116, 142, 125, 169, 180, 193, 197; ORBIS archives pp 2, 5, 8, 19, 25, 27, 48, 53, 99, 119, 129, 134, 144, 146, 153, 168, 198; Oleg Homola pp 6, 57, 64, 126, 157, 159; Oldřich Egem pp 9, 52, 133, 137, 145, 150, 172, 214/5; Jon Olney pp 10, 55, 58; Milan Racek pp 13, 104; Karol Demuth pp 16, 169, 175, 177, 180, 190, 192, 195; Sláva Vaneš pp 21, 93, 109; Andrej Šťastný pp 29, 32, 77; Frant. Maleček pp 31, 88, 97, 122, 126, 155; Jos. Ployhar p 42; ČTK p 47;P. Horník p 51; J.Molín pp 59, 73; Igor Zehl pp 80, 135; Lad. Sitenský pp 81, 121, 161; Frant. Zahradníček pp 83, 139, 156; B.F. Dusík p 92; Jiří Poborák p 131; Václav Ostádal p 141; Václav Fuchs p 146; Zdeno Vlach p 157, 167, 176, 178; J. Čeněk p 163; Mir. Vlček p 164; E. Čeňková p 182; Alex. Jiroušek pp 184, 187, 189.